EROTIC WELFARE

Thinking Gender
Edited by Linda J. Nicholson

Also published in the series

Feminism/Postmodernism
Linda J. Nicholson

Gender Trouble
Judith Butler

Words of Power
Andrea Nye

Femininity and Domination
Sandra Bartky

Disciplining Foucault
Jana Sawicki

Beyond Accommodation
Drucilla Cornell

Embattled Eros
Steven Seidman

EROTIC WELFARE

SEXUAL THEORY AND POLITICS IN THE AGE OF EPIDEMIC

LINDA SINGER

EDITED AND INTRODUCED BY
JUDITH BUTLER AND **MAUREEN MacGROGAN**

ROUTLEDGE
NEW YORK LONDON

Published in 1993 by

Routledge
An imprint of Routledge, Chapman and Hall, Inc.
29 West 35th Street
New York, NY 10001

Published in Great Britain by

Routledge
11 New Fetter Lane
London EC4P 4EE

Library of Congress Cataloging-in-Publication Data

Singer, Linda, d. 1990.
    Erotic welfare: sexual theory and politics in the age of epidemic
/ edited by Judith Butler and Maureen MacGrogan.
      p. cm.—(Thinking gender)
    Includes index.
    ISBN 0-415-90201-0 (CL). ISBN 0-415-90202-9 (PB)
    1. Feminist theory. 2. Feminist criticism. 3. AIDS (Disease)—
Social aspects. 4. Sex and law. 5. Social history—1970–
I. Butler, Judith P. II. MacGrogan, Maureen. III. Title.
IV. Series.
HQ1190.S46 1992
305.42′01—dc20   91-44472
                                          CIP

British Library cataloguing in publication data also available

Contents

Editor's Introduction   1

Part I. Erotic Welfare   17

1.   Author's Introduction   19
2.   Sex and the Logic of Late Capitalism   34
3.   Disciplining Pleasures   62
4.   Regulating Women in the Age of Sexual Epidemic   83
5.   Reproductive Regulations in the Age of Sexual Epidemic   88
6.   Hospitalization and AIDS   100

Part II. Selected Writings   109

     Editor's Introduction   111
1.   Bodies–Pleasures–Powers   113
2.   Interpretation and Retrieval: Rereading Beauvoir   131
3.   True Confessions: Cixous and Foucault on Sexuality and Power   145
4.   Defusing the Canon: Feminist Rereading and Textual Politics   163
5.   Just Say No: Repression, Anti-Sex, and the New Film   177
6.   Feminism and Postmodernism   187

Other Works by the Author   199
Works Cited in Part I   201
Index   205

Editor's Introduction

If there are ties that bind, she is the one tying the knot.
Linda Singer, Author's Introduction, *Erotic Welfare*

Linda Singer sought to complete this book in 1990, but that year she became increasingly ill with cancer and died in early August. She did leave significant portions of the manuscript in completed or almost completed condition. This book is composed of two parts, the edited version of *Erotic Welfare,* and selected essays she wrote on feminism, postmodernism, and cultural theory between 1987 and 1990.

What is the best way to present this work to a readership under such circumstances? A personal introduction is not easy here, but neither can it be avoided. Although Linda Singer was against the personalist and confessional character of some work in women's studies, she gauged the success of any feminist inquiry by its power to transform women's lives. What she sought to compel, and what she did compel, was a rethinking of those issues most proximate to desire and power within a framework that gave them wider meaning, indeed, that gave them radical philosophical consequences. In this sense, she would not abide by a purely personalist discourse. In fact, a "discourse" is what she would have called it, and in that appellation she would have taken her distance from the personal at the same time that she would have installed it as her most passionate object of inquiry.

So, in this introduction, how loyal can I be to Linda Singer's method? Clearly, I will not try to reduce the intellectual breadth of her work to her personal life: that is impossible in any case. But I cannot write of this text without letting you, the reader, know something of the kind of person she was, from what struggle this work emerged, and how she took her illness as an occasion for intense speculation, radical critique, and a sympathetic connection with those who suffer from AIDS. What she wanted most passionately in her final months was to be able to write, to write of illness, the ways in which it is managed, crafted, extended, controlled; to write of bodies, how they are determined within the dense web of medical power regimes; to connect the medical and legal control over women's bodies and their reproductive freedom to the medical management

1

of the AIDS epidemic and, hence, to provide a systematic link, a coalitional frame for these demanding and mournful times.

To do some of this, I need at least to explain the place of the personal in this life, Linda Singer's life, which was in such a rare and compelling way a life *in discourse,* a life that came alive again and again in talk, in writing, in lecturing. And a life which even in its final gestures sought to make use of power as resistance, defiance, transgression, as a critical affirmation in the face of power understood as control, regulation, discipline.

In a sense, her intellectual task was to understand what structures of power *inhere* in what is conventionally circumscribed as the personal. As she left for Texas to receive treatments for her kidney cancer in the summer of 1990, she brought along one book: Baudrillard's *Fatal Strategies.* I know she took some defiant comfort that this title would appear under her arm as she waited in the doctor's office, arguing with nurses over protocol and equipment. On the occasions in which we talked over the telephone during that time, the conversation turned to death and, in particular, to Camus.

I remember how often the words "contingency" and "choice" entered her talk, and how she would refuse to accept at face value what any of the medical authorities told her she had to do. She resented those proclamations of necessity and insisted that every medical imperative finally be a choice that she made. And in the final months she raged against the choices she was forced to make; the treatments available to her threatened to make her feel more ill and unable to work and write, and yet without these treatments she faced the prospect of a quick death. This was for her a choice between, on the one hand, a productive clarity that would give her some final weeks and months to write, to conclude her business with the world, to be with her friends and family, and, on the other hand, a loss of clarity and consciousness for the sake of saving a life, her own, a prospect for which she sustained little hope. She distrusted the optimistic scenarios that others tried to offer her about the chances of her survival if only this or that treatment were tried, and she considered such scenarios to be part of the inflated narcissism, the self-congratulatory rationalizations that the institution of medical research handed out freely and cruelly. And she would repeat often how cruel she thought holding out the prospect of hope could be. She tried to find and adjudicate the grounds, the reasons, for deciding for or against any given treatment, and in the face of every stark dilemma she would stall the decision and produce an array of choices and possible trajectories of consequences which often startled and disoriented her friends and family. Why wouldn't she simply opt for the treatment that promised an off-chance at life? What could be more important than that?

What appeared to be more important to her was to sustain a sense of her own power to make a reasoned decision in the face of a medical apparatus and its discursive regimes that sought to deny to her any sense of agency. She insisted that the various proposals of medical treatment be addressed to her as possible decisions for her to make. And she would take her time in making those decisions, rework conceptually the ways in which those decisions were framed for her, reframe them, refuse them, resist them, and eventually come to accept some form of treatment with her ambivalence intact. What she reflected on in those final months was the "absurdity" (her word) of making a choice for which no definitive justifications could be found and no certain consequences could be predicted. She wanted to be able to find a guarantee for the rationality of her decision, to know that in the face of this monstrous difficulty, she was still a rationally choosing being; and yet, that demand could only meet with frustration because there was no way to predict and because the most certain of any of the possible consequences appeared to be death. She would muse ironically over this picture of herself, dwelling within the central trope of existentialism: choosing at the limits of rationality in the face of death. But there was something in this site of tension that most absorbed her, not the final act of consent, but the elaborate reflections and ratiocinations, the discursive production that the demand for a decision incited and sustained.

Death was for her that which called for a strategy. It was that against and toward which she thought; it troubled and stalled her thought, but also incited her to heights of discursive resistance that took everyone around her by surprise. As much as she wanted to recapture the belief in herself as a deliberate agent who might be able to sustain reason in the face of death, she would also pursue every path of reason to its limit—the unknowable, the unforeseeable, the unpredictable. It impressed me that at such a moment she would invoke Camus—not Kierkegaard, not Heidegger, not Sartre, but Camus—the most affirmative of the existential philosophers, the one who insisted that that ungrounded choice at the limit of rationality was precisely the affirmation of life. It was this unreasoned affirmation that Camus understood as *hope* in Kafka, a strange description of that writer who, like Linda Singer, documented everywhere the radical circumscription of the will by institutions indifferent to human life. But this was perhaps Linda Singer's circuitous route to hope: not only a hope that she would live, that something would arrive in the future to undo her fatal illness, but, rather, an ungrounded hope—'wild' in the sense that Merleau-Ponty intended—that emerged precisely at the moment when all such predictions are exposed in their full contingency. It was as if precisely at the moment in which life exceeded the possibility of being controlled, planned, predicted, that life itself, the teleologically unconstrained being of her life, opened itself to a non-instrumental affirmation.

The theme of regulation and control pervades her work, as does the problematic of resistance. If life is to be affirmed as that which exceeds the efforts by which it is rationalized, constrained and subordinated to some teleological goal, then life can be the locus of an affirmative power that opposes regulation. One of the insights that Michel Foucault's work offered Linda Singer was a complex view of power, one which allowed her to maintain an opposition to regulatory operations of all kinds at the same time that that opposition is itself conceived as *part of power*. The task for her was to distinguish between disciplinary modes of power and the kinds of resistances that they occasion and spawn. For Singer, power could not be restricted to that which disciplinary regimes *produce*, tactically or inadvertently. The resistance to a disciplinary regime is not merely the inadvertent production of that regime, a peculiar way in which that regime produces the possibility of its own self-defeat. Rather, for Linda Singer, power-regimes are themselves formed and sustained through certain radical erasures, constitutive exclusions, and this was nowhere more evident to her than in those masculinist regimes constructed through the subordination and exclusion of women. On the one hand, women are excluded and erased from such a system, and on the other hand, they are everywhere recirculated *within* that system as fetishized objects, phantasmatic sites of erotic investment. This way of understanding the contradictory strategy by which women are subordinated (as outside the very system and as a highly invested commodity within the system) is taken in part through the work of Hélène Cixous, but also from feminist critiques of the traffic in women within the structuralist economy of exchange. As a commodity that must be exchanged between male owners in order to consolidate masculine authority, women are essential to the very economy from which they are (perpetually) excluded. For women, then, to begin to move outside of this economy is to threaten that exchange relation with a radical and unassimilable contestation of authority, a break in the founding relation of exchange, what Singer often called "a rupture" with and within the economy of masculinist power. This excessive status of women, the way in which they are marked as both outside *and* constitutive of the exchange relation, provides for Singer a specifically feminist locus of resistance. Here she radicalizes and rewrites the Foucaultian notion of resistance in a specifically feminist modality.

This insistence on figures of excessive femininity as those which mark a radical departure from disciplinary power regimes becomes clear in her prefatory discussion of authorship. Patriarchal power regimes preclude the very possibility of the production of a feminine subject or a feminine author. The terms "feminine" and "female" in Singer's work are never reductively biological, but function as cultural markers of gender; the argument is that insofar as an author is marked as feminine, that author ceases to be an author within the economy of the patriarchal disciplinary production of authors. Erased and yet writing, absent yet assertive, the feminine author occupies this contradiction as a "rupture" in the masculinist regime of power.

In her preface, Linda Singer theorizes the problematic of the feminine author through the figure of Scheherazade. But shortly after that figure is introduced, she is repeatedly referred to in the text as "S." Like Kafka's everpresent "K." Singer here substitutes herself ambiguously for the figure she analyzes, authorizing perhaps the uncertain sliding that I perform here between what is personal in her work and what in her work transforms the very meaning and consequences of the category of the personal. Significantly, however, she writes that this "S" is, enacts, a principle of excess in relation to the disciplinary operation of control: "S's power is not that of the rebellious slave nor the seductress. Her power is that of performing the spectacle of difference which cannot be mastered."

What Linda Singer found in Camus as a resistance to control under the name of unreasoned decision and which, in that context, became the occasion for an affirmation of life, reappears here in a specifically feminist opposition to patriarchal power regimes. If the feminine is that which cannot be accommodated by the masculinist production of subjects, then the feminine is, strictly speaking, not an identity, but *a difference from* that which counts as identity, the wild and untamable, the specter, the sign of that power regime's fundamental limitation, that which exceeds its control. For Singer, the opposition to control is itself a powerful opposition and, in that sense, a reworking of power against the apparatus of control. The discourse that emerges from the site of that difference will constitute a rival and contestatory configuration of power; it will mime and dislocate the master's words, rework his discourse, work his discourse against him to compel his defeat.

In a sense, this was her strategy in the face of death. Death never appeared as a simple existential possibility, for in the final year, it was incessantly articulated in and through the discourse of medical decisions. Death emerged as a possibility that might be realized if certain kinds of actions weren't taken. That possibility came to exist for her through the sometimes admonishing and exhortatory utterances of medical personnel, authorities who wanted to lay claim to her body in order to make it live, but whose claims signified the kind of disciplinary exercise that signaled for her a different kind of death. If one of those doctors or experts told her, "you *must* do this in order to live," the "must" took away from the very "living" it sought to sustain. When she entered the hospital in Texas, she was told that the drugs she required could be administered only if certain intravenous pumps were available. She was given a room and required to stay there even though it appeared that there were no pumps to facilitate the administration of the treatment. Constrained in a hospital room without reason, she demanded that they get the pumps immediately or she would simply check out. No docile body, Linda Singer scandalized the hospital staff and ended up procuring the pumps that gave some rationale for her confinement.

That scene reappeared for her in a final set of dreams. In a tormented sleep, her last, she reiterated out loud the terms of that confrontation: she rehearsed the scene of entering the hospital, and with her final words, she addressed the imaginary doctors, all of them: "Get me those pumps or I'm checking out." The pumps she needed, were they the pulsions from her heart which at some level she knew to be threatened? And that threat to "check out," was this her way of orchestrating and refiguring the submission to death as a self-willed act of defiance?

Introduction to the Manuscript

Linda Singer's manuscript *Erotic Welfare: Sexual Politics in the Age of Epidemic* is not primarily a book about AIDS, although she mentions the illness throughout the text and had intended to write more on the cultural effects of AIDS. It was her view that the sexual panic prompted by AIDS has pervaded the political and cultural life of the United States in recent years and has spawned a *a logic of contagion,* "a panic logic," in her words, an upsurge in regulatory power that extends itself through the proliferation and production of more and different sites of erotic danger. The fear of contagion which in some sense locates itself in relation to AIDS far exceeds the threats posed by that illness; hence, Singer notes that there is a veritable "outbreak" of new "epidemics," such as teenage pregnancy and drug abuse, which are figured within cultural discourse as threatening social phenomena with the capacity to spread.

The cultural and economic production of "epidemics" reroutes political attention and resources away from the task of providing the concrete services that those who live and suffer with AIDS require: increased funding for research, extended insurance benefits, hospital and medical services, both in-patient and out-patient, and an increased educational program in safe sex practices, among young gay men, intravenous drug users, prostitutes and their clients, especially in non-English-speaking communities within the United States and among the poor whose access to public services are limited.

In the place where those essential services ought to be expected to emerge as what Singer calls the "beneficent" effects of power, we are witnessing the intensification of regulatory regimes centered on phantasmatic sites of erotic danger, those cultural sites of erotic exchange which threaten the hegemony of the traditional family within the political imaginary: women's bodies, pornography, prostitution, gay and lesbian sexuality, children—figured as vulnerable to sexual exploitation by forces outside the family. The regulatory or disciplinary apparatuses that emerge ostensibly to counter or "wage war" on these epidemic conditions are themselves invested in sustaining and reproducing the very social phenomena they seek to control. In her chapter "Regulating Women in the Age of Sexual Epidemic," Singer remarks that "contagion becomes a major figure in social relationships and in social production." For Singer, "the age of epidemic" is in part an industry of discourse. The emergence of AIDS has, she argues, forced a radical remapping of sexual boundaries, of the terms of sexual exchange, of the constitution of sexuality as a disciplinary object and commodity fetish. The epidemic condition is no longer localized but has, according to Singer, become the very paradigm of power, the disciplinary matrix by which bodies and pleasures are invested with social and economic value. As Singer phrases it, "disciplines function as enabling forces for inciting and stylizing that which they also come to regulate."

The cultural and economic implications of the epidemic are far-reaching, since the regulations that have emerged to control prostitution, intravenous drug use, bath houses and other public and private spaces for gay male sexual encounters, are forms of power that both produce and limit sexuality. One way that this productive constraint operates is to divide the field of sexual possibilities into the normative and the pathological. Over and against the subculture of drug addiction, for instance, there is the construction of a culture of "healthy" bodies; over and against the construction of "high-risk" or dangerous sex, there is the production of the family as the exemplar of sexual safety and health; over and against the ostensibly degraded and risky life of prostitutes, the construction of the good wife and professional woman whose life represents fulfillment; over and against the woman bound to a pimp, the construction of the good mother whose subordination to male authority is thereby rendered invisible. Indeed, for Singer, the production of these binaries is always a deployment and dissimulation of power, for if the first term in each of those binary oppositions is negatively marked, then the negativity—i.e., the workings of oppression—that inheres in the latter term is effectively concealed. Singer maps out the dynamics of these constructions in her chapter "Sex and the Logic of Late Capitalism." In her view, a critical approach to the epidemic does not consist in affirming what the culture offers as sites of erotic safety, health, and autonomy, for those concepts more often than not reinscribe a disciplinary subordination at the very moment that they claim to be its alternative.

In a sense, Singer is interested in how the recent heightening of sexual regulations that is in some ways prompted by the AIDS crisis comes to exceed the bounds of AIDS and to establish a contemporary regime in which epidemic conditions rationalize the augmentation of regulatory apparatuses beyond any justifiable or instrumental purpose. These disciplinary procedures, however, are not simply irrational: they are the deployments of hegemonic social structures by which male privilege as well as racial and class privileges are insidiously reasserted. Moreover, this disciplinary production of pleasure produces the very sites of resistance to and reinscription of those hegemonic structures; hence, it is not possible to do without discipline, especially the disciplinary apparatus of self-care.

The various ways in which hegemonic privilege makes use of regulatory apparatuses to produce and control pleasures, bodies, and sexualities risk failure, according to Singer, precisely because hegemonic power tends to produce an *excess of value* that it cannot fully control. This appears to be the function of commodity fetishism for Singer: the construction of an object in and through an over-investment of value. This last insight is crucial to understanding Singer's notion of the construction of the feminine as a site of erotic over-investment, which then can be occupied and redeployed in reverse to show those who wield hegemonic privilege precisely that which exceeds their grasp. Women's sexuality occupies this place within masculinist power regimes. For Singer, "sexuality emerges in the capitalist discipline as that which is both to be disciplined and that which remains as excess or resistance to discipline and, therefore, must also be pacified, accommodated, indulged." This has specific meaning for the construction of women's sexuality.

Under capitalism, she argues, regulatory and disciplinary practices are invariably taken up to fortify and recirculate hegemonic structures. The notion of "safe sex," she argues, has been appropriated by culturally conservative critics to argue that the nuclear family is the safest sex around: "In an era of panic sexuality, the family is being repackaged as a prophylactic social device." This vulgar expropriation of the call to "safety," which originally developed within the context of gay men's outreach and self-education projects in progressive health work, implies that homosexuality itself is unsafe, a notion that is directly counter to the original meaning of the phrase: gay male sex can be made safe. Hence, gay men and others within the AIDS community who have issued the call for safety in sex are transfigured by this reappropriation into the very site of erotic danger from whom protection is required; indeed, the list of sites of erotic danger targets an array of sexual minorities and marginalized communities in whose interests the call for safety was originally made.

Singer, however, emphasizes another dimension of the discursive production of "safe" and "healthy" sex. Throughout the book, she repeats that sex has never been safe for women, and she notes with some irony and anger that the contemporary valorization of the patriarchal family returns women and children to a "private" family structure conventionally pervaded by sexual subordination and sexual abuse. But Singer is critical of the ways in which various institutions have made use of epidemic conditions to recirculate and reconsolidate hegemonic social structures that are detrimental not only to a variety of marginalized sexual actors within the cultural and economic field, such as gay men and lesbians, single mothers, prostitutes, and other sex workers, but to the transformative promise of various non-hegemonic cultural practices (those that have survived the recent repudiation of sexual arrangements of the 1960s) that attempt to find satisfactory ways to produce and sustain pleasure, especially for women, outside the parameters of the nuclear family.

One of the central questions posed by *Erotic Welfare* concerns the viability of alternative sexualities in a post-liberatory erotic climate. Knowing that no return to a liberatory space or "politics of ecstasy" is possible, but refusing as well the pessimism which would foresee hegemonic privileges totalizing the cultural and political field, Singer predicts and affirms a difficult kind of cultural labor: "It will take a certain kind of discipline to live and work without appeal to a political imaginary dominated by figures of apocalyptic transformation and the utopic possibilities of liberated pleasures." Pleasure is never liberated or capable of liberation under current regimes of power; in fact, both the notion of "freedom" and that of "pleasure" are strategically deployed by hegemonic power to produce the effect of greater autonomy precisely at the moment when the individual is being sutured into the logic of regulation: "pleasure becomes a crucial currency for social control in a post-scarcity economy." And yet pleasure is never fully subordinated to control precisely because this is a cultural and erotic economy which is characterized by panic logic and whose primary tendency is to produce and multiply the very phenomena it seeks to control. Inasmuch as the proliferative capacity of this economy outstrips its regulatory means, it creates sites of excess value, mentioned above. Insofar as these sites of erotic value are constituted discursively, they become cultural positions from which a certain eroticized speaking and agency emerge. Constituted as excessive, outside the economy and yet as the very currency of exchange, women, for Singer, are in the non-systematizable position of being both inside and outside disciplinary structures; they are both a subject of discipline and always in need of further discipline; hence, they are that which exceeds every effort at discipline, discipline's limit, the site where it produces its own cultural psychosis.

Singer follows the Foucaultian position that pleasure can no longer be understood in opposition to power, for power is the discursive matrix by which pleasure is produced and circulated. The disciplinary apparatus that emerges with the ostensible purpose of limiting or even abolishing certain forms of sexuality can work only by becoming itself the site of the production of a new set of sexualities. Hence, the disciplinary or regulatory move of power *against* certain kinds of pleasure becomes effective only by becoming *itself* a site of erotic investment, recirculating pleasure in different forms of prohibition and displacement. The regulation of pleasure is always in some sense the (re)constitution of pleasure as and in regulation. As a result, there is no sexuality "outside" of the disciplinary apparatus through which that sexuality is produced, although there is always the possibility of an *excessive* production, the creation of a surplus which then can operate as a critical lever on the system from which it is spawned: in Singer's purposefully ambiguous formulation, "The law will also always produce that which stands outside it."

With her concern with late capitalist dynamics, Singer's own position moves with startling originality from Foucault to Baudrillard; indeed, one might argue that among the most important non-feminist theoretical texts in her work, apart from Herbert Marcuse's *Eros and Civilization,* are Foucault's *History of Sexuality,* volume 1, and Jean Baudrillard's *The Mirror of Production.* Baudrillard offers a theory of discourse and, more specifically, a political account of cultural *signs* that locates significatory value as a joint investment of economic and erotic relations of exchange. This becomes crucial for Singer, who transfers that Baudrillardian insight back onto the object domain marked out by Foucault: bodies, pleasures, sexualities. But Singer's originality exceeds that deft transfer of discourses precisely through subjecting both theoretical languages to a feminist reinscription. Singer notes that sexuality is always figured as an economic exchange, a form of *social currency,* and that the bargaining power of each partner in the heterosexual exchange is marked by a power differential from the start.

This claim will have far-reaching consequences for her analysis of prostitution, marriage, and questions of surrogacy. More generally, for her, over and against both Foucault and Baudrillard, bodies, pleasures, and sexualities are always already marked by sex, that is, their value and significance are produced (differentially) through the axis of sexual difference.

The few but important references to Lacan in her work, and the specific use of the category of sex as always already linguistic, work to support the view that subjects produced and controlled through power are always positioned in a differential relation of sexual difference. I gave a paper once on Beauvoir and the sex/gender distinction with Linda Singer in the audience. Beauvoir's formulation "One is not born a woman, but rather becomes one" came under consideration. I mistakenly reiterated Beauvoir's grammatical confusion, postulating the possibility of a "one" who is in some sense *prior* to its gender. In the course of the discussion, I confessed to the audience that I almost always read the signs on bathroom doors marked "men" and "women" as offering normative and anxiety-producing choices, delivering a demand to conform to the gender they indicate. After the talk, Linda rose from the audience, hand on hip, and explained to me that what I had figured as a choice was not one at all, that "one," she said, "is always already inside the door." Her criticism, which I quickly came to accept, implies that there is no human "one" prior to its marking by sex, but that sex— i.e., the differential relations that produce sexed positions within discourse— produces the very possibility of a viable "one." This feminist critique of humanism reappears throughout her analysis here, which means that the discourse on epidemic and sexuality is grounded in an analysis of sexual difference.

The reader may be surprised at first that a book which purports to address the problematic of epidemic focuses on questions of discipline, pleasure, late-capitalist forms of sexual exchange, prostitution, pornography, medical regimes of regulation, reproductive freedom, and almost everywhere returns to a central concern with the status of *women* within the era of epidemic. In a sense, this is Singer's point: that the disciplinary response to the epidemic of AIDS does not work primarily to alleviate or abolish the epidemic condition; on the contrary, it presumes epidemic and extends it throughout the social field, transforming "epidemic" not only into a readily transferable or "contagious" figure, but installing the presumed proliferative logic of epidemic as an abiding epistemic matrix for the disciplinary production of cultural knowledge about bodies in general.

The disciplinary response to AIDS, according to this analysis, can be read as a refusal to address AIDS that engages instead a panic logic that proliferates phantasmatic sites of erotic danger. This is a form of regulatory power that refuses the possibilities of an enabling or "beneficent" response in order to project, produce, and police its own phantasms of danger, thereby letting the more pressing dangers of dying with AIDS proliferate. Precisely through deflecting the productive dimensions of power away from caring for those who are suffering, those vulnerable populations are constituted as the very site of danger from which protection and safety must be secured. The regulatory apparatus that is meant to cure the disease thus enters into an epidemic logic by which that apparatus "immunizes" itself against the very populations it is supposed to serve, thereby letting the disease spread without intervention—one might even say "producing" the disease.

Singer's thesis, that the epidemic has become an epistemic and disciplinary matrix, a contemporary knowledge/power regime of the erotic, has far-reaching consequences for contemporary social and cultural analysis. A cultural critic of the Baby M case may not think that the manner in which the issue is framed, the legal judgments articulated and adjudicated, has anything to do with the prevalence of epidemic logic. But Singer's grammar is instructive here, for it is no longer a matter of referring to "a" or "the" epidemic, for "epidemic" has lost its article; it is no longer an issue, a fact, a phenomenon. It has lost its discreteness and specificity and become a condition, no longer an object of knowledge, but a contemporary epistemic condition of articulation. Hence, the effects of epidemic are to be found throughout contemporary discourses on bodies, pleasures, sexualities, sexual arrangements, forms of erotic exchange, the production and marketing of zones of erotic safety, the juridical construction of bodies in relation to the state, the rightful relations among family members, the delimitation of what is a family under the law.

Singer is interested in the effect of this heightened regulatory climate on the reproductive rights of women, on how questions of surrogacy are framed and settled, on pro-family sentiment and policy and its effects on women, on the media's circulation of certain highly invested signs of femininity and how the state and the market seek to regulate and domesticate non-hegemonic forms of sexual exchange and reproduction. Epidemics appear to justify radical interventionist policies on the part of the state to regulate not only the exchange of fluids, but the larger relations of exchange within which sexuality occurs. The Baby M case, which Singer analyzes in her chapter "Reproductive Regulations in the Age of Sexual Epidemic," lends itself to epidemic logic, and can be read not only as a proliferation of discourse incited by the juridical status of semen and ovum, but as a discursive production that attempts to ward off a sexuality that is figured as proliferating outside the domain of the traditional family. Hence, Singer's critical practice is "to read the language, logic and contagious effects of the Baby M [legal] decisions as strategic discourses, operating within the hegemony of sexual epidemic."

In her final chapter, "Hospitalization and AIDS," Singer makes clear that the routinized modes of regulating bodies within hospital environments can be *resisted* through forms of patient advocacy. She calls for a *politicization* of cancer along the lines that AIDS activists have organized a politics of advocacy. Central to the kind of advocacy that she envisioned was the implementation of those conditions which would secure the effective articulation of patients' *demands*. She sought through cultural analysis to articulate the experience of mute and isolated suffering into that of a demand, an address, and thereby to transform a docile body into a linguistic actor in a social exchange. She knew as well that simply giving voice to suffering would not suffice, for the discourse within which one gives voice is a mode of exchange constituted in hierarchy that implicitly recirculated the regulatory apparatus. Hence, she sought to bring other discourses to bear on the medical regime—feminist, philosophical, political. And while she called into question the consumer model of patient rights as a late-capitalist device of power, she also sought to affirm the notion of patient agency implied by that model. She brought a number of discourses into the medical circuit of discursive exchange, jamming the system, disrupting its regulatory rhythms, performing criticism until the end.

Singer's mode of philosophical and cultural criticism redeploys strains of phenomenology (especially Merleau-Ponty and his account of style and the body), existential philosophy (Camus, his meditations on contingency and on the plague as a condition), radical feminism (Ti-Grace Atkinson's critique of heterosexuality as an institution as well as feminist critiques of patriarchy as a system), Foucault (discipline and pleasure), Baudrillard (the economy of signs), Laclau and Mouffe (the notion of hegemony and suturing) and French Feminism (especially Cixous and the question of how to generate feminist critique as/from the figure of excess). She also read widely in contemporary cultural and media criticism, and was committed both to film studies and cultural studies more generally.

But perhaps most important to her work was the situation of being a feminist philosopher, one who was grounded in the continental tradition but found her intellectual audience among those women and men who attended the sessions of the Society of Women in Philosophy, the Society for Phenomenological and Existential Philosophy, and the Radical Philosophy Association. These were forums in which she thrived, in which her work constituted a radically original and provocative contribution, in which she was an enormously respected member of the intellectual community. Within that subfield of philosophy called philosophy and feminism, at the time Linda was publishing and giving lectures, there were perhaps no more than twenty women philosophers in this country who were publically seeking to work philosophical connections between feminist theory and the philosophical figures of the continental tradition (Hegel, Nietzsche, Sartre, Merleau-Ponty); the same numbers were actively involved in writing about or through French Feminism, and even fewer were concerned with making connections between that tradition, feminist philosophy, and poststructuralist thought. Linda was one of the few who worked through Nietzsche and Merleau-Ponty, Foucault and French Feminism, and brought all this to bear on feminist politics and concrete economic and political issues of power and pleasure. Her eclecticism was a deliberate intellectual promiscuity, one which fit with her understanding of the postmodern complexity of power. She would impress and provoke her audience; the verbal and theoretical complexity of her performances was disarming and galvanizing. She was a fiercely committed teacher and insistently generous, and saw her task as that of radical empowerment. Her political anger was palpable, as was her desire to advocate, and to secure the conditions for effective advocacy, for women, but also for a wide range of subordinated groups. She sustained belief in the power of language, but she also insisted on working language, not merely for its power to communicate or to persuade, but rather for its potential as political spectacle and erotic scandal; she produced a verbal fire, on and off stage, that could not be contained. As a woman, she knew that it was already a scandal to become a philosopher, and to become one without forfeiting the precarious and enabling positioning that being a woman entailed within that profession and other social institutions structured by male privilege.

In Singer's opening discussion, she considers the double-bind of the woman philosopher who, as woman, is such a site of semantic and erotic excess, who is both outside the regime and of it, and who works that position of both/and to delimit the power ruse that sets and destabilizes the boundaries of philosophy's own possibility. If women are produced as that which is outside the disciplinary apparatus of philosophy *and* as that which must be radically subdued within philosophy (as a figure for the passions, the body, irrationality, social and political chaos), then women have no proper place within that profession, are always that which exceeds the propriety which that discipline insistently reinvokes. To be in the discipline as a site of excess is, then, both the effect of a certain complex ruse of subordination and the occasion to articulate a subversion and a resistance to that discipline itself. Singer remarks at the outset of her introduction, an introduction that I found in the form of drafts and notes, that her words on the page record an absence, that the words on the page are traces of an absence. What I think she meant by such words was that a woman performs a certain self-erasure to enter the discourse of philosophy, and that that absence persists in and by the words, resounds as an echo in the words, offering the words as signs whose meaning is always already at some remove from what appears. For what does it mean to speak or write within a philosophical discourse that presumes and produces the woman philosopher's exclusion and erasure? This was a hermeneutic problem that claimed Linda's attention, and she responded to that fix by speaking double, by insisting on the rhetoricity of philosophical discourse, and by stylizing almost every constative claim with irony.

She could not have known, I think, that the words which predicted and contained her absence would also be those which preserve her for us, and which mark the failure to preserve her, the irreplaceable loss.

Editing the Manuscript and Acknowledgments

Maureen MacGrogan at Routledge and I compiled the segments of the manuscript that Linda Singer had left. Throughout the academic year 1990–91, Maureen and I decided that the book ought to be divided into two parts: the first would be edited as the manuscript "Erotic Welfare: Sexual Theory and Politics in the

Age of Epidemic"; the second would be a selection of her recent writings on contemporary cultural politics and the status of feminism in relation to both conservative pronouncements of its demise and the challenge of postmodernism. We also decided that I would edit and write the introduction to Part I, and Maureen, who had encouraged Linda Singer to sign a contract for this book and who worked closely with her as friend and editor, would write the introduction to Part II.

Two chapters were near completion: "Regulating Women in the Age of Sexual Epidemic" and "Reproductive Regulations in the Age of Sexual Epidemic." There were two versions of "Disciplining Pleasures," one which appeared to be more finished than the other; they appeared to constitute two separate essays that did not overlap. They are edited and published together here as "Disciplining Pleasures." The "Author's Introduction" consisted in a series of drafts with some marginal notes written by Linda Singer indicating what ought to go where. On almost every occasion in which a decision presented itself on whether to include writing that did not appear directly to follow the preceding discussion or whether to omit that writing in the interests of coherence, we opted to find a way to include that writing. In some cases where the digression seemed pronounced, we chose to include the material as an endnote. No endnotes were supplied with the manuscript, and I know from conversations with Linda Singer that she imagined a book with a minimum of citations. We have tried to respect that wish at the same time that we have tried to provide some minimum guidance to those materials that are central to her analysis and to clarify some of the allusions to authors or texts. We have included a list of texts cited or mentioned in *Erotic Welfare* at the end of the book. The endnotes for Part II include complete bibliographical information at the end of each essay. On some occasions—e.g., the discussion of "addiction" in "Sex and the Logic of Late Capitalism," the final section of Part I, "Hospitalization and AIDS," and the section on "technology" in "Reproductive Regulations in the Age of Sexual Epidemic"—Linda Singer left notes that were not yet made into full sentences. I tried to work carefully with the material in each of these instances to replicate her style and grammar. For the most part, my additions consisted in supplying subjects and/or verbs to phrases which served as elliptical notes to herself.

The final section of Part I, "Hospitalization and AIDS," appears to be the last of her writings. She left notes indicating that she wanted these two sections to converge at the practical question of how to politicize patienthood. I organized the material in order to conform to what I understood and imagined her wishes to be. I told her before she died that I would make sure this work was published, and I have no way of knowing whether she would have wanted me to do this differently. She didn't want to talk about it.

I do know that Linda Singer would have wanted to thank her family, her colleagues, and her friends for their encouragement and support. And though it is surely a risky business to try to name those who were there for her as she undertook this project which meant the world to her, it is perhaps more risky to refuse the task. Her parents, Vivian and Eugene Singer, were loving to her, admired her and her work, were proud of her achievements, and encouraged her in ways that were profound and enduring; and then there were her friends who continued to love her in the face of her occasional protestations: Frances Bartkowski, James Creech, Dion Farquhar, Nicole Fermond, Carol Remond, Corien DeGong, Scott Kegelman; her brother, Paul; her editor at Routledge, Maureen MacGrogan, who supported her enthusiastically throughout. Her colleagues and friends at Miami University, especially William McKenna, Susan Jarrett, Peter Rose, Roy Ward. I imagine she would have thanked as well those feminist colleagues who have supported her work: Sandra Bartky, Judith Genova, Shere Hite, Jana Sawicki, Iris Young, Elizabeth Weed. And Martin Dillon, her mentor in the Department of Philosophy at SUNY-Binghamton, with whom she learned to speak philosophically about the body. And her students, who gave her enormous satisfaction, who taught her, and whom she empowered radically through her political pedagogy. And I'm sure there are scores of others to whom I apologize and explain that, although I try to speak for her here as I imagine she would want me to, I know that I err as I go. I have tried to be an advocate on the model that she called for, but my reading can never be the same as her writing.

Judith Butler
1992

I
Erotic Welfare

1

Author's Introduction

One remains loyal to the tradition because one has nothing to say about the doctrine itself.

Lacan, "Function and Field of Speech and Language," *Ecrits*

Writing a book is an act of presumption, assumption, and to that extent an act of hubris, a gesture that assumes that all that has come to represent orthodoxy and authority is somehow incomplete, in need of transgress, transcendence, and supplementation. A book always emerges from a lack, whose transitivity migrates between the world that seems to call for it and the writer whose lack invests the call with some kind of mobilizing significance. Although a book represents a condensation of a process of labor and struggle offered to readers for whom those struggles will never be visible (and if they are, it's a problem), hence an object of self-effacing sacrifice, it is also a gesture that already comes in the form of demand—a demand for time, energy, attention, advocacy, and maybe sympathy, from strangers for whom the author, if present is all, is so only as a structuring absence, the trace of a voice, a fictive persona, a point of view that recedes and is recast in each act of reading, yet whose name also becomes the place where failures, gaps, and errors are laid to rest.

The reader's decision to open the book, in some sense to activate it, is, despite the phenomena of synoptic reviews and word of mouth, essentially an act of faith which must trust or at least anticipate the very promise that the unread text represents. As a writer reflecting on the ironies of her own process and of the larger forms of exchange operative in the system of reading and writing, I both depend on those promissory protocols, but also find myself anxious in the face of them, anxious about the possibilities of fulfilling promises, or at least not making false ones. This opening somewhat polemical preamble is an attempt at least to circumvent some of those, by saying enough that those who should spend no further time here will be spared the temporal expenditure at the same time that I clearly hope to seduce others, in part by employing some of the strategies I have learned from a real master, the woman who uses the telling of stories to keep herself alive, the figure who has come down to us with the name *Scheherazade*. The figure of S is known to us, and this is not unusual, only through the representations produced by a member of her audience, i.e., only from the point of view of her addressees, her interlocutors, and her targets. That her effect, dare I say her power, is represented primarily through the figure of seduction is not surprising under the circumstances, nor is the tendency to emphasize her exoticness, her singularity, and her otherness. S certainly is an extraordinary figure, at least to the extent that she occupied a rather extraordinary position, namely, that of being a woman performing in and for the seat of power, a woman whose position was to perform power in a way that the powerful then simply could not do without. In this moment, S has produced the position from which she is no longer simply the object of the male gaze and its functional economy. Her stories, dances, performances also have the effect of dislocating or decentering power by capturing it in the shifting veils of its own misrecognitions. S's art was that of producing the story of how to disempower the resistances of that power to the very forms by which it itself is contested and resisted. Even though her feats are recounted from one who has already been figured by their effects, S does give us some clues, if one knows how to read this meta-story, i.e., against the grain, or between the veils.

One of S's major tactics, according to the legend we've received, was her dance of the seven veils. In this moment, S can be imagined exploiting the ambiguities of the play between the presence that has since seduced and produced Western metaphysics, and the discourses of its deconstruction, as evolutionary repetitions of the rituals of mastery still baring the pleasures of the fort/da game, the delight in differences. But S's reversal comes from the way in which her specular performance of difference also makes a difference in the economy of difference. This difference is neither that of the episodic reversals outlined in the master/slave dialectic in Hegel, nor in the seduction theory of Sartre. For Sartre, the transitivity of power is exchanged between positions that, although different, are different symetrically—one is a negation/denial of the other, hence the subtext of mutual dependency. The positions of men and women are different. They are opposite but they are opposite asymmetrically. Women in patriarchy cannot simply figure their transcendence in the death of the master, as the slave can. Nor is the moment at which they episodically capture the other by capturing his gaze, his body, his desire, the kind of act that has much negotiable currency beyond itself. S's power is neither that of the rebellious slave nor that of the seductress. Her power is that of performing the spectacle of difference which cannot be mastered. This disruption works, at some level, by confounding the anticipatory structures of a masculinist scopophilia and voyeurism, in which the truth is seen, illuminated, optimally and in the most neutral medium. S shows that the antinomies of this economy can be exploited in a way that disappointment is recoded as pleasure and as a perpetual promise. At one level S is a tease, but certainly one with whom her audience is more than complicit. Her success and their enjoyment depends on a mutual and unspoken compact of deception that not only willingly, indeed, desirously suspends or brackets disbelief, but also renders inoperative the categories of beliefs, warrants, and grounds in the world veiled by and through S's dance. The dance is a strip-tease, a ritual in the production and dissimulation of femininity. It is the performance of a feminine masquerade that promises but never unveils itself to its unseen producers, its audience, the men screened by the veils to the point where they are no longer the masters of presence and absence, no longer the markers of difference, the choreographers of the masquerade but rather, those whose expectations are constantly defied by the force of the spectacle to which they are now being subjected. S's genius was not only to make them want her by precisely never giving them what they wanted, but to do this in a way that made them only want more of the same. S's genius was that she perfected her craft under the gaze of those at whom she aimed without ever tipping her hand. Each one of those thousand and one nights, she could entertain them with the stories of the strategies by which she kept herself, and many other women after her, alive.

Now, S is probably not the most apt figure for appropriation by a philosopher, even or maybe especially if that philosopher is also female and a feminist. Seduction, the strip-tease, the veil are not traditional philosophical tools. Philosophers are supposed to be the voices that remove men from the realm of caves and shadow into the light. Not a compact of deception, but of truth. But in many ways S is a very apt figure for the woman philosopher, who is bound to need different figures with which to decorate her space. Because S does produce a truth, a truth about difference and power and stories—and it is partly the truth of strategics and the subtleties of performance, particularly the performance of stories that are always also seductions, and therefore the situations in which the performer must always be other than what is performed. It is that very difference that kept S, and many of us since, alive.

So, for my part, I want to try to put in play the lesson of S, by performing some of what I see as my difference, without tipping my hand. It begins with my recognition of the different addresses I intend or imagine for this work, and what might be read, or projected on one's anxious days, as radically differing sets of expectations and demands. Sartre says, I think rightly, that to write is first to choose for whom one writes. Speech, writing are to and for and from the Other(s). Who those others are likely to be, particularly for a book of this kind, are already to some extent predetermined or over-determined by traditional divisions of knowledge and the institutionalization of disciplinary differences. In this respect, the book is written by someone who was trained in philosophy and wants to be read by philosophers, at the same time that the effect of this reading is intended to destabilize and contest the contemporary constitution of philosophy's boundaries and conventions. Of course, I also want this book to be read by people not trained in philosophy, including many feminists, I imagine, who may be actively hostile to philosophy insofar as it marks a particularly conspicuous example of masculinist hegemony. The question of audience, the kind that becomes a real issue in writing, however, is not one of market sociology, but rather is played out in the question of language, voice, position, and context.

In this respect, I am engaged in the ultimately paradoxical project of trying to seduce those whose business it is to steel themselves against seduction. I propose to tell stories of a difference that will exploit the very power they aim to contest or destabilize. In terms of textual strategies, this means that much of this discourse will speak from or on the basis of that which has been taught to me as "the history of philosophy," but will do so in a very unorthodox way. Such confrontations with the law are encoded in a figure of anxiety, that is part of what the law is for; and hence my opening evocation of an erstwhile father from whom it is also easy to maintain an ironic distance and a kind of authorization for my enterprise of intervening in what another superlative tactician, Hélène Cixous, calls "the chain of fathers." Because times and especially the instruments of power have changed significantly since S's days, I will need more than veils to do the work, especially because I also lack her grace and other charms. Only some of that charm can be passed along in a discursive chain between prospective adoptive mothers, fathers, and their children. Hence, a need to produce/perform a dance of self-authorization, like Scheherazade, a masquerade of masking and unmasking. The mobilizing fiction here is that of the bandita.

The bandita is a fiction born, like the fiction of a discourse of truth opposed to fiction, from lack, desire and demand. The bandita fiction is the mobilizing myth of successful transgression, the figure whose legend and mystique lie precisely in her abilities both to transgress its boundaries and to escape capture by eluding the logic of the posses that pursue her. She has no proper name—she is the figure of impropriety. She keeps moving in and out of the shadows. Unlike S, she is not confined to a single space. She can appear anywhere, and we can learn much here about the tactics of quick movement and surprise and movements of resistance to capture by law. Her performance, unlike S's, works best when there is no one watching, since she supports herself, as many dispossessed people do, as a trader, in this case, of the relics she has ruthlessly appropriated by robbing graves, taking that which can be translated into negotiable currency, i.e., that which has or is of value, and leaving the remainder. She does not seduce her pursuers through veils, she lassoes them, encircling with a force that can be instrumentally immobilizing. She stuns first and asks questions later. Her aim can be uncanny, and her life depends on it.

The bandita is successful in transgressing and eluding the law because she understands and in some sense identifies with it, albeit from the other side. She is an outlaw only through and by its office. It is from the side of the law that her legend is produced; as compensation for its own lack, this legend learns to produce pleasure in the subversion of the law. But living as she does at the frontiers, crossing and traversing borders at will, unimpeded save by the limits of her energy, her very mobility is also a source of anxiety, a terrorist in the kingdom where the dead and private property are supposedly sacred. The bandita survives outside the sphere of domesticated stabilized identities. It is not that she has no attachments, but that her attachments are polymorphous, outside the fixed economies of exchange of family and kinship. Her way of life represents a form of refusal, specifically, a refusal of the role of object of exchange in favor of a position from which she can at least cut her own deal, and if there are ties that bind, she is the one tying the knot. Such adventurism, when it is female, is often recoded as promiscuous and, in this sense, the bandita is a figure not of too little loyalty but of too much, preserving the effective surplus from all those she has encountered in her travels, a surplus that is both gift and compensation for a life lived always on the way.

All authorial personae, and perhaps authors themselves, are constructions. Such constructions are both chosen and found, happen to us as we happen to them, and are therefore also overdetermined. They reveal, disclose, represent, seduce, offend, symbolize to and for a reader, or better, in a more hopeful mode, readers. There they work, or fail to, within a differential calculus that no construction could consciously anticipate, much less try to accommodate. Maybe personae, or voice, as Malraux said of style, really emerges only in and through the other. But voices are not accidental, and these days they also cannot really be unselfconscious. Too much theory from too many places has killed or at least ironized any claims to textual innocence, as readers or writers. Even if all that is written here is only a proliferation of signs, we are the products of their manipulation and, therefore, how one writes this matters.

What does the trope of the bandita imply? Playing with the remains of dead men, ruthless pillaging, taking what's needed and leaving the rest. The bandita recycles these remains, rather than recasting them as reliquary objects of display, under glass, protected from desecration. They are already desecrated—and also embalmed by others. The remains recycled make a different map, and mark new intersections between discourses, disciplines, forms of "knowledge." The bandita, according to legend, is promiscuous, and this book is not only intellectually incestuous but paradigmatically promiscuous, bedding with many, remaining with none, loyal to no single woman or man. The bandita cannot stay on the main roads but has to find her own way. Even if others have been this way before, the trails are not clearly marked. That might very well defeat the purpose (there is no honor amongst thieves, and probably less amongst their pursuers). Not all routes are the right ones. There is digression, and indirection, in part because one never knows where one is safe, especially when administrations change so often. Sometimes the problem is that one is not sure where one wants to go, or one only knows how to get to places one can or no longer wishes to be. The bandita moves quickly. She has to. Often this speed works to her advantage, there is so much ground to cover. Sometimes not, and something is missed along the way. But even though she moves alone or in small bands, the pace of her progress is not entirely self-determined, although it is determined by what she is pursuing, and what is pursuing her. This cannot be helped. It comes with the territory.

Banditas take risk, and despite their well-deserved reputation for bravery and brazenness, they also get scared sometimes. Such fright is certainly not entirely unfounded. Not all silence is comforting, not all surveillance is sympathetic. At such moments, they wonder why or when they stopped being dutiful daughters, and try to retrieve the desires that brought them to this place. Most of the time we can remember.

These fictions of feminine authority represent my effort to find/construct a way to speak as one identified as/with the problematic fiction, "woman philosopher." My reflections on this problematic are offered in recognition that this possibility is one with a certain historical specificity, and that until recently that conjunction, as problematic as it is, could not have been made at all, a designation withheld as a means of denying whatever legitimacy or inscribed authority that term now contains to the works which offer the thinking of women. The position of a woman philosopher is structured by the space between—a space of contradictions to be spanned by attempting precisely to try, to dwell or, at least, to work in a place from which one is also always already exiled, dispossessed, a space of difference produced by/as a consequence of the difference between the frontiers that give the territory its particular labyrinthine shape.

These complications, moreover, are not only structural, but proliferate in the form of ambivalence and conflict that are operative at the epistemic and existential levels, the nexus of which is often coded as the dilemma of the postmodern. The postmodern economy is one in which systems and currencies of exchange and linkages between them have so proliferated that any notion of fixed identity dissolves in the momentum and range of these exchanges, a technological extension of the bandita's life on the roads between. That the text that follows is postmodern is likely only in the sense that it takes the postmodern to be the place from which one writes, the place that is precisely not a place, but a network of places linked by the movements by which they become places along the way. The text is the process of linking that which has not yet been mapped in quite this way or is the fiction by which the lack is being specifically put into play in my performance. This linkage will involve a transgression of the traditional frontiers and borders by which the map of Western knowledge is usually drawn. This redrawing of the map is not a matter of or in the manner of a simultaneous projection. It does not presume or assume the integrity of the space it enters, an integrity that emerges only for a point of view at a distance and at great height. The kind of mapping I propose is more in the manner of producing tales that precisely are designed not to end, to perpetuate the telling as a way of staying alive, and to do so by moving through a space that one is not mastering, but moving through, because it has not been thoroughly mapped, projected, surveyed by the eyes of the law.

Juggling may be the best metaphor for what I'm doing—juggling, depending on one's paradigmatic affiliations, signs, referents, contexts, ideas, events, theories. On the one hand, I want to talk about historical specificities—sexual epidemic in the 1980s and its implications for contemporary sexual politics. On the other hand, I want also to exploit this as an occasion for a (again depending on one's paradigm) broader, more conceptual, theoretical, abstract, visionary, speculative discourse on the relationship between sex, power, and philosophy. Already a problematic if not to say presumptuous concept, certainly one that is likely to be hard to market. Where to place such a book—inside or outside philosophy, the women's section, sociology, speculative metaphysics? This is no small consideration in a historical moment where the division and production of knowledge is not unrelated to the structures of the commodity.

From the other side, where does this text place itself—already problematic—whom does it address, from where, for what end? And why should anybody care, and who wants to be just another false prophet on the remainder table, if one's text gets that far? What justifies such an undertaking?—i.e., the expenditure of at least my time and resources, and presumably, should this make it to print, the time and energy of the readers, as well as of those who will print, edit, market the product of my labors. Who am I and where am I in writing this—from what voice, syntactic and otherwise? Why the first person to begin, when the question of identity is at stake? Am I the associate professor tenured at a midwestern university, trained in the history of philosophy, or the teacher of feminism and women's studies? Or am I the child who learned to command attention through words? Is mine a position of privilege or vulnerability—the privilege that follows from being white, middle-class, educated, tenured, the vulnerability that comes from being a woman, in a marginal area of a marginal discipline and the position of isolation that often induces? There are other privileges and vulnerabilities that could be stipulated—some in fact are likely interchangeable, others ambiguous (where does one place being heterosexual, for example?). What is the fiction that seems both to necessitate and to undermine the process of disclosing, confessing one's position, and why is that relevant?

As I write this, I find my mind inhabited by two different tropes of the feminine writer—Beauvoir's "dutiful daughter" and Gallop's notion of "the daughter's seduction." In some sense, the strategy and construction of this text will occur within an economy of ambivalence with respect to these tropes. Like the dutiful daughter, I will confess, I will labor to demonstrate my entitlement, dare I say my authority to speak by showing that I speak in light of what others have already said. Ideally, that intertextual edifice ought be distinguished by its breadth, depth and selectivity—I should have read a lot, or at least "enough" (already a rather elastic category) and "the right people." This already raises the question of audience, and by extension politics—textual and otherwise. Who is right depends on who is speaking and who is being spoken to: the profession of philosophy, feminists, activists, the impulse book buyer? How much is enough—and too much? The dutiful daughter worries about such things. They often keep her from writing. Whence rises the image of seduction? The sense of never being good enough produces the intellectual siren, Scheherazade seducing with her stories, the dance of the seven veils and seven theories, a perpetual play of simulations. This book is nothing if not intellectually promiscuous, an exercise in paradigmatic polymorphous perversity. It is either jargony or allusive. It is certainly "intertextual." But it is so in what are admittedly perverse and problematic ways which I both cannot help but try to anticipate and, if you will, defend or at least explain, as the dutiful philosopher is trained to do.

Beyond the problematics attached to my speculative scope and presumptions, many of the terms of my analysis—like sex, power, the body, male and female—are always already reifications which can and perhaps should be deconstructed, subjected to an analytic of difference or avoided by virtue of their hegemonic surplus. Each term, no matter how carefully defined and used, will suffer from both vagueness and compression which will both deflect and reflect further specification. Closely related is the problem of relevance, which is context-specific and, hence, variable. Because my text will draw from a range of current and not-so-current theories, without using/privileging one as a regulatory scheme for the others, the text will likely operate in a sustained spirit of transgression of paradigmatic codes and etiquette. Further related is the plurality of voices that accompanies this proliferation of paradigms. My analysis will operate both at the existential level of the first person as well as at the level of historical and structural discourses of the third person. Given the nature of my subject matter, I find this strategy of syntactic slippage unavoidable. Nonetheless, in spite of the formidability of these obstacles and problematics, I choose to proceed (existentialist origins rearing their heads).

Why use the occasion of sexual epidemic for reflecting on the relationship between sex, power, and philosophy? Is the juxtaposition of the noble claims and tropes of philosophy—truth, knowledge, logic, order—with the random movement of contagion between sweaty bodies itself a heresy, an indication of my transgressive perverseness? Clearly the question is posed from the assumption, for which incidentally I have some anecdotal evidence, that there are those in the discipline with which I am primarily identified who would answer in the affirmative. Two lines of defense can be offered for this position. The first is the view that philosophy is situated in or operates from a "presuppositionless" position free of prejudice, bias, allegiance, or identification with any particular socially identifiable affiliation—including gender, race, class, and ideology. A revisionist version of this position has emerged in response to the critique lodged on the basis of the sociology of knowledge argument, namely, that to the extent that such affiliations do infiltrate philosophical process, they factor in as contingent rather than necessary elements. Hence, the equation of "philosophy" with the thought of white privileged males is mere coincidence, rather than an essential element establishing both the credibility and legitimacy of the philosophical enterprise, and hence in no way essentially connected to the influence and power, at least in discursive circles, that philosophers traditionally assume for themselves.[1]

I have chosen to write in the name of "sexual epidemic" as a rubric under which to link a range of theoretical and political questions that have emerged around sexuality in a variety of registers. It is a discourse prompted by, speaking after, the circulation of AIDS as a social signifier, but it is not a text that means to dance around the graves of the dead.

The subtitle of this text situates the writing in a historical moment in which sexual theory and politics are being yet again transfigured by their mediation through the construct of epidemic. The impetus for the emergence of such a signifier is of course the condition that has come to be known as AIDS, but it seems equally obvious that AIDS is not the site of anxiety, not the only form of unregulated proliferation which has been represented as epidemic. Indeed, as metaphors of sickness and health come to dominate the representation of the social, we are confronted by an ever increasing number of cancers, viruses infecting the body politic through mechanisms of contagion and communicability. In order to represent a phenomenon as socially undesirable, be it divorce, drug use, single motherhood, teenage pregnancy, one need only call it epidemic. In doing so, one not only engages in a kind of rhetorical inflation, but also mobilizes a certain apparatus and logic, a particular way of producing and organizing bodies politically. An epidemic is a phenomenon that in its very representation calls for, indeed, seems to demand some form of managerial response, some mobilized effort of control. To the extent that epidemics come to function as a ground for the mobilization of social resources, they operate as more than metaphors of the social. They also function as political logics, forms of social rationality. It is the historically specific operation of the logic of this sexual epidemic that I hope to elaborate.

In considering the contemporary sexual epidemic as a political construct, I do not mean to imply either that there exists some singular origin or intentionality behind this design, or that the strategic apparatus it generates and makes use of is unilateral, consistent, or coherent. There may be tenuous consensus that the situation calls for changes, but the nature and direction of those changes are very much a site of contest and discord. It is also a struggle that is taking place on a variety of fronts and on terrains that are neither comparable nor necessarily compatible.

One site of struggle for the sexual epidemic is certainly bodies, bodies already inscribed with regulatory encodings like gender and race. These regulatory devices are revised and contested, not only by subjects identified with those bodies, but also by competing disciplines and techniques of body management. At this juncture the boundaries of bodies have become liminally engaged by the culture of simulations, the terrains of representations and images, disciplines and practices, gestures, ideologies and institutions. The polymorphous proliferation induced by the epidemic situation is a consequence of its destabilizing effects. An epidemic is already a situation that is figured as out of control, hence at least indirectly a recognition of the limits of existing responses, hence a call for new ones. Because the destabilization effect is also represented as a threat, a threat to the very order of things, epidemic conditions tend to evoke a kind of panic logic which seeks immediate and dramatic responses to the situation at hand. As a consequence, epidemic logic tends to promote the proliferation of opposing forms of response— those which depend on extending and intensifying existing regulatory schemata (what might be called the conservative agenda), and a tendency to ironize or otherwise supplement those existing forms, using the crisis as an occasion to demonstrate critically their limits, and by extension to take this as an occasion to introduce other items into the societal agenda.

The notion of "erotic welfare" toward which this text represents some move-ment, some desire, intention, proleptic imaginary, entails a rethinking of the socio-psycho material constitution of the realm we have collected under the term "desire." It will entail a consideration of how we come to know, feel, represent, produce, reproduce, exchange, and authorize what we want, what gives or is pleasure, what constitutes the thresholds of necessity, scarcity, and surplus. The use of the term "welfare" is intended to allude both to the sphere of value, ethics, specifically an ethic of benevolence, and to the sphere of political economy and social utility. It is a way of reopening the questions of whether what we want (or say or feel or think we want) can also, in some sense, be good for us. It is an attempt to interrogate the frameworks in terms of which such judgments or determinations might be made. This is, therefore, a strategic discourse, tied to, enabled, and prompted by conditions that help to construct a "sexual epidemic" which are not necessarily transferable and which, in some sense, this text works, in true postmodern fashion, to render obsolete.

Because the notion of "welfare" is intelligible only in terms of social systems of production and exchange, the question of erotic welfare already engages the sphere of political economy—sexual and otherwise. Given the hegemonic apparatus of genital condensation and phallocentric primacy in the inscription of bodies, that sphere consolidated under the term "sexuality" will be a primary component of our consideration. Given, however, that that which is consolidated by the term "sexuality" is also displaced and proliferated by that term, any attempt to analyze the construction of desire will necessitate engaging related semiotic systems: e.g., production and consumption, life and death, health and disease, necessity and excess.

Within the framework of a logic of sexual epidemic, images of erotic access and mobility shift registers from those associated with freedom, surplus, choice, recreation to those of anxiety, unregulated contact, and uncontrolled spread. Communication has become communicability; access is now figured as an occa-sion for transmission and contagion. The early phases of this sexual epidemic display those symptoms: countries, including the United States, reconsider conditions for admitting tourists and immigrants and other measures designed to limit the mobility and contact of people with AIDS. Indeed, one early narrative of origins attributes the importation of AIDS to the US to a particularly promiscuous airline steward who is said to have contracted the disease during one of his frequent trips to the Caribbean. Within the imaginary of the sexual epidemic, such images of erotic access and mobility are cathected with desire and *ressentiment*.

In light of this contradictory logic, one might consider that for Camus, the plague signifies a rupture in the order of things; it stalls and limits liberal optimism, especially the proliferative notion of choice, the expansive logic of progress. Now the plague functions as a rupture in the (optimistic) sexual political economy, specifically in the progressive logic of the sexual revolution. Now we see the contradictions that structure the logic of a liberalism that at once promotes the progressive expansion of choice but also establishes limits to tolerance, pluralism, choice, and utility.

The sexual epidemic is rife with opportunities for conflicting political inscriptions. The anxiety induced by the regulatory production of the epidemic is conducive to conservative political agendas. The anxiety that becomes mobilized around the connection of sex to death in AIDS entails an increased fetishization of life as such. Hence, the anxiety produced through the epidemic is displaced and condensed in the regulation of sexual reproduction and the promotion of the family as the supposedly exclusive site of safe sex.

Epidemic logic depends on certain structuring contradictions, proliferating what it seeks to contain, producing what it regulates. The logic of epidemic depends upon the perpetual revival of an anxiety it seeks to control, inciting a crisis of contagion that spreads to ever new sectors of cultural life which, in turn, justify and necessitate specific regulatory apparatus which then compensate— materially and symbolically—for the crisis it has produced. Although epidemic logic is not unique to the social construction and approach to questions of disease and health, the emergence of AIDS has provided, or has become an occasion for, its reinvigoration and spread to areas far afield. Now there are "epidemics" of child abuse, pornography, teenage pregnancies.

Epidemic logic works through a strategy of regulated production. In this case, the production of anxiety follows from the isolation of some phenomena which have reached quantitatively undesirable proportions, anxieties which are then to be allayed by specific measures or larger strategies aimed at addressing the problems so named. Hence, epidemic logic interpellates its subjects, not only through rational persuasion or empirical induction, but by exercising a kind of control through incitement. In this sense, the force of this logic's credibility is much the same as that by which advertising and marketing discourses establish their own authority.

Advertising and marketing are crucial supplementary apparatuses in a capitalist political economy that depends on ever-increasing production. The purpose of advertising is, needless to say, to incite patterns of ever-increasing consumption, where that consumption is no longer tied to potentially regulating devices like need or material necessity. Advertising works either through the mobilization and displacement of desires onto commodities—the girl on the car hood—or by generating problems and crises for which it can then offer a palliative commodity. The ideal of advertising is the creation of surplus demand as well as brand-loyal repeat purchasers, i.e., consumers for whom consumption has become a necessity.

Advertising depends at once on both the mobilization and proliferation of desire and its restriction to a particular object or commodity (the desire not just for a car, but for an Oldsmobile). This explains in part the military tactics of "targeting" markets (which involve tactics of proliferation and specific targeting of force). This also explains the multiple encodings of the same message, designed to appeal to already established patterns and conditions of consumption and reception.

Concerns about health can be used to justify any number of interventions into the lives of bodies and the forms of exchange in which they move as well as to provide an occasion around which to mobilize social assets and resources. The epidemic inscription therefore functions as a socially authoritative discourse, which also both draws upon and generates mechanisms for its own legitimation. This point is supported by Foucault's analysis of the regulatory force of epidemics, which, he argues, could only exist with supplementation by the police, and an apparatus of surveillance. Under the logic incited by epidemics, forms of regulatory intervention into the lives of bodies and populations which might, in other circumstance, appear excessive can now appear as justified forms of damage control and prophylactic protectionism.

We can see symptoms of this aspect of the epidemic logic operating in the increasing public calls and sympathy for a range of interventionist and regulatory practices, including mandatory AIDS testing, calls for quarantining those with AIDS, proposals about mandatory notification of sexual partners, and the suggestion that those who have tested positive be tatooed in order to indicate their condition to others. Although such measures can be seen as and are often argued to be violations of privacy, a notion central to liberal ideology, the authorized panic induced by epidemic conditions can be and, in this case, has been used to justify and rationalize what would otherwise be rejected as intolerable interventions and interference with freedom of choice and expression. Hence a regulatory apparatus legitimated by its utility as an anti-contagion device can itself become contagious, and circulate to other sites in other forms. In a climate induced by epidemic, it becomes reasonable to intervene into the bodies of others. In the name of protecting the health and well-being of the social body, it is only logical to try not only to close gay bathhouses and clubs, but also to test employees for drugs, athletes for steroids, and to restrict further the situations in which alcohol and cigarettes may be purchased and consumed.

Because epidemics justify and are in fact constructed in order to necessitate a complex system of surveillance and intervention, epidemic situations often provide occasions for the reinstitution of hegemonic lines of authority and control (Risse, Patton, Brandt). With respect to this sexual epidemic in particular, there is much evidence that it has provided conservative forces with a unique opportunity to re-market their own rather specific and rigid social agendas. The ideological surplus mobilized and organized by epidemic logic may help explain why it is that the forms of discourse primarily responsible for circulating this hegemony have come not from medical or public health officials, but from political and ideological advocates. Conservative groups with a range of interests as diverse as those of Lyndon Larouche and Jerry Falwell have been able to exploit the anxiety operative in plague conditions as a basis for support not only for regulating the bodies of those in the high-risk groups, like gays and drug users, whose bodies are fetishized as vials of contagion and death, but also for controlling the processes by which life is generated, in the form of a proposed constitutional amendment against abortion, limitation on support for sex education and contraception, and opposition to the development of reproduction technologies.

The New Right has been successful in exploiting the AIDS phenomenon for its own purposes, at least in part because such discourse recognizes that plagues are never just medical problematics, and the anxieties they help foment far exceed those of self-preservation and prudence. This explains their success in mobilizing anxiety and concern among those populations, like heterosexual Christians, who are at the least risk of contracting this sexually and intravenously transmitted virus. That is because, as another theorist of plagues, Albert Camus, points out, plagues are never just medico-bureaucratic problematics. They are also world-transforming moments of ontological crisis which permeate the entire logic and fabric of a community's existence by calling it into question in a fundamental way, i.e., within the currency of life and death. A plague, according to Camus, always marks a radically anxious point of rupture in the economy of the everyday and its system of stabilized and sedimented significations. Faced with a plague, one can no longer simply go on with business as usual. One is forced to call one's habits, values, and pleasures into question, precisely because the world in which they had a place is in the process of slipping away, disrupted in a way that always feels like an imposition, and seems unjustified, senseless.

Part of the appeal of the conservative position is that it offers a radical and totalizing form of explanatory closure. The sexual epidemic is given sense, treated as a retributive consequence of past transgressions, which now return to consume the sources of pollution themselves, as well as claiming what are represented as "innocent victims." In the social imaginary offered, AIDS is but a symptom of the loss or erosion of authority, i.e., absolutist, religious, paternalistic authority, which was better suited to organize energies for socially useful purposes like reproduction and consumption. The failure to heed that authority, in the name of "liberalization," "tolerance," or "sexual liberation," lies at the root of the crisis as we now suffer the consequences of sexual proliferation, which threatens not only our physical well-being, but our spiritual health as well.

The establishment of a connection between epidemic and transgression through a consequentialist logic of judgment is certainly not a strategy unique to this age, and is as old as the story of the plagues from the Old Testament. It was certainly a central element in the medieval social logic. Its recapitulation in recent papal documents confirms its longevity and hence, at some level, its utility. As Camus' narrative ironically demonstrates, such discourse does give sense to what seems without reason, gives form or order to what otherwise seems an impersonal and indifferent movement of contagion. What is specific to this epidemic is the way such a logic is being used, not only as ground for conserving hegemonic forms of authority, but also as a basis from which to engage in revisionist interventions and initiatives designed not to conserve but to reverse the direction of public policy in a variety of areas, as well as to serve as the basis for a critical revisionist reading of the sexual revolution as a way of marketing an alternative ideology centered on buzz words like "family values."

Notes

1. Surely what I have come to recognize as the figures of my eternal return—power and desire—are those of which I have been in perpetual pursuit and those which have motivated and continue to motivate philosophy. Philosophy, as a historically enduring enterprise, has a great deal to do with power and desire, albeit in many senses indirectly.

Some relations which come to mind:

1. Philosophy is one of the powers of masculinity; it excludes and marginalizes women; it exercises conceptual domination over women and sexual difference through the constitution of its various spheres of relevance and forms of construction.

2. Philosophy is constantly marking out its turf; it is perpetually in a struggle with skepticism, against which philosophy asserts its territorial imperative on behalf of knowledge and truth; philosophy is impelled by a desire to know, a desire to know what can be known, a desire to know when/that one knows.

3. Philosophical knowledge can thus be understood as possible formations of desire, a desire in philosophy and for philosophy; this is desire as possession, i.e., to possess the logic, laws, generative grammar of all that is, to encompass the world within boundaries of mind and system; this is a desire for a demiurgic and procreative power: to be the origin of the explanation of the world, to reproduce its genesis discursively and conceptually.

4. There are counterformations within philosophy, derived from the Kantian tradition of self-criticism, apparent in the work of Derrida, in which there is a setting of limits to what can be known and experienced, in which there is a pleasure in limits.

Texts have varied and strange beginnings—if not grounds. To write a text which demands of readers (i.e., strangers) an investment of time, energy, and attention on the basis of some vague and unstatable promise is already an act of some presumption. To write/speak of things so highly charged as power and desire is worse still, or maybe better—in any case, it is a risky endeavor. In light of this risk, I am prone, on occasion, to retreat/regress to a desire for a myth of origins—a rephrasing/rewriting of the child's question "Where did I come from?" which now emerges as "Where does this/it come from?" So far, there are no stories with which I play.

The first question is easier, but perhaps less significant, because it is more easily isolated as a discrete event, although its significance emerged only retrospectively. Sometime in the summer of 1985 I was engaged in a getting-acquainted conversation with a man and a woman who have since become good friends (and cohabitants). At one point, they were engaged in an animated discussion of their experiences with meditation, to which I found myself listening with only half an ear. Although (or perhaps because) both are engaged in mentally demanding professions—he is a lawyer/arbiter, she a college professor—they each valued the cleansing effects of meditation, which they described, as I recall, as a process of emptying or silencing of the mind, which brought them both a real measure of pleasure. At this point, as I remember, I found myself erupting with an uncontrolled urgency usually reserved for intimates. In retrospect, I believe my outburst to have been fueled by a certain anxiety/horror: "Empty the mind?! I just can't relate to that. I spend all my time desperately trying to fill mine up." As I now read this, the outburst marked a point of difference or distance which was for me most revealing. It was a moment in which I got some sense of location within a psychological economy of power and desire that both distanced me from the meditative personality and also helped to re-explain the series of choices I have made as an adult. The most significant of these choices is, in this context, my decision to study and pursue a career in philosophy, to wit, a profession of perpetual reflection and self-criticism.

2

Sex and the Logic of Late Capitalism

A few words about the chapter title. It should be clear that when I invoke the term "sex," I am not referring to some innate or ahistorically given set of biological or instinctual predispositions, but to a set of practices, techniques, behavior, language, signs that are already, from the very outset, social, i.e., they presuppose or are emergent with reference to the Other. The conjunction of terms in the title should not, therefore, be read as a promise to produce that which might emerge by a separation of the two terms conjoined, i.e., as a retrieval of some pristine sexuality from the grips of capitalist logic, or the re-invention of some post-capitalist form. By use of the conjunction I hope to call attention to what I read as a relationship of reciprocal constitution between them, i.e., the terms opposed then conjoined are really correlatives, like play and work, each of which comes to take on its signification in and through this relationship, a relationship that, as I hope to show, is not seamless, i.e., is not without its points of contradiction, opposition, and contest.

There is an extensive literature documenting this dynamic with two key figures circulating prominently within it, the philosophers of play and work, Freud and Marx. There are the various re-readings of their intersecting points and divergences (Reich, Fromm, Marcuse, Slater) and those that seek in some sense to inaugurate a post discourse (Althusser, Lacan, Nancy, Lyotard). Although this work depends and relies on this literature, my aim here is far less ambitious; i.e., I am not attempting to give a systemic or genetic account of this relationship, but rather, I intend to focus on some specific contradictions emergent as a consequence or as strategic responses to the sexual epidemic.

One of the linking tropes derived from the literature is that of economy—i.e., sexuality or libido can be thought of as a political economy, a systemic grid of differences which produce, circulate, and order value. In a capitalist logic, the primary value to be produced and accumulated is surplus value or profit. Late capitalism, by which I mean the historical form now operative in first world industrial and post-industrial nations, represents a specific development of this logic, and is a system of such significant complexity that I cannot do justice to it in this context. But from this complexity I am interested in extracting certain agenda, priority, and strategies following from the transformation of value to that of profit, and to show how sexual epidemic provides both occasions for its extension and points at which the contradictions which are also produced provide special problems for the projects of sexual management.

In late capitalist economies, profit is generated less from the primary production of material goods, and far more from the production of services—a move from an economy geared toward production to a knowledge and service economy, or, as Baudrillard claims, simulation. Furthermore, the basic strategies for maximizing profitability (i.e., cost-effectiveness) are now being applied to the accumulation of capital as such (the intensification of profitability through the manipulation of the markers of profitability: currencies, stocks, foreign exchange, etc.). The aforementioned shift can be explained vis-à-vis this kind of cost-effectiveness, i.e., primary production is no longer the most efficient way to accumulate profit.

Because the accumulation of profit depends upon extracting the value of what the worker produces and transferring it to someone else, and because work is organized in a way to make the most profitable use of the worker's time (that is, it is already alienated), capitalism has always demanded a disciplined work force, a body of workers capable of working their bodies in a way responsive to social demands and utilities.[1] Following this logic through the strategic mediations provided by Foucault, sexuality emerges in the capitalist discipline as both that which is to be disciplined, and that which remains as excess or resistance to discipline and therefore must also be pacified, accommodated, indulged. It is also, consequently, that which must also be socially managed and coordinated to maximize its social utility, i.e., its profitability.

Logic of capitalism depends not only on control over surplus or production, but also on the production of scarcity, or controlled scarcity. The notion of scarcity is crucial to capitalism—both as its justification (there's not enough, especially now, of what we need to survive; therefore, let's control it so that the maximum number of people benefit by it—production of surplus) and sometimes, at least, as that for which capitalism is the remedy. Without scarcity, there would be no value. But scarcity must always be articulated: it must be constructed usually by reference to a nexus of needs and desires. Hence, capitalism must also be perpetually creating needs—and here later capitalism, not of primary production but reproductions and simulations—has developed in a way that significantly diverges from the classic form represented in Marx.

When the profit logic is applied to sexuality understood in this sense, a clear difference emerges as two separable but not necessarily oppositional profit centers useful for generating negotiable social currency, sectors I will summarily term the reproductive and the erotic. The utility of reproduction for a system dependent upon perpetual expansion is obvious. Profit accumulation will always depend upon the production of workers, preferably more than are necessary at any given time so as to keep wages down, and upon an ever-expanding body of consumers and heirs. The development of sciences like demographics, fertility and contraceptive technology, and population control provide clear evidence that this crucially vital social function is not being left to chance. But profitability is not limited to a question of numbers and distribution. Following the principle of both multiplying and extending profit centers, reproduction is organized to be done in the most profitable way, i.e., with the least investment of social resources. Where reproduction generates profits in the form of commodity consumption, this results in a shift in the signification of the reproductive unit (the biological family) from a site of production to that of consumption.

But this strategy depends on mobilizing that which is excluded, namely, the erotic excess, the non-utilitarian dimensions of sexuality which are often summarized under the sign of pleasure. As many thinkers from Marcuse to Foucault have pointed out, capitalism works not only by opposing itself to the pleasure principle, but by finding strategic ways to mobilize it, a form of control by incitement, not by the repression but by the perpetual promise of pleasure, i.e., of that which is denied by the profit-producing process. The genius of late capitalism is the development of strategies for managing and profiting by its own excess. Two basic strategies are condensation and displacement, which correspond to genital primacy and commodity fetishism.

As a consequence of its success, late capitalism has largely succeeded in establishing the articulation of needs and desires along two basic axes—genital gratification and satisfaction through consumption. These two elements converge in the construct of leisure, that sphere of time which is not work. In the contemporary organization of time, leisure functions as that which is both compensatory and inciting, viz., work (when one is unemployed, one is not at leisure). But as the product of discipline, it also functions as a site of resistance. Leisure time is certainly a major profit sector.

Although the logic of late capitalism would demand an enlargement of erotic and reproductive commodities, this logic does not operate seamlessly but finds its limits regarding an oppositional profit logic in terms of which sexual labor, reproductive and erotic, must also remain the only form of labor which is unpaid and uncompensated. This opposition and the contradictions it produces are not without strategic value, a value that is both economic and psychological/ideological. Although that value will become clearer as things proceed, one point of contradiction proper to capitalism needs to be emphasized from the outset: on the one hand, paid labor under capitalism marks that labor as alienated; on the other hand, capitalist sexual political economy seeks to preserve the status of sex work as unalienated labor, allowing the disciplinary dimensions to recede or be displaced by its mobilizing functions as a mechanism for resistance, transgression, opposition to the sphere of demand. As a consequence, sexuality functions in a late capitalist economy as a prototype or emblem not only of alienation, but also of freedom, and that in the name of which demands can be made of an alienating social system.[2] But this depends precisely on setting limits to the process of commodification. Sexual commodities depend for their value on the existence of a sphere of uncommodified sexuality, as the demand for the segregation of sexual work from the compensatory economy of wage labor only makes sense once sexuality has been constituted as that which is always subject to the logic of the commodity.

The management and construction of these boundaries has always been a complicated process which has generated any number of systems of knowledge, surveillance, incitement and punishment. The management problems posed specifically by a sexuality that is constituted as epidemic are significant, and my intent in this chapter is to try to trace out some of those that emerge from the attempt both to expand the ways and forms in which sexuality both reproductive and erotic can be commodified and to preserve sexual labor as that which is ideally unpaid.

Because epidemic conditions arouse concern about the exchange of bodily fluids, various strategic agendas have been offered as inducements to genital de-intensification, to which one should, under most circumstances, "just say no." In this sense, as I have previously suggested, the epidemic sex-pol economy might currently be described as being in a state of recession or stagflation, discouraged by a prudential logic in terms of which genital sexuality is a high-risk investment, prompting a move toward libidinal diversification. Not surprisingly, one form of diversification/displacement will be perpetually offered in the forms of commodities, many of which are being marketed rather explicitly as compensatory, safe-sex substitutes. (I will discuss some of the particulars here shortly.) But one ironic consequence of the sexual epidemic is that sexual services and commodities have been a real growth area in the 1980s. At a time when uncommodified sexuality has been constituted as a high-risk zone, the zone of sexual commodification expands as a profit center.

Within late capitalism, there exist strategic connections between advertising, marketing, and pornography; each represents and enacts a strategy of seduction. Although advertising and pornography are differentiated by their strategies and styles, they exist in a relation of mutual incitement. Within the contemporary erotic economy, it is necessary to trace the transformational logic and grammar that effect the transferential network by which erotic desire is constituted as commodity fetish.

These connections are necessarily made at the level of language, signs, spectacles. The effectivity by which advertising creates erotic needs demands a reinscription of the body, where the body in question is designed precisely to be spectacle, on display—a mirroring simulacra—another site for induced misrecognition (*mésconnaissance* in the Lacanian sense). Such representations constitute sites of erotic satisfaction and release. In both advertising and pornography, the goal is to incite arousal and satisfaction serially, that is, to displace erotic investment on to other commodities, other items within the genre. Both modes of incitement depend on signs and reading; they are phantasmatic constructions, images, whose value consists in not being real (in the Lacanian sense). Here we encounter the limits of any narrow sociological or representational theory of reading, for the power to incite, to produce erotic need, here depends on the incestuous slippage of signs, the variability of positions in a system of ungrounded differences, i.e., language. In this sense, then, pornography is not the discourse by which one body is represented to another body: it is a phenomenon of literacy, addressed to a reader of signs. Advertising is the mechanism for mobilizing this transferential network in the direction of particular commodities. In pornography, the commodity is a sexual semiotic, that is, a phenomenon of sex without bodies. This is part of what makes pornography an appropriate site for erotic investment in the age of sexual epidemic.

Advertising depends on marketing, which is the science of constructing, dividing, targeting, and mobilizing consumers. Marketing entails the transformation of an audience from one of potential to actual consumers. This is accomplished through a series of interrelated strategies, most saliently, market segmenting and establishing tactical specificity, which involves recognizing, producing, and proliferating differentiated needs in the service of profitability. The goal of marketing, to facilitate consumption, involves the intensification and extensification of profits. This means to create for (of) the commodity an existential necessity which, in many cases, does not pre-exist the commodity and which is inseparable from it. In light of this logic, then, the production of addiction serves as the ultimate success of marketing strategy. For the addict is the most loyal of customers, one of whom the provider can be sure will be a repeat purchaser. For the addict, the object has become quite literally an existential necessity, an object or commodity which functions both to satiate and to expand the needs it also creates (one has to have had a drink or a cigarette in order to need one). Addiction can be read as the ultimate extension of the logic of discipline—the production and regulation of needs—through this double-gesture of incitement and enslavement in the name of pleasure.

The regulatory or disciplinary mechanisms of the market seek to control and cure the very addictions they themselves have produced. There are specific sites of addiction that are produced and controlled by the regulatory mechanisms that have emerged to address the epidemic of AIDS. One site of strategic intersection is the war on drugs, since intravenous drug usage is one medium for the transmission of the virus. In the name of health, we are witnessing the remobilization of sentiments in favor of regulating the ingestion of substances of various kinds, which appears not only in the crackdown on those substances already under legal control (illegal recreational drugs), but in the proliferation of testing for an ever-expanding list of prescription drugs: tranquilizers, steroids, hormones. What constitutes acceptable addiction is now subject to redefinition. We have seen a switch from policies which encourage addiction to tobacco to policies designed to limit tobacco consumption through prohibition. This prohibition has been extended spatially to include planes, restaurants, and the workplace. Both sugar and caffeine have been produced as new controlled substances.

The prohibitions against addiction, however, are strengthened by the preservation of the very addictive behavior they ostensibly seek to limit. Addictive behavior helps to produce a disciplinary subject; addictive behavior is routinized and repetitive and, to that extent, predictable. Addictive exchange structures are also useful insofar as the agency of control is displaced onto the object; regulations are dissimulated and rewritten as the language of need and desire.

The convergence of marketing, pornography, and epidemic logic produces now widely distributed images of sickness and health as new forms of pornography. We get the double production of AIDS photographs contrasted with new versions of the body beautiful. The logic of addiction also encourages the routinized and repetitive behavior of the "health addict," the workaholic who makes sure to make time for that morning workout at the gym. This disciplinary logic of addiction works in yet another direction to intensify the phenomenon of ritualistic repetition in domestic work and childrearing practices.

Many factors not specific to epidemic conditions also contribute to motivate this expansion. In some sense, sex work has specific characteristics that would make it attractive as a source of potential profit intensification. Excluding from consideration for the moment reproductive technology, most forms of sex work are rather capitally de-intensive, relative to other industries. Here profitability is also intensified by its resistance—i.e., most forms of sexual wage labor are also considered taboo. This allows for a higher profit margin, a lower paid and more manipulable/vulnerable labor force, and a particular set of expectations, viz., satisfaction from its clientele. Those ways of capitalizing on sexuality that have been most enduring are those which maximize this margin most efficiently. (Not a long time has to be spent training workers, designing/maintaining complicated equipment, or any real concern given to quality control.)

Three major institutional forms for capitalizing on sexuality as the marker of desire in late capitalism (though not specifically its inventions) are *prostitution, addiction,* and *pornography.* All three are strategies for maximizing and consolidating the socially useful, profitable excess produced as sexual energy, excess desire. These institutional forms have dual functions compatible with the dual strategy of discipline and incitement. They function as strategic safety valves, compensatory indulgences, selective circumscribed sites of transgression on the one hand, while they also function as limits against which coordinated and acceptable forms can be mobilized and maintained. In other words, the existence of commodified forms of sexuality capitalizes both by turning sex into capital, and by preserving sexuality from it.

These three institutions are certainly not specific to late capitalism. Not for nothing is prostitution referred to as the oldest profession. If we are to believe Lévi-Strauss, prostitution was the original form of exchange, where the objects exchanged are the bodies of women. But in the phase of development described alternatively as one-dimensional (Marcuse) or the consumer society of simulations (Baudrillard), these institutions take on connotative and productive values that are specific to that mode of organization. Further dynamics of overdetermination are induced by conditions of sexual epidemic which encourage, at least at the level of prescriptive ideology and prudential reason (which are obviously not the whole story), a more wary relation to other bodies, suggesting sublimatory strategies of displacement onto objects, images, commodities. Those in our culture are already commodity-competent. We cannot help but be. The socially inscribed circuitry which allows for the displacement of erotic significance onto subjects has already been well trained by advertising and the cinema. In the age of epidemic, however, what had been a system of subliminal seductions has now been promoted to the status of an explicit prescription, and not only from marketers.

The point is that epidemic sexuality has been constructed not coincidentally as a window of opportunity for capital, a period of growth, producing new and enlarged mechanisms for commodifying the sexual body, erotic and reproductive, and for profit by the fact that in catastrophic conditions which place the sexual body in question, value is intensified. The panic induced by the epidemic construct induces precisely the kind of free-floating anxiety that, precisely because it has no object, can be transferred onto any object, and from object to object in series. The kind of symptomatic hysteria that expresses itself through intensified consumption is the kind of hysteria that is good enough for business to become hegemonized as rational prudence.

The lesson that late capitalism has chosen to draw from its own production can be summarized by the slogan "Sex costs." AIDS provided an occasion for the cost-benefit logic in which sexuality had been constituted as the sphere of primary satisfaction to become an explicit articulation. It is not that sex has not always had its price. It is just that in the age of sexual epidemic, which is also the age of late capitalism, the joint efforts of the commodity system, the medical profession and the media have found a way to make that ideological construct profitable. At one level this is a moment in which capital seems to be tipping its hand, but it is more like the dance of the seven veils. This cost-benefit logic leaves in place the profit and possession logic underlying that which is offered as the alternative— monogamous marriage.

Entrepreneurs like Hugh Hefner found ways to package promiscuous sexuality as an occasion, indeed, a rationalization for conspicuous consumption. Now its opposite, i.e., the risk of sexual promiscuity, is also represented in a way that necessitates consumption. Codes of opposition have now become interchangeably a rationalization for consumption and for accumulation as profit.

The surplus produced by this neutralization takes on particular strategic value given the intensification of affect operative in epidemic conditions. In this context, the homogeneity and substitutability of commodities takes on the added connotations of safety and comfort. The very attention to surfaces, the temporality of perpetual seduction, the slick and glossy thinness of the image take on added appeal when the depth of the body and history have come to be thought of as explosions ready to happen, a depth which is a phenomenon now linked with despair and with death. The distraction induced by the sheer speed with which the series of commodities is presented can in this context come to seem the most innocent and least threatening form of seduction. Absence of finality becomes a virtue. Disappointment is never irrevocable. If it's bad, just throw it away.

The sexual epidemic in which the prospect of "liberated spontaneous sexuality" is represented as no longer possible, or in the process of slipping away, provides a context in which the myth of scarcity, so central to the creation of needs and demands upon which capitalist production depends, can be rewritten and recirculated. If "free sex" is scarce, one will have to pay. Sex costs. If the cost of contact with bodies is too high in the currency of risks, one will have to pay in another currency for something else. The myth of scarcity circulating in this epidemic is not only a tale of the scarcity of bodies, it is a tale about the scarcity of time as well. The sexual epidemic temporalizes the erotic and eroticizes the temporal in the direction of profit intensification, similar in strategy and effect to the profit intensification of spatiality in the 1970s under the name of the "condominium," where space is divided into the smallest marketable units and then sold as equity investments. The foreshortening of time provided by dyadic linkage of death and desire is conducive to the incitement of multiple episodic consumption encounters. Why not now, since you can't take it with you? Brevity is conducive to seriality and the patterns of repetition upon which the market economy depends.

The isolation induced by epidemic conditions, symptomatized by the fear of contagion, is also conducive to seduction by commodities. As Baudrillard suggests, "consumption is primarily organized as a discourse to oneself." Indeed, a number of advertisements for sexual services address a consumer explicitly constructed at home, in bed, alone—e.g., the phone sex industry. What is produced here is an auto-eroticism mediated by objects or, better, telephonic projections which are at once commodities and services on the market. (One calls in, as it were, to gain access to a discourse that one fantasizes is for oneself; in other words, one pays to turn erotic discourse on/for oneself.)

The hegemony of the sexual epidemic is instructive in the ways it induces the very anxieties it also promises to allay, constructs the deprivations for which it can then rationalize its productions as compensation. Baudrillard points out the ways in which "consumer society substitutes a social order of values and classifications for a contingent world of needs and pleasure."[3] This substitution is facilitated by the hegemony of sexual epidemic in which the possibility of such contingent pleasure is also represented as slipping away, dying out.

Baudrillard remarks, "It is not political will that breaks the monopoly of the market . . . it is the fact that every unitary system, if it wants to survive, has to evolve a binary system of regulation . . . power is only absolute if it knows how to refract itself in equivalent variations; that is, if it knows how to redouble itself through this doubling."[4] Within contemporary epidemic conditions, regulation works through the installation of a set of binary relations that entail the legalization and normalization of some practices at the same time that others are criminalized. This binary system of regulation functions to fetishize and target specific institutional forms for regulation by leaving the larger structures of power to circulate and proliferate. That which is prohibited works to sustain hegemonic social structures: the regulation of prostitution preserves marriage and the sexual and reproductive exploitation of women; pornography preserves advertising; addiction preserves brand loyalty and repeat-purchasing consumer patterns. Regulation inescapably takes place within a system of capital, commodities, and the asymmetrical figuration of differences, including sexual difference, that reproduces hegemonic lines of privilege, dominance, and power.

Although criminality is regularly figured as that which threatens the smooth functioning of this system, criminal behavior is itself the paradigm for behavior which maximizes profits. Criminality generates profits directly in the form of a higher profit margin, i.e., higher prices, lower labor costs, no taxes, benefits, deductions. As the paradigm for profit making, criminality assumes its most public form in the way that international capital "launders" its "dirty" drug money. Here the system which creates and seeks to manage a criminal class turns out to be the most blatant criminal. The crimes of international capital—e.g., laundering drug money through international transfers—work the possibilities of capitalism for its own constitutive criminality. Moreover, crimes of such global magnitude— e.g., the U.S.–Noriega affair—justify the production of a discourse of outrage that also allows for the maintenance of homologous forms of exploitation under other names. Most important among these latter forms is the institution of marriage as a form of sex work, legalized prostitution, which remains largely unpaid and not for profit. That social form makes sure that women do not control or profit from the surplus value already imposed on them by the construction of "woman" as eroticized commodity. Indeed, that social arrangement makes sure that any negotiable profits derived from her work go somewhere else. The other way that such value-laden social forms get put into false contrast with criminality and exploitation is through the circulation of a notion of "safe sex" as synonymous with the family, preserving and protecting incest and intra-marital rape as forms of safe sex. The profitability of illicit sexualities and institutions that provide services and commodities, regulation, therapy, punishment, offers further justification for surveillance. One of the consequences of sexual epidemic is a kind of social urgency about discovering sexual criminals—most notably those that sexually exploit children. There seems to be an epidemic in reported cases of child sexual exploitation—by parents, child-care workers, babysitters, as well as strangers. What social surplus is produced in these search-and-destroy missions? This is also an era of high visibility sex crimes—Jennifer Levin, Tawana

Brawley. Certainly the twenty years American feminists worked to increase public awareness and sensitivity to the very ubiquity of sexual assault, as well as the context they provided for reinterpreting its significance, are partly responsible for the attention which the public has been willing to give to these incidents. But as the media attention given these two particular cases has clearly shown, the pursuit of legal or social remedies for such offenses also always has the ironic effect of producing two victims, while placing both parties to the encounter on trial.

What is the ideological/social utility that results from the production of surplus victims and defendants?

Certainly, one immediate and proximal result of the number of child abuse cases recently making headlines is to raise parental and especially maternal concerns regarding day care and the safety of their children. Compounding an already existing social guilt, these recent cases help to reinvent the myth of the nuclear family as the optimum social space for children and, by contrast, any collective social alternatives are correlated with implicit risk and danger.

Attention to criminal sexuality is also useful as part of the larger effort to minimize recognition of class difference. Sex crimes do cut across classes. One of the reasons so many of these cases have received coverage is that it was middle-class women and children, like Jennifer Levin and Lisa Steinberg, who were victimized. Publicizing social problematics that seem immune to class differences has a certain utility in reducing class resentment, and in inducing more sympathetic reactions toward social regulations, even when these are class-differentiated (issues like abortion). This publicity allows also for social coding of the private as a sphere of greater control, protection, and safety, which will have serious implications for social issues like day care.

The creation of a criminal class conceived as outside the system of capital and regulatory management justifies the mobilization of social power as militaristic force, e.g., fight crime, war on drugs, wipe out porn. There seems to be at work here a figuration of criminality as disease, and a reverse association of disease with criminal—i.e., high-risk—activity (crimes like drug addiction are likened to diseases like cancer, where AIDS appears to be the unnamed associative link between them). Both criminality and disease are conceived as outlaws, invaders with secret ways, as well as forces of disorder. Both criminality and disease (and their postulated equivalence) are used to rationalize forms of power in the name of maintaining a healthier, that is, crime-free and disease-free, society. Both rationalize power as management. As Susan Sontag remarks, "Society is presumed to be in basically good health; disease (disorder) is, in principle, always manageable."[5]

Criminalization normalizes that which it opposes—it also creates a highly marketable excess. Hence, we witness the proliferation of sex-crime dramas on television and on film, the blurring of fictional and informational genres, the "typing" of such narratives: day care abuse, child abuse, incest, family murders,

murders of parents by children, violence against women who have strayed outside the marital norm.

As in the production of addiction, then, regulatory power preserves and increases the very criminality that it claims to oppose, becoming the paradigm for the contagious criminality that justifies its own interventionist strategies ad infinitum.

Part of the point of this whole discussion is that the revisions, reconsolidation, and expansions of these institutions also change or ought to change the political issues surrounding them—what is significant about these phenomena gets recast, as do the terms of contest. Specifically, they decenter what have been the primary competing social agendas/discourses in terms of an opposition between a logic of repression, prohibition, and punishment (criminality) and those which seek to mainstream, normalize, enlarge the scope of such practices. Questions tend to center either around a juridical rhetoric (legalization vs. criminalization), or a moral one of sin and sanctity, or a political one of rights and freedoms. The limits of legislative and prescriptive approaches to these institutions dramatically show the limits of prohibition as a strategy. They also miss the obvious strategy value of the attempt at prohibition to the intensification of their profitability (exhibited focally in all the cases where being banned in Boston prompts increased sales everywhere else). Criminalization also reduces protection for both service providers and customers. Transgressiveness comes at a high price, and is indeed part of what contributes to its market value and high profit margin.

Political questions regarding these institutions ought not to be posed in a way that misrecognizes or confuses the socially constructive with the legislatively elective. The question in late capitalism cannot be whether or not there ought be prostitution, as though such a matter could be decided. To pose the question this way is to miss what prostitution is, and in some sense, if one is prone to speak this way, what is wrong or at least problematic about it. Part of what is problematic is the hegemonic utility of that which it mobilizes as resistance—like the fetishizing of sexual labor as unpaid, the noncompensatory economy which maintains reproduction as alienated and undervalued, and the system of heterosexist and male domination it justifies. The excess represented by these institutions also tells us a great deal about the lack constituting that which is situated as the prescribed, the normal, the acceptable.

It is also to assume the suturability of needs to the social. A better strategy would be to see needs as that demand which can never be socially accommodated, hence a site of resistance to regulatory seductions. These are desires which are explicitly placed in a sphere of transferable differences that are available only through explicit efforts of articulation and contestation. To see pornography as some special set of representations is to miss the extent to which pornography is the master genre for late capitalism, the literature for a society of perpetual incitement. In this sense, pornography is not an aberration, but an intensification of its productive logic, its generative grammar. Similarly with respect to addiction—it is not an aberration, deviance, but a success story, a model for modifications and transfer.

In an epidemic context, the limits of frontiers/boundaries legislative and otherwise are obvious. Epidemic is defined by its indifference to those boundaries and prescriptions. It is that which cannot be willed away, individually or collectively. In this sense ours is the age of epidemic prostitution, pornography, and addiction, or these have become epidemic and not by accident. Hence these forms are neither marginal nor optional, but are the modes by which sexuality is historically institutionalized in our age. They are that against which the hubris of elimination logic shows itself. The law will also always produce that which stands outside it. Sexual epidemic mediated through the logic of late capitalism operates to produce contradictory ideological, institutional, and technological effects, viz., the project of sexual management. On the one hand, there is the attempt to market "selective refusal" as a preferred social response—e.g., the "just say no" campaign, which is both an official campaign, and a recurring motif available through a variety of popular cultural outlets, in film, popular fiction, television.

At the same time that this foray in the aesthetics of discretion is being designed and circulated, the range, availability, and outlets for producing and marketing sexual apparatuses and services proliferate. Needless to say, the commodification of sexual services is not itself a new development. Prostitution and wet-nursing are practices that have long and extensive histories. There is also an extensive tradition of cultures producing apparatuses designed either to facilitate or to stimulate sexual contact, enhance its pleasures while precluding pregnancy or sexual contact (chastity belts, genital mutilations). Such apparatuses, as well as the workers who produce and or use these items in the performance of sexual services, may be classed into two basic categories: *reproductive technology* (contraception, abortion, birthing instruments and services) and *erotic technology and services*. Whereas neither category is a product of capitalism per se (such practices predate its emergence historically), strategies and mechanisms specific to late capitalism have helped contribute to the fact that sexual products and services are a growth area in the contemporary economy even at a time when there is an explicit cultural agenda to limit sexual circulation. Indeed, one of the ironies of the contemporary situation is that many products and services are being marketed as safer alternatives to genital sex, or as safeguards against epidemic conditions. Correlatively, the expansion of sexual services facilitated by technological developments (in areas like medical, communication, and other technologies) expands the number and nature of sexual workers, especially expanding the numbers of workers outside the sphere of primary production (which in this case would mean genital contact). Reproductive and fertility technology expand the potential reproductive and medical brigades. Expansion of the therapeutic sexual service areas has also opened new occupations as sexual counselors and surrogates. New forms of erotica—phone services, special-interest sex clubs (S & M, swapping), the current trend for clubs catering to women (Chippendales)—

expand the forms sexual work can take, and therefore the potential sources of profit.

Expansion of the profitability of the sex industry has been accomplished, in part, by incorporation of strategies and mechanisms that have been successful in maximizing profit in other areas. These strategies (which will be discussed later and in greater detail) include mass-marketing tactics like advertising, market segmenting, specialization of functions, deskilling of labor as a consequence of its division into relatively anonymous, interchangeable functions (the essential characteristic of any call girl or phone sex operation, as well as of the porn theaters which run features continually throughout the day with the audience entering and leaving at will). As an example of the strategic utility of mass-marketing techniques, consider the ways in which strategies of mass marketing and market segmenting have been used to expand the audience for pornographic films and texts. The traditional pornography audience was overwhelmingly male, and the usual conditions for spectatorship (which usually involved going to a specialized zone where such publications and theaters were housed) meant that men usually indulged in pornography either alone or at male-dominated events, like stag or fraternity parties or gay male clubs. The relative inaccessibility of pornographic publications, traditionally concealed in brown paper wrappers in stores with blacked-out windows, and the clandestine conditions under which they have been sold, presumably contributed to part of their transgressive appeal—outside the mainstream mass market, so hot they have to be kept under wraps. This aesthetic has not been entirely displaced. But it is now supplemented by subsidiary forms and outlets aimed at other audiences—most notably, heterosexual women—which make pornography available in home video form (therefore available for viewing privately in a domestic context) or marketed through mail order in women's magazines. Barbara Ehrenreich also points to an emerging genre of "Christian fundamentalist" erotica, sex manuals, and marriage guides designed to eroticize relationships within that moral and normative framework. Some particular items like Marabel Morgan's *The Total Woman* are given the full benefit of advertising and promotion through the mainstream media. Erotic paraphernalia are now being marketed like Tupperware, to women in their homes, where they are presumably more at ease, and where exploration of such products may occur under conditions more discreet than in a store. Erotic material can also be sampled on cable television stations, which are also major outlets for advertising phone sex, call girl, and other services and establishments. The marketing of such material in the home and through conventional media like television not only increases the potential market saturation for such messages but also alters the signification attached to them. Taking sexual services out of the red light district and bringing them into the home has the function of normalizing and destigmatizing them, encouraging the viewer to consider them as commodities like any others that are also advertised in such formats. With the expansion of in-home buying services, the decision to respond to an advertisement run by one of the numerous "escort services" that advertise in New York City is accomplished in the same manner as one buys a lawn mower, with the added benefit that one's companion will arrive far more quickly than the lawn mower. In this instance, we have a case of a new marketing strategy for a fairly traditional sexual service.

But part of the proliferative genius of late capitalism is to find ever more profit-intensive areas of investment (more profit-intensive than the weekly importation, as one service promises, of "submissive oriental women right [sic] trained to fill our every need and desire"). The latest and most ingenious development in the area, from the perspective of cost effectiveness, are the new series of phone sex services known as "party lines." Such services, which charge the caller by the minute, differ from services in which the caller is connected with a paid employee of the service (usually female) with whom to converse. The new services, by contrast, are not nearly so labor-intensive, since the caller pays only to talk with other paying callers. The obvious benefit here is that such ventures are relatively capital-deintensive, with costs limited to setting up the telephone system, and labor-deintensive, since the only employee with whom a client is likely to come into contact is an operator, who, at least it is claimed, monitors calls, eliminating abusive or offensive callers, and in some cases is able to arrange private lines for two parties who want to speak free from auditory surveillance by others on the line. For the most part, however, the clients entertain, solicit, titillate one another. In this case, the sexual service for which one pays is really the technology that allows callers to contact others, often anonymously, privately, without being seen. This is the perfect cost-effective enterprise for the society that Foucault has dubbed the society of "talking sex."

Telephonic promiscuity is marketed as a safer and more discrete alternative or compensation in an age where other forms of sexual contact are being represented as far more risky. It also makes possible a form of social contact appropriate to mass culture—reaching out and touching someone telephonically—highly mediated, simulated, coded, anonymous, and expensive. For the consumer, such services have the advantage of being easily accessible and easy to use, as well as being malleable enough to accommodate a range of agendas, styles, and presumably outcomes. There are special services for gay men, lesbians, teens, blacks. Such services can also be enjoyed under conditions that are relatively discreet, and involve no advance planning and relatively little risk—conditions of use can be controlled by the user (one can hang up when one wants to, one can speak or not, etc.). Such services expand the range of consumers to those classes of people—teenagers, single mothers, housebound women, for example—who would not be likely or even able to enter the sexual commodity system otherwise. The obvious benefit from the viewpoint of the service provider is that the users are also the show. The service is made profitable by low labor costs and high profit margins.

Market segmenting has also been a useful strategy for expanding the market for sexual services. Part of this involves a logic of specialized sexualities, each of which can then be fetishized in its differences through a capital- and commodity-intensive erotic aesthetic. Barbara Ehrenreich remarks on the popularity of S & M as a particularly capital intensive form of sex (requiring elaborate paraphernalia as well as technical discourses and service providers, tops, bottoms, clubs, magazines, etc.) The economic advantage of specialized sexuality is not only proliferation (more kinds of sex, more kinds of supportive instrumentation), but the creation of a differential economy of access and availability, a kind of erotics of supply and demand, which allows certain sexual practices to be preferred at premium prices, given their presumed relatively limited availability.

Here, again, the culture of sadomasochism is a good example, but other contemporary practices come to mind: specialized dating services that place a premium on very young prostitutes—male and female—or so-called secret or special practices. The multiplication of erotic possibility also maximizes possibilities for demand and desire. The very division of sexualities becomes an erotic mechanism of perpetual stimulation and incitement and also maximizes sites of profitability, positions within the economy from which profits can be made: experts, aesthetes, procurers, and prosyletizers. Such mechanisms also work to produce a kind of compensatory optimism. At a time when certain sexual possibilities are being cut off, the market economy can always promise satisfaction in the form of next year's model, the market's way of producing a "revolutionary" development and sustaining a sense of apparent freedom through the proliferation of a range of erotic options, styles, and scenes.

Mass marketing of sexual apparatuses and services, not only erotica but also contraception devices, sexual accessories, and hygiene products, helps normalize the commodification of sexual functions and the integration of sexuality into a capitalist market system. One of the linking figures which helps to accomplish this social suturing is that of power, which is easily transferred from the economic to the sexual realm and back again. It is the very strategic versatility of this figure that allows those who pay for sex to feel empowered in that gesture: one can always get some sex by paying for it, one can be in control of the conditions for satisfying one's needs, desires, and thereby be less vulnerable. Those who receive payment also feel as though they have the upper hand precisely because they are in the position of benefiting in a clearly marked social way from this transaction, and hence are less vulnerable. The irony here is in the way that the mediation by the economic, specifically the monetary, is linked or recoded in the currency of personal control and autonomy.[6] Self-employed prostitutes, for example, often represent this explicitly as an occupational benefit, and as a positive distinction between their position and that occupied by most other women, who are disempowered by having to give it away for free (or the price of meal, or in concert with unpaid domestic labor). On the other hand, it comes as no surprise that one of the pleasures of prostitution for many men is precisely their feeling of superiority to those whose services they consume. In this configuration, power is associated precisely with not having to sell oneself, but rather in being so vested with excess that one can use it to elicit what one wants from another on demand. When one pays the piper, one can also call the tune.

The figure of the female prostitute, especially, also helps to empower men not only by testifying to their superior economic position, but also because such a figure is used, in reverse, to discipline "straight" women in a way that also works to male economic advantage, by normalizing or valorizing the dispensation of women's sexual services (erotic and reproductive) without economic compensation. If men can represent prostitution as the debased and exploitative form of sexual exchange, the appropriation of women's services without compensatory benefit can be sold to women in the name of their own autonomy, dignity. The same forms of economic privilege which have always sustained prostitution are also those which sustain it as a segment of sexual forms, and a relatively marginal one. The maintenance of this relative marginality is crucial for maintaining a larger economy in which the majority of women can be said to choose to do sex work for free. By maintaining sex for money as a distinct segment or sexual subset, the largely "free market" in sexuality, which would include all forms of uncompensated sexual exchanges, is hegemonized and naturalized in a way that sustains dominant class and gender interests, and is ultimately exploitative of its practitioners, especially relative to the consumers. This differentiates sex work from most other industries, where laws tend to favor the producer.

The figure of the prostitute can also be used to manipulate women psychically as a regulatory device in relation to other women: she is available as the ever-present, threatening other. If his needs are not accommodated at home, he can easily pay for sex elsewhere. This figure also produces a kind of sentimentalization which obscures the dynamics of the sexual political economy, and encourages women strategically to misidentify the nature of their interests in such transactions. One is debased by the receipt of some kind of clearly discernible and negotiable currency or benefit. Love, appreciation, admiration are not, in this context, considered negotiable currencies, though they could and certainly are marketed as not only compensatory but superior benefits. Gold diggers, women willing to use sexual liaison as a vehicle for improving their economic and social positions, are usually, most amusingly, represented as dumb rather than as particularly canny, clever readers of the heterosexual market system, strategic investors of their own sexual and social capital for maximum benefit. Part of the paradox of prostitution is that its mechanisms work not only to place women but also to lead them to identify with positions negatively, oppositionally defined (regarding other women), while preserving without question the entitlement of men to occupy both. Women are ultimately both self- and socially defined in terms of an opposition in which the best sex is both paid and unpaid.

Another paradox raised by the figure and institution of prostitution (in its contemporary incarnation) concerns contradictory relations between power and knowledge, and between economic and sexual value. Although the routes by which women enter the institution vary widely, from explicit coercion[7] to explicit choice (as a preferable occupation to others considered), it is an occupation in which there are no standards of certification, valuation, accreditation, norms of expertise. At most, there are informal reference networks, recommendations from consumers, and the pimp's or prostitute's promotional discourse. But the very economic transaction transfers to the prostitute the signification attached to being a professional, i.e., of being expert, up on the latest developments, providing the quality of service for which others are willing to pay. She must be good if she can get people to pay for it.

It is important to discuss prostitution as a specific set of social practices and institutions which are socially coded as marginal, discrete in the sense of being determinate, ghettoized and thereby or therefore carrying the markers of transgression and to a certain extent, taboo—witness the Jim Bakker episode. It must also be emphasized that prostitution certain exists, in another sense, on a continuum with other ways of socially organizing and transacting sexual relationships where relationships are already mediated by a logic of profit and loss. Radical lesbian critiques of marriage (like Ti-Grace Atkinson's) and of heterosexual relationships in general (as in Firestone and Beauvoir) depend on a linkage between traditional bourgeois marriage and courtship with prostitution. The similarities are that of exchange of sex for some form of material and/or in many cases softer currency—like love, romance, social legitimacy or recognition.

In the traditional male-female exchange, women are in the position, often emphasized only for a short period of time, of having to barter their social currency—sexual attractiveness and fertility—for the prospect of economic support/security and legitimacy for their offspring. Just what is objectionable about this transaction varies with particular feminist theorists, but central to all of these is the assumption that the very conditions which necessitate/encourage such transactions are already sufficiently asymmetrical as to disadvantage women in such exchanges. Disadvantages are coded in multiple currencies. Because a woman's future in patriarchy is so much a function of the man with whom she is officially linked through marriage, women's affectivity and eroticism are always infused by strategic considerations that infringe upon the spontaneity of her eroticism, and which impose upon the very structures of her desires a dependency that abridges her autonomy and capacities for self-transcendence (Beauvoir). Like the prostitute, her linkages are based not on a calculus of desire but rather on the basis of the best exchange rate. Considered in this light, marriage and prostitution come to look less different and more structurally similar. In both cases, social necessity demands that women put themselves on the market, present the most attractive packaging possible, and wait for the bids to come in. Success in either enterprise depends in different degrees on the woman's willingness and ability to incarnate the desires of the other with superior purchasing power (or some other currency in which the woman is invested or intending to invest), to provide those services which he is willing to support materially. In both cases her value is determined relationally, i.e., by her exchange value assessed in terms of the market, even though much of the labor in performing such services demands precisely autonomous creativity, imagination, cleverness, and craft.

Further linking their situations are the conditions that make questions of choice and autonomy highly ambiguous and problematic. On the one hand, the choice between mother and whore is one of the primary figures of differentiation for women. The difference between the good and the bad, the respectable and the illicit, the revered and the exploited. Feminist analysis, however, which emphasizes the exploited condition of all women, forces a reconsideration of the political economy of heterosexuality in a way that problematizes the nature and the significance of these oppositions. If prostitution is objectionable, as many liberals and feminists argue, it is because it is exploitative (either of women or the sacredness of sexual relationships, or of the clients), especially under conditions where men such as pimps and club owners end up with the lion's share of a woman's earnings, and where her work only enhances the forms of control he has over her. Many Marxist and lesbians-feminists have argued that marriage operates, especially economically but also psychologically, in much the same way, and therefore that marriage, motherhood, even heterosexual relationships as such, are paradigmatic cases of the alienation and exploitation of women's labor.

The traditional marriage contract, and the conduct of contemporary marital relationships, assumes and in fact depends upon vast contributions of women's unpaid labor. This includes domestic service which, as survey after survey indicates, is still women's responsibility whether or not they are also engaged in wage labor. (Women who do not do their own household tasks are more than likely to be paying another woman to do it for them.) Reproduction is also similarly organized so that the majority of labor not only in birthing but more importantly childrearing falls disproportionately to women, as does the burden of economic support in the growing number of cases in which fathers either do not acknowledge paternity, divorce the child's mother, or fail to marry her in the first place. Whereas cases of elective paternity are socially rewarded, there has been historically very little effort made to hold men economically accountable for the children they produce. If they choose to, men can use their children, and by extension the women who produce them, as legitimate heirs, points for consolidating or marking their social wealth, authority, and power. If not, women are often left, as divorce statistics indicate, economically impoverished by the children whose absent father's name they still carry, often leaving that same man free to begin the very same process with another woman. Ironically, in light of the contemporary statistics on the longevity of marriages, the rate of paternal child support, the number of single mother households, one of the primary benefits of marriage over prostitution, namely, the prospect of legitimacy, economic support (at least partial), and a coparent for one's children, is rapidly eroding. Given statistical probabilities, one of the strategic considerations that enters choices about marriage and childbirth is the prospect that as a woman one is likely, at least at some point and for some period of time, to do this alone, with male participation largely elective and selective.

What has also been called "the displaced homemaker syndrome" is another example of the ways in which the political economy of marriage parallels the more exploitative dimensions of the prostitutive exchange. Much of the currency that women both invest in their marriage, and more importantly in the context in which they are paid, is the relatively non-negotiable currency of love, affection, nurture, and attention. Through such transactions, men are able to exact from their wives vast amounts of unpaid and often unacknowledged labor as typists, researchers, translators, editors, secretaries, etc., that not only enhances their professional status and work, but also puts them in a better position to abandon their wives when their services are no longer necessary or are available elsewhere.

There is also evidence that men benefit professionally and economically from the attention wives give to their husbands' needs, not only by creating a comfortable environment in which he can work or retreat from work, but also by giving him the psychological nurturance and space to concentrate on his work, knowing that his daily needs are being taken care of, leaving him more available and open to the very possibilities of which women in performing these functions are deprived. Given the current ways of organizing the biological time clock, women are often in the position of interrupting or abridging their careers to raise families at the very time that men are most professionally active, and are likely to be making the most rapid advances in their careers. Given this, it is not surprising that even in cases where both parties engage in wage labor, women are still the ones economically disadvantaged by divorce. The position of many divorced women is like that of the worker in the company town whose one plant has just closed. Paid in the company scrip of affection, she is now left with a bunch of worthless investments because the contract in which they had some currency no longer exists.[8]

Feminist analysis of the sixties and seventies has the effect of both problematizing and making more complex the question of what prostitution is and, by extension, what if any sexual exchange, given the logic of late capitalism, mediated through a sexual politics of male and heterosexist privilege, could be non-exploitative, non-commodified, not productive of some alienated stratification of dominance.

The effect of this kind of feminist analysis is radically to disrupt the logic of stabilized opposition by virtue of which the category of prostitution is socially constructed as some unique sphere of a specifically commodified sexual relationship, thereby allowing for the implication that all other forms of sexual exchanges are not commodified, do not exist, operate, function within a market economy. By extension, it calls into question not only just what/where prostitution is not (if not marriage, then maybe romance) but also just what the nature of such non-exploitative relationships is supposed to be.

When Ti-Grace Atkinson made the claim that marriage was legalized prostitution, that statement forced a reconsideration not only of prostitution, but also of marriage and of the legal system which constructs and enforces a materially reinforced symbolic difference between the two practices. Several lines of questioning and construction are prompted by this crucial insight, but none of them take what might be described as the hegemonic interrogation of oppositions—either marriage or prostitution, yes or no to prostitution, particularly on the basis of the opposition of good and bad. The productive effect of the irony operative in Atkinson's statement is both to elicit the embedded social investments in these signifiers, and at the same time to problematize the moral and evaluative mystifications that divide these choices and the women who identify themselves and one another in terms of their relationships to them. In doing so, it displaces judgmental considerations with strategic ones of relative and situational advantage, while at the same time pointing toward the limits of such strategic machinations in a context already organized in a way to secure their circumscription and domination.

One obvious line following from Atkinson's conjunction of marriage and prostitution is a very definite critique of marriage and of the assumptions which both produce and condemn prostitution as an institution. If, as one line of argument suggests, prostitution is wrong because it exploits sexual desire, degrading it by turning it into a material exchange, marriage is wrong for the same reasons. Men are still forced to pay for sex and women to sell it. If prostitution exploits women, especially their youthful bodies and spirits, often leaving them with very little to show for their efforts, married women are often in the same position. The differences that prompt the morally self-righteous superior positions often underlying critiques of prostitution must get recast in light of the recognition that, in relation to economic exploitation, good women, women who marry, are frequently not that much better off. Considered strategically, as a response to what is an essentially exploitative heterosexual politics, it might be argued, as some feminists have done, that at least in principle the prostitute may very well be in a better position, economically and otherwise, than the married woman (especially if she is in a position to control her own money, i.e., works freelance). As against the situation of the married woman, her services are compensated in negotiable currency rather than in more mystical forms like love and affection. The transaction is therefore more straightforward, demystified, honest. Furthermore, because she is on the open market (or at least on a market with multiple points for consumption of her services), she is in a better position both to barter and to increase the profitability of her assets, making not one deal, but many.

What is considered obligatory behavior for a wife, and is thereby often entirely uncompensated, becomes for the prostitute one more occasion for negotiations and profit potential. She can charge separately for each sexual act she performs, with other amenities like costume or talk-time charged at separate rates. Rather than being trapped in the impossible project of attempting to fulfill the needs and desire of a single person on whom one depends for one's very survival, the prostitute can often profit by the very *unfulfillability* of those needs which both motivate her clients to seek her out, and allow her to profit, whether or not at least most of the promises she makes are ever fulfilled. If he is not satisfied with her performance, he will simply find someone else, as will she. The prostitute may be also thought to be advantaged by being divested of much of the romantic mythology that mystifies other women. She, more than other women, is clear about what she wants from such an encounter, and in most cases is more likely to get it—up front. She is also in a better position than most women, especially wives, to determine the time, circumstances, and conditions under which the encounter will take place, as well as to be in charge of establishing its limits, temporally and substantively. What she will and won't do is much more subject to explicit bargaining. Furthermore, while her performances may often be rather theatrically elaborate (a tactic, ironically enough, that Marabel Morgan recommends for wives to keep their husbands home), she is also more discreet and performatively specific about what is expected from her, in contrast with wives, who in addition to performing sexual functions are also expected to meet psychological and emotional needs for nurture.

In what was probably a largely unintended irony, the liberal feminist advocacy of the pre-nuptial contract stipulating the precise terms and conditions of exchange (popular in the 1970s) was an effort to secure some of the benefits of the prostitute's situation for married women. And while both kinds of agreements can be and are often breached, it can be argued that at least the durational limits of the prostitute's connection with her client offers some measure of self-protection. Precisely because such contracts have no legal status, they are also easier to escape.

Atkinson's statement therefore gives a different picture of the alternatives, at least for women who take themselves to be heterosexual. It is not a choice between selling or not selling oneself, being exploited or not, but rather a question of the form and social valence given to the form such exchanges take. A woman can sell herself to one man (or at least to one man at a time) or to many. She can trade sex or fertility or nurturance or domestic service. She can do her work in the kitchen, or on the street, in a bedroom or a bathhouse. But the larger conditions which alienate labor are the same, empowering men both because they do and do not have to pay for sex, and they control and have far superior access to the currencies of social value.

What does separate marriage and prostitution, and by extension the women who identify themselves and one another in terms of these markers, is the legal mark of difference which establishes these institutions' identities within a differential calculus of value. Marriage is that form of alienated heterosexual exchange that is not only legally sanctioned but also socially rewarded, celebrated, and promoted. Prostitutes, by contrast, are selectively harassed, punished, and forced to run the risk of those in marginal enterprises, often having to pay for protection both from the regulations and from the risks of clients and pimps whose behavior is also unregulated. Although there may be strategic advantages in presenting oneself as available to any man rather than as the possession of one, there are also clearly risks and dangers precisely in that availability—the risk of being raped, hurt, killed, or ripped off with little likelihood of any legal remedies or social compensation for one's losses. Furthermore, the moral surplus attached to the differences in legal status functions both to dismiss the harm done to prostitutes, either because they are bad women or because they have somehow gotten what they deserve, and to induce women to enter into what Dworkin calls the protection racket of the heterosexual couple. In this racket, women, to some extent like the figures in Hobbes's imagined social contact, agree to give up some of their mobility and autonomy in exchange for the protection of one man against the exploitative intrusions of other men. The debased fate of the prostitute is then used as a part of a construction in which marriage can come to be seen by many women as the strategically preferable choice.

The question now becomes, which strategic utilities are being operationalized in the legal distinction between marriage and prostitution? What is it specifically about marital relationships that, from the point of view of the masculinist capitalist legal system, make them the strategically preferred social arrangement? One way to begin to answer this question is to remember that the purpose of the legal system is to protect the consolidation of hegemonic interests. Considered from the point of view of a cost-benefit logic, marriage is the most cost-effective way to maximize the profit potential of women for men, while maintaining a ceiling on the level of male capitalization. The marriage contract institutionalizes the expropriation of women's labor and love (or at least conjugal duties), along with an asymmetrical series of rights and obligations. Considered by heterosexual men, marriage is constructed less as an either/or alternative to prostitution than as a strategically and situationally beneficial alternative to it. The benefits are for men who can pay for sex when it suits them while otherwise having greater access to a woman from whom they frequently receive far more extensive and higher-quality service at a much lower price. The utility of this construction is both that it mobilizes a majority of women into what is from their standpoint the least advantageous exchange system, and subjects them to a logic of opposition, psychologically and politically, that men are and always have been free to cross. The occasions for prostitution are numerous, considered from both the sides of supply and demand, and the needs or desires it activates are those which have been represented as relatively foundational or basic. The very limits of this kind of arrangement, temporally and functionally, are also instrumental to its proliferation as well as to the promise embedded in this institution.

That is why the logic of repression is ultimately both inadequate and uninteresting when it comes to discussions of the politics, value, or utility of prostitution. Such discussions are often misleading, homogenizing what are rather diverse enterprises, and depending upon a set of assumptions, both about social particulars and about larger epistemic issues like the status/possibility of free will and choice. Arguments that attempt to advocate for prostitution through the language of legalization miss the point of what prostitution is for. Strategically, given the existing local logic, legalized prostitution is something of an oxymoron. It fails to get at the heart of the issue in terms of exploitation, since, as has been argued, legality and selective exploitation are certainly compatible, as evidenced by the legal construction of marriage, and the capitalist definition of free employment.

Arguments made in favor of legalizing or decriminalizing prostitution often depend upon the kind of strategic analysis I have been talking about. According to this position, given the relatively limited opportunities available for well-paid work open to most women, choosing to sell sexual service which is more highly valued than a woman's other skills can be seen as a reasonable strategic option, and certainly should not be socially precluded or punished, especially without similar treatment being given to those who choose to avail themselves of it. Precluding sexual service as an occupational choice is therefore not only arbitrary, but also reflects a basic and intolerable social hypocrisy by virtue of which sexuality is that which is both most highly valued in women, and also that which can never be activated in a way that enriches or benefits the party who is valued. The argument is therefore based on a situation that assumes choice—with the decision to enter prostitution a strategic determination of where an individual's best opportunities lie—and therefore should, like other occupational choices, be protected. Furthermore, since money is a primary currency of social value, there is no prima facie reason to exempt sexual exchanges. In capitalism, workers are constantly in the position of having to exchange their bodily capacities for wages or marriage. Given that the moral differences between these economies are negligible, there is no good reason to punish women for behavior that in other circumstances would be socially rewarded and recognized—namely, the activity of maximizing one's powers and capacities for one's own benefit through the accumulation of surplus value. If heterosexual relationships in patriarchy all have the effect of exploiting women, women at least ought to be in a position to decide how best strategically to navigate this situation. Prostitution thereby becomes defensible as a choice which women ought to be able to make without fear of organized social reprisal, especially on the grounds of moral self-righteousness.

While such arguments have the effect of restoring to the prostitute some dignity beyond that of the hapless victim, as well as pointing up the connection between prostitution and other socially exploitative exchange systems, such positions ultimately depend upon a set of assumptions precisely about choice that may be true for some women who find themselves in the sex industry, but are certainly not generalizable as a model. As a number of feminist works, including *Female Sexual Slavery*,[9] have shown, the strategic model is simply not descriptive of the conditions under which many women end up as prostitutes. There is certainly much documentation of the various forms of coercion used to procure prostitutes, including abduction, sale by parents or husbands (mostly in the third world), violence or the threat thereof, and various forms of chemical and psychological manipulation, as well as the exploitation of women in vulnerable positions—because they are poor, or young, runaways, abandoned, addicted, etc., which leave them without other choices in any meaningful sense. Hence, while it may be important, at least within the limits of a capitalist patriarchal sexual economy, to argue for the rights of women to choose to sell their sexual services, it is a mistake to think that this is coextensive with a defense of prostitution as such. Legalizing prostitution would do little more than provide conditions that would support, encourage and likely multiply such coercive practices by legalizing and normalizing them. Legalizing prostitution because marriage is legal is to miss the point of what is wrong with both of them, while creating further conditions that will allow social responsibility for its fallout to be placed yet again on the backs of its victims.

On the other hand, any effort to limit/eradicate prostitution through the imposition of increased punitive measures flies in the face of the larger developments in both technology and marketing which allow for an expansion of the possibilities for making sexual exchanges economically profitable. This is especially clear in the area of reproductive technologies, where it is already possible for a man to sell his sperm (a right which has never been contested or claimed to be exploitative) and where a woman could, although recent legal developments suggest otherwise, conceivably be in a position either to sell eggs for implantation in the body of another woman, or to sell her egg and uterus for artificial insemination, or just her uterus for carrying another woman's fertilized ovum. There may also very well be a market in eggs for medical research or for any other medical or other benefit that may be extracted from them. Certainly, the commodification of reproductive functions is not an entirely unprecedented phenomenon historically. The practice of kings with infertile wives taking mistresses or disposing of wives for other ones has a long history, as does the practice by which economically privileged women contract the services of wet-nurses. But developments not only in technology but also in ideology, the legal system, and social expectations about the nature of families, maximize the occasions and the sheer number of such transactions.

Beyond those factors encouraging wider use of such services, the fact that such procedures are profitable for those with control of the technology and professional expertise means that it is likely that such tendencies will intensify. Such practices, buttressed by supportive marketing and promotional techniques, are likely to reduce whatever resistance might exist in the marketplace to paid sexual services, both erotic and reproductive.

These circumstances, I believe, change the shape and nature of the questions and of the discourse that seeks to resist the exploitative consequences of sexual commodification, forcing a strategic consideration of just what exchange forms can be legitimately juxtaposed to it—in other words, what would non-exploitative sexual exchanges be like, how would they function, and what would be the prospective consequences of such transactions, especially in light of the histori-cally specific conditions brought about by the hegemony of sexual epidemic, which preclude or otherwise change the terms of what had been culturally figured as the model of liberated sexuality?

One significant pre-epidemic vision of sexual freedom consisted in the promo-tion of a series of multiple encounters considered non-exploitative by virtue of resisting the model of monogamy, possession, commitment and by remaining without expectations, episodic, an exchange in kind of sex for sex. Not only have conditions of epidemic made such strategies less viable, but so has feminist critique, which has problematized this vision of liberation by asking whether it is not a different modality of regulation, given the ways in which these sexual exchanges are sutured into a logic of profit and loss. (This may be the place to recuperate the critique of models of sexual liberation founded on the non-commit-ted multiple ejaculatory economy of adolescent males.)

Prostitution, the selling of recreational sexual services, related products and accoutrements, is only one dimension of the capitalization of sexuality—its social mobilization and organization for the production of profit. Sexuality is also organized through other disciplinary mechanisms—like the medical and the thera-peutic which also allow for further interventions by the commodity system.

As a recent article in the *West Side Spirit* by Janet Grady Sullivan announces, the "AIDS business" is "booming." Out of a situation of death and despair, cagey entrepreneurs are developing services and technologies designed precisely to address these new circumstances, including "drugs for treatment and prevention, blood storage centers, detection techniques and nutritional supplements." One might also add, dating services that provide contacts with only pre-screened clients as well as other kinds of social services designed to reduce risks of random encounters. AIDS also has had an effect on how existing products like condoms are being marketed—television ads are now aimed at women. Another social service: a Long Island–based Safecom aimed at gay men—which offers clients "safe company cards" after they have had two negative test three months apart.

The AIDS epidemic was certainly not the first intersection of the medical commodity and sexual market systems. Selling sexual aids and services—contra-ceptive devices, aphrodisiacs, and love potions—has a long history. But the capital intensification of sexuality began in earnest with the medicalization of sexuality at the end of the nineteenth century, which generated, along with a catalogue of sexual dysfunctions and diseases, a series of medical, psychological, and pharmaceutical technologies, therapies, and therapists with which to address them, along with a supportive research and scholarly apparatus as well as a popular (self-help) literature. Whereas the imposition of the medical discourse has had profound effects on the social structures of sexuality, I want to concentrate here on those which show how this historical process has helped to manage and transform the social currency of sexual exchange in a way that maximizes profit, both in terms of the consolidation of economic capital, and in terms of social profitability, i.e., its utility. This is important because such logic affects and will affect the social strategies developed for addressing the AIDS epidemic as well as the forms such therapeutic technologies and the discourse about them will take.

Both Foucault and Marcuse addressed the intersections between sexuality and the dominant strategies imposed by hegemonic institutional utilities. Foucault's discussion emphasizes the strategic utility of sexuality as a site for intervention into the lives of populations and individuals. Dominant utilities include those of producing populations (and regulating that production) and coordinating the lives and behaviors of individuals. Marcuse's analysis (as well as that of feminists like Diana Dinsmore) emphasizes the specific utility of sexuality for two other crucial social functions—one of which is the creation of socially useful desires, i.e., desires which the existing social system is designed to meet, and the fulfillment of which will serve to enhance the power and authority exerted by the hegemonic forms of organization, most notably, the organization of social labor for private profit, and the organization of reproduction and kinship in patrilineal, male-dominated forms. What increases the ideological potency of sexuality as a mechanism of social control is that regulation ultimately becomes translated into the currency of self-regulation, because sexuality has already been constructed as that which is or belongs to the realm of the private, i.e., opposed to the social. The regulatory force is represented and enacted through a currency not of coercion but of desire, in a way that encourages its individuation or personalization.

If desire is paradigmatically sexual, and the sexual is paradigmatically private, then individuals are far more likely to project expectations for their own fulfillment (and resentment over the lack of it) onto the private sphere than to articulate those expectations as an organized social demand, a demand for an organized social response, such as the redistribution and reorganization of basic institutions. The social logic which propels the cultural tendency (at least in the last one hundred years) both to talk more about sex and to increase the desire for it (control by incitement), can be attributed at least in part to its success as a mechanism of both pacification and mystification. That is, it provides a way to provide satisfaction to individuals in a way that not only preserves existing power structures, but also entails a minimum of capital or social investment to maintain. (Though there are indications in the recent and ongoing discussion of day care that the social cost of maintaining the nuclear family may very well be going up. In the resistance to day care, the existing assumptions about low costs are made obvious: why pay for what we've always gotten for free and, to show the beauty of this tactic, have freely chosen?)

Mechanisms work both to reduce the demands individuals are likely to make on the social and to encourage paradigmatic identification of themselves with a private rather than class affiliation, a move which works to mislead individuals about the source of much of their distress. One of the great ironies that feminists, especially American, drew from the so-called sexual revolution was that human tragedies follow from the discourse which made sexuality, especially genital sexual contact, the primary bearer or marker of human well-being, a burden it could not and does not bear well. Over-investment in sexuality is also a way of avoiding or minimizing the demand for investments in other areas, specifically the demand that other enterprises, like work, also be organized with an expectation of the possibility of satisfaction.

One of the other strategic benefits of over-investment in sexuality and the consequent centrality of notions of sexual identity is that it encourages divisions that make populations ultimately easier to regulate (gay ghettos, red-light districts) and also easier to target as consumers (market segmenting). The phallus is the primary commodity fetish.

Sex being so central to the very conception of human well-being, mechanisms are now in place and being mobilized which will justify (or be represented as justified by) the concern for protecting this very sexuality (and its freedom) from the threats imposed by disease. In the name of sexual health all sorts of means to control populations that would ordinarily seem unacceptable now seem to be justified as lesser evils: recent suggestions for quarantining, tatooing people with AIDS, and other proposed legislation which would treat the disease as a justifiable cause for denying citizens what would otherwise be their rights.

These issues force a consideration of the ways in which the AIDS epidemic is producing a social surplus, negotiable even though it is not only or primarily monetary currency. The AIDS epidemic also provides justification for the state's intervention into the bodies of all kinds of individuals—gays, military recruits, pregnant women, prisoners, maybe applicants for federal jobs, and IV drug users. Clearly, AIDS discourse is supplemental to an existing trend by virtue of which social control and surveillance of the behavior of human beings is progressively normalized and rationalized by increased use of routine screening of potential employees for drugs and alcohol, no-smoking legislation, changes in liability laws regarding drunk driving. All of these procedures are designed to intervene in cases where the self-regulatory logic of "just say no" has failed. Such practices share a common justification in the terms of benevolence—either paternalistic ("We want our employees to get help or protection") toward clients and others, or, to a much lesser degree, punitive. More important than the substantive effects of these particular procedures is the social recoding of practices that have been understood as the invasion of privacy, surveillance, intrusion, to what is currently regarded as benevolent protection.

Notes

1. See Freud, *Civilization and its Discontents,* ed. and trans. James Strachey (New York: Norton, 1963); Marcuse, *Eros and Civilization: A Philosophical Inquiry into Freud* (Boston, Beacon Press, 1955).

2. One might consider in this regard the sexual politics of Wilhelm Reich, and the theory

of pansexualism. See Wilhelm Reich, *Sex-pol, Essays, 1929–34*, ed. Lee Baxandall, (New York: Vintage, 1972).

3. Jean Baudrillard, "Consumer Society," in *Jean Baudrillard: Selected Writings,* ed. Mark Poster (Stanford: Stanford University Press, 1988) p. 43.

4. Baudrillard, "Consumer Society."

5. Susan Sontag, *AIDS and its Metaphors* (New York: Farrar, Straus, & Giroux, 1989).

6. *Sex Work: Writings by Women in the Sex Industry,* eds. Frederique Delacoste and Priscilla Alexander (Pittsburgh: Cleis Press, 1987).

7. Kathleen Barry, *Female Sexual Slavery* (New York: New York University Press, 1985).

8. See Shulamith Firestone, *the Dialectic of Sex* (New York: Morrow, 1970).

9. Kathleen Barry, *Female Sexual Slavery.* (Englewood Cliffs, N.J.: Prentice-Hall, 1979).

3

Disciplining Pleasures

It should come as no surprise that the AIDS epidemic and the cultural discourse surrounding it have produced, at least for the time being, a change in the terms of sexual exchange, and with it a change in the erotic climate. The eighties have ushered in a new sexual aesthetic, which Richard Goldstein of the *Village Voice* has dubbed "the new sobriety," and which postmodern theorists Arthur and Marilouise Kroker have somewhat more dramatically characterized as "panic sex." The emergence of these historically specific hegemonies not only marks shifts in how sexuality is culturally valued, represented, and circulated; it also points toward a rupture in the order of things, or at least a displacement, an optimistic threshold of possibilities represented by the discourse of sexual revolution, and the politics of ecstasy which promised a universe of pansexual possibilities for experimentation and exploration that the current risk of epidemic contagion seems radically to foreclose.

Since the sexual revolution spoke to issues beyond genital behavior, we can also expect to see the symptoms of the current sexual epidemic inscribed on bodies other than those infected with HIV virus. Indeed many of the more hysterical symptoms have emerged from segments of the population least likely to contract a sexually transmitted disease. That's because the sexual epidemic I'm speaking of is more than a health or medical problematic; it represents a kind of rupture in the sexual/political order of things. Just as the discourses and practices mobilized under the rubric of "sexual revolution" recast the relationship between the personal and the political, the epidemic construct allows for and in fact seems to justify a reconsideration of the politics of the personal, and more particularly the politics of pleasure that emerged from it. Because the prospect of contagion raises the social stakes attached to individual behavioral choices, and because in an epidemic situation such latitude carries the signification of threat and risk, epidemic conditions can and in fact are being represented as occasions necessitating organized efforts to coordinate the behavior of individuals through the generation of new forms of sexual discipline and management.

The strategic interest in coordinating populations through the disciplining of pleasure is certainly not specific to this sexual epidemic. As any of a number of critical historians like Peter Gay and Michel Foucault have argued, Western culture can be viewed as a series of problematizations, each of which justifies and mandates the deployment of regulatory formations over the lives of bodies. If Lévi-Strauss is right, the emergence of culture is coextensive with the development of disciplinary symbolic practices which regulate bodies through systems of exchange. In both constituting and regulating the play of socially relevant social differences, disciplinary mechanisms emerge as correlates of the problematics they promise to resolve, and problematics formulated along the lines suggested by the disciplinary strategies that are already in place. Drawing upon these analyses (and there are others I could cite as well) my use of the term pleasure assumes it to be a disciplinary construct—rather than an ahistorical, organic phenomenon. My concern is to consider how pleasures are constructed within the hegemony of sexual epidemic and how their placement within this discipline formation recasts the political problematic of pleasure. In the old days, that which functioned as a limit on the pursuit of pleasure was cast either in the psychoeconomy of guilt and shame or in a moralistic discourse which posited harm—to others or oneself—as the limit. Just when post-Freudian discourse seemed to proffer the prospect of pleasure without guilt, epidemic conditions forced the confrontation between pleasure and finitude.

One of the historically specific consequences of the sexual epidemic has been the emergence of a managerial calculus in which pleasure is evaluated not within a differential economy of rights, privileges, and relative utilities which has been dominant in liberal logic since utilitarianism, but in the more highly charged and hysterically invested currency of life and death, health and disease.

Christianity, of course, also made this linkage, which may help explain why epidemic conditions have been conducive to the resurgence of fundamentalist discourse and have helped resuscitate its political currency. (And its absolutist dimensions are likely comforting in light of the ambiguities and complexities of the current situation.) But because this linkage had to bridge the infinite abyss beyond the phenomenal and the eternal, the connection between worldly excesses of the flesh and the ultimate fate of the soul which survived the death of the body could only be demonstrated indirectly through a calculus of cosmic probabilities. This, however, also left room for alternative cost-benefit logics. The very mechanisms by which soul was privileged over body and the sacred valued over the profane could also be reversed in a moment which Nietzsche described as the transvaluation of value, the moment of turning the tables and casting one's fate with the life of the body and its order of things. Because the Christian discourse draws so much of its currency from the economy of eternity, and because that currency differs fundamentally from that which dominates in the sphere of the phenomenal, its disciplinary formations leave open different strategic choices with respect to the prescriptive necessities that follow from that difference, including the choice of denying or discounting that difference altogether, and as any of a number of post and anti-Christian paradigms have done, of rejecting the logic of absolutist prohibitions and recasting evaluative differences within a logic of existential consequences of relative benefit, recuperated in the valorizing language of autonomy, privacy and individuation, and transcendence.

Because Christianity problematized pleasure, especially pleasures of the flesh as sins of excess, in need of continual regulation, and because so much of its disciplinary force followed from the prospect of punishment in the form of eternal damnation, it is not surprising that those discourses which sought to challenge both its hegemony and authority chose to focus their analyses on the repressive dimensions of this disciplinary apparatus, as well as on its own tendencies toward excess in the form of what Marcuse termed "surplus repression." What was repressed, according to this analysis, was pleasure, especially the pleasures of private immediate engagement which in late capitalism tend to be sacrificed or denied in favor of some overriding set of economic or cosmic utilities. As a consequence of this critique, the prospect of pleasure, and an expansion of the sphere of entitlement to pleasure, became key signifiers for critical discourses which sought to mobilize populations in resistance to the hegemonic orders of power and authority which sought to deny or arbitrarily restrict the forms of gratification to which everyone has a right. Because the political problematic of pleasure offered by the left was initially figured as a problematic of repression, and because the pursuit of pleasure was assumed to be intrinsically beneficent, the strategies of resistance that tended to suggest themselves privileged tactical transgressions of restrictive norms as a primary way both of undermining their authority and of exercising entitlement to that which had been arbitrarily denied. In this alternative social calculus, cultivation of difference rather than coordination was the primary rule, with success measured, to a large extent, in the very proliferation of erotic economies and stylistic divergences. Such stylization served both to individuate and to draw people together in affinity groups. This is the logic which helped produce the climate of sexual pluralism and tolerance associated with the period of sexual revolution, and which is now subject to revisionist critique. It is also a logic which, given the current sexual epidemic, seems to have reached a dead end.

The situation of sexual epidemic helps point up the limits of a critical logic which, though it sought to challenge notions of individual interest and entitlement at an economic level, nevertheless maintained a liberal model of pluralism when it came to matters of sexual and libidinal autonomy. Given the atomistic aesthetic which tended to dominate discussions of sexual liberation, any discourse which attempted to set disciplinary limits on the pursuit of private gratification tended to be regarded as a pernicious imposition to be resisted in the name of freedom, individual autonomy, and self-regulation. Out of this configuration emerged a variety of enterprises. It is not that the limits of this logic went unnoticed or unchallenged, especially although certainly not exclusively by many French and American feminists, who sought to move beyond tolerant permissiveness toward a political critique of the strategic dimensions of pleasure—which eroticize domination, misogyny and the social/sexual abuse/exploitation of women. But as long as repression could be figured as the major threat to pleasure, and as long as both capitalism and Christianity could be represented as disciplinary mechanisms opposed to the pleasure principle, the private pursuit of pleasure could be represented as a form of resistance to oppression, and an assertion of the powers of the life of the body over the economy of death.

The problem is that under epidemic conditions, the relationship between pleasures of the flesh and the prospect of death is not limited to the set of probabilistic relationships postulated by Christianity in the form of punishment after the fact. In a contemporary context, that relationship is also mediated through medical discourse and theories of contagion, in terms of which that relationship is one of material causation transacted between bodies, the consequences of which will also express themselves in material terms in the language of symptoms, disease, and deterioration. This discursive framework entirely recasts the context and terms of strategic judgments, at both the individual and social levels. For one thing, the choice is no longer one of allying oneself with the fate of the body rather than of the soul, but is rather a matter of differing probabilistic corporeal destinies measured against the possibilities not of salvation in the next life, but of deterioration and death in this one. Furthermore, the calculus of risk is significantly different. The threat or risk is no longer primarily the threat of disembodied divine judgment, but rather comes to take root in the body of the other, a body which carries with it the history of its own prudential calculus of choices.

The hegemony of sexual epidemic has redefined the site of struggle in the politics of pleasure. That which threatens pleasure is not a disembodied figure from without, but rather a risk embodied in at least some of the processes and activities in which it is pursued. Given the demonstrated correlations between certain activities (unprotected anal intercourse, IV drug use) and relative risks of infection, it is no longer possible unilaterally to advocate the deregulation of pleasure as a life-sustaining strategy, any more than one can reject all disciplinary interventions of limits as gratuitous puritanical excesses.

This is not to say many of the responses proposed to combat the current epidemic are not puritanical and excessive. It is rather to suggest that the traditional terms of analysis and critique used to challenge the hegemonic exploitation of pleasure, especially sexual pleasure, are inadequate to the demands of the contemporary situation, where the choice is no longer between regulated and unregulated sexuality, but is rather a matter of strategic choices between disciplinary mechanisms. This means that one cannot assume, as theorists like Ellen Willis seem to, that any progressive critique must proceed with the assumption that existing disciplinary mechanisms are intrinsically anti-sex, and thereby to be opposed on those grounds. While the prospect of pleasure without limit had provided an imaginative site from which both to criticize existing arrangements and to envision more utopic possibilities during the era of sexual revolution, the sexual epidemic has forced a radical restructuring of expectations and priorities, such that disciplinary realignments of behavior can now be represented not as a limit on pleasure, but as a way of protecting and securing it.

The current sexual epidemic presents us with a drama different from the struggle between liberation and repression, and therefore casts questions of discipline within a different register. It also means that the disciplinary impulse can no longer be assumed unproblematically to be symptomatic of a hegemonic political agenda. Therefore, the political alliances proceeding on that basis will need to be rethought. Consider as an example of the new political problematic of pleasure the debate that ensued within San Francisco's gay male community in the face of the proposal to close the bathhouses as a way of limiting the spread of AIDS. This debate received national attention in part because, as commentators like Dennis Altman point out, this debate was taking place in the city that had been regarded as the capital of gay culture. The terms and tenor of this debate were certainly colored by the fact that bathhouses had been a key site for mobilizing gays in defense of their turf when it was threatened by earlier attempts to close them. By 1984, however, it was gay activists who introduced a city-wide referendum to restrict sexual activities in bathhouses. One of the effects of this initiative was the creation of political ruptures within what had previously been constituted as a relatively homogeneous community of resistance to regulatory interventions from outside, i.e., from homophobic heterosexual interests. The debate over the baths moved the site of political struggle from a struggle with the outside to a struggle within a community that had previously understood itself to be founded on common interests. Despite certain ad hominem critiques, the impulse behind regulatory intervention could not be dismissed as homophobic, since they emerged from and were advocated on the basis of genuine concern for the preservation of the health and well-being of the members of that community, for whom the bathhouses were said to constitute a real health risk. Conversely, those who argued against closure did so out of concern that what was at risk was not only the health of individuals, but the very gains gays had made in securing social and symbolic space free from the intervention and regulation of the state.

One of the reasons this struggle took on such vituperative and intense proportions is that both sides could claim the indigenous authority to determine what was beneficial, or at least better for the group as a whole. In such a context, differences over strategy and tactics could be read as failures of loyalty and gestures of betrayal, especially in a community in which mutual advocacy and support was regarded as a central survival strategy. The debate over the bathhouses was complicated because it forced the introduction of supplemental considerations beyond that of advocating and protecting homoerotic pleasures. The bathhouse debate forced consideration of just what tactics and practices best served that function, and provided occasions for political realignments which cast doubt on the homogeneity and modes of linkage between members of the gay community.

Much of the difference between the two positions centered on the question of whether paternalistic intervention best served the gay community, or whether efforts were better spent in educative efforts to encourage self-regulation and voluntary behavior modification. One of the most significant factors to emerge from this debate was the series of disciplinary theories and practices now circulating as the discourse of "safe sex." In examining the emergence of safe sex as a specific sexual political hegemony emerging from the sexual epidemic, certain strategic complexities of the contemporary politics of pleasure become more apparent.

For one thing, the speed with which what was a local discourse of a marginalized community was integrated into official social policy represents a significant shift in the configuration of social authority. The appropriation of techniques of safe sex for mass consumption is tantamount to acknowledging the authority of the gay community, rather than restricting that community to the role of victim, not only to regulate itself, but also to serve as an instructive frame of reference for heterosexuals. As a result, the politics of sexual epidemic has produced some strange bedfellows, as the Reagan administration finds itself taking the bulk of its prescriptive discourse from a community that in other contexts has been represented as a threat to the forms of moral authority it has taken as its mandate to defend (most specifically, the hegemony of the monogamous heterosexual couple and the nuclear family).

This is but one small irony among others. Consider, for example, the differential social responses given to the primary prescription of safe sex practice— namely, the recommendation that condoms and spermicides be used during genital intercourse in order to inhibit the exchange of bodily fluids. When Margaret Sanger attempted to distribute condoms to make sex safer for women who were dying from having too many children or from illegal abortions, she was arrested and jailed for obscenity. When that same device can also be presented as a way of protecting men from absorbing these same fluids, however, their use is advocated by the surgeon general as a public service.

What is particularly ironic and chilling about the campaign to market safe sex as the latest disciplinary innovation is the implicit assumption that circulates along with it, namely, that sex was safe before AIDS. Sex was safe, it seems, as long as it was mostly women who died for and from sex in childbirth, illegal abortions, faulty contraception, rape, and murder at the hands of their sexual partners. For men, sexual safety may simply be a matter of wearing a condom. For women, however, sexual safety is not so easily achieved because the risks for women who engage in sex with men or with other women outstrip the risks of contracting a sexually transmitted disease. How safe it is to be a heterosexual or a lesbian will be materially determined by such factors as the nature and availability of contraception, abortion, and fertility technology, the social organization of the family, and the repertoire of social responses to sexual violence.

One of the strategic utilities of the campaign for safe sex is the possibilities such a discursive framework offers for remarketing the nuclear family as a prophylactic social device. This strategy again takes on an ironic cast when viewed from the history of women's and children's position within the family. That history reveals that the family has never been a particularly safe place for women and children. Most violence against women occurs within the family, as does the sexual abuse of children. Whereas defense of the family was not an explicit element in the generation of safe sex practices, its disciplinary logic leaves such practices open to mobilization by discourses which offer differing and competing visions of just what constitutes sexual health and safety, as well as competing senses of the utilities to be preserved and protected.

The discourse of safe sex has also more recently been incorporated as part of a larger campaign to discipline pleasures expressed in the form of the demand to "just say no"—not only to genital sex without prophylactic mediation, but also to an ever-proliferating range of objects including alcohol, nicotine, and other drugs, as well as any practice or substance that is represented as unhealthy. This campaign to encourage elective refusal is, however, also being institutionally buttressed by legislative and other mechanisms like the promised "war on drugs," the raising of the drinking age, and the normalization of drug testing and other forms of surveillance into what had previously been considered areas of private discretion. Such changes are accompanied by a shifting set of utilities, as evidenced by changes in the institutional and social responses to the consumption of tobacco. Historically, the tobacco lobby has been extremely effective in its mobilization of social resources for the purposes of encouraging consumption. More recently, however, the protection of the pleasures of smoking has been progressively eroded by concern about the health risks of such practices, not only for those who consume the product directly, but also for those who can now be characterized as victims of ambient smoke. As a consequence, the regulatory practices protecting the consumption of tobacco are progressively being replaced by more legislation designed to limit the space of entitlement enjoyed by smokers. Here again we have an example of the malleability of disciplinary mechanisms regulating pleasure in response to shifting social utilities, and therefore a case disclosive of the limits of associating the advocacy of pleasure with any particular political agenda or strategy.

The specificity of its prescriptions not withstanding, the recent "just say no" campaign is but a particularly bald and conspicuous case of what Freud argued was the essence of the social contract—namely, the demand that individuals learn to discipline and regulate their pleasures in relationship to the reality of social demands.[1] Because these demands are neither individuated nor optional, that contract is always accomplished with some ambivalence, the effects of which, according to Freud, tend to return in the form of compensatory symptoms, fetishes, and fixations. Although the mechanisms which regulate desire achieve their effects in part through repression, punishment, and through the threat of loss, such laws do not eliminate the desires they regulate, but instead work to produce them in the most socially useful form as defined by the dominant configuration of social interests.

The productive dimension of disciplinary mechanisms is also emphasized in Foucault's analysis of modern power mechanisms which, he argues, depend less on the powers to withhold and punish than on control by incitement, i.e., by the capacity to produce and circulate a system of desires and objects that fulfill them. The productive dimensions of disciplines operate to stylize pleasures relative to the specific institutions and practices through which they are actualized, and in terms of which their differences acquire value and significance. Because the relationship between disciplinary formations is non-continuous, any paradigmatic shift will be experienced as a rupture by those subjects who find themselves subject to what is, in this transitional moment, a series of conflictings desires, expectations, and demands.

In the contemporary situation, many of us find ourselves caught between the discursive figures of sexual liberation and sexual epidemic, and what often seems to be the unbridgeable gap between the aesthetics and forms of life associated with each. In light of the temporal and historical dimensions in which these disciplinary mechanisms operate, the gaps and contradictions between them cannot be simply sutured by a logic of supersession, in which an earlier untenable position is abandoned in favor of a more enlightened or realistic one, especially since there is no basis upon which such determinations could ever be made.

The challenge presented to a progressive politics of pleasure is to articulate a way to live in light of the contradictory evidence that our desires and pleasures have been strategically constructed, but that they cannot also thereby simply be reconstructed in relationship to a rewritten set of utilities, regardless of the position from which or the intention with which such rewriting is undertaken. As Camus has said of plague situations, they force us to live with tapped resources. The sexual epidemic forces us to live with our socio-libidinal contradictions, without appeal either to myths of their inevitability, or to their malleability to direct/immediate legislative intervention, at least insofar as those are designed to produce unilateral coordinated results.

The capacity to live without appeal takes discipline—both in the sense of a willingness and a commitment to reengage the repetitive dynamics of struggle, and in the sense of a redeployment of our powers of invention. The existing literature on the sexual epidemic is filled with calls for such inventions—the invention of new erotic imaginaries, new aesthetics of pleasure, new narratives capable of inscribing our bodies with alternative desires and choreographies. More specifically, as Simon Watney suggests, one of the challenges to the current ideological apparatus is to develop images, languages, and practices which eroticize safe sex. Such a possibility depends, in part, on a disciplinary realignment in which such practices are not positioned as compensatory resignation, but operate within a larger aesthetic which invests them with stylistic value and institutional support. The prospect of such tactical reinventions is facilitated by the strategic assumption of the productive relationship between discipline and pleasure, those moments when disciplines function as enabling forces for inciting and stylizing that which they also claim to regulate.

The political reformation of pleasure is tantamount to the invention of a new discipline, which will demand from its subjects a certain kind of discipline, particularly political discipline. One of the vectors of difference introduced by sexual epidemic is that the terms and aesthetics of sexual political struggle have become distinctly less sexy than they were under the aesthetic which promised ecstasy and liberation. It will take a certain kind of discipline to live and work without appeal to a political imaginary dominated by figures of apocalyptic transformation and the utopic possibilities of liberated pleasures, to engage in a struggle that will lack the dramatic clarity of revolutionary struggles waged in the name of sex, pleasure, desire against forces that seek its annihilation.

The rhetoric of social action in our age, be it medical, political, or theoretical, is largely dominated by militaristic metaphors of combat, enemies, positions, support, and defense. Such metaphors work to produce a set of expectations about the dynamics or forms such struggles assume, as well as suggesting strategies of response and modes of resolution. In this culture, we tend to wage war on our social problems, and from this formation follows the tendency to invent what one writer on AIDS has called the magic bullet, which works by annihilating that at which it is aimed. The political struggle of this epidemic is to develop strategies without appeal to the figure of the magic bullet aimed at a clearly defined enemy which its action eliminates. Such a configuration is inadequate to a situation in which the enemy is neither clearly defined nor stable in identity, and may very well be an enemy within. The politics of pleasure in the age of sexual epidemic will lack the righteous pleasures of great crusades and grand gestures, and are more likely to be waged in the trenches of institutionalized disciplinary practices. What we need is to find, invent, retrieve a form of discourse and practice capable of inciting those mobilizing energies which can take pleasure in the struggle without appeal and address a situation for which there is no quick fix.

II

In beginning any discussion of pleasure, one enters a field that is already structured by a certain ambivalence, especially in the Western phallocentric tradition. That ambivalence, which may for the moment be summarily characterized as the difference between discourses of advocacy and critique (pleasure has always had its supporters and detractors), very well may be a consequence of certain slippage within the sign, a slippage similar to that which Elaine Scarry shows operates with pain. Pain, according to Scarry, shatters language. The inexpressibility of pain pushes language to its limits. The very inexpressibility of pain has political implications, leaving it open to two mutually exclusive operations of power, which Scarry terms making and unmaking. The absence of a language for pain allows pain to be transferred from its originary site in the body and reappropriated to substantiate fictions of power. As Scarry shows in superb detail, the project of giving voice to pain, bringing it to language, can serve two very different sets of utilities. Giving voice to pain can work either to alleviate pain or occasion more of it. Scarry then goes on to argue that civilization can be seen as the effort to stabilize these conflicting potentials. This is accomplished, in part, through the disciplining of pain and its representations through the mechanisms of war and torture, and through the development of the language of human agency and truth.

Scarry's analysis shows that torture and war operate, as Foucault suggests about disciplines, as mechanisms of proliferation and regulation. Part of the purpose of both war and torture is to formalize procedures for how pain may be inflicted, so that the pain produced can be reappropriated to substantiate the regime of power that produces it. The idea I wish to entertain here is whether there are anything like comparable disciplines of pleasure, and if so, how they operate. This is a first stage of asking the question, paralleling Scarry's: what sorts of ways of working pleasure might constitute a remaking of the world, a mobilization of pleasure for liberatory possibilities?

No discourse about the liberatory potential of pleasure can go on without a certain dose of irony and realism, which already restricts any grandiose utopian pretensions. The factors contributory to the production of this postmodern hindsight are multiple and overdetermined. They are part of what distinguishes the contemporary discussion from that of the '60s, when it was more possible to talk in optimistic terms about the liberatory potential of sexual pleasure and self-expression. Such factors include AIDS, Marxist critiques of consumer culture, gay critiques of mandatory heterosexism, feminist critiques of pornography, phallocentrism, Foucault's critique of the repressive hypothesis—one could go on. The point is that contemporary theorists are confronted with a situation in which the problematic is not that of liberating pleasure from repression by traditional moral regulations, but a situation in which modern power works at least as much by the mobilization of pleasure, what Foucault calls control by incitement. Pleasure, like pain, is that which operates in significant enough slippage between bodies and the power apparatus which represent them, so as also to be appropriable for the purpose of substantiating the hegemonic figures of domination, be they regimes, institutions, or economies. Most critical traditions—Marxism, feminism, post-whatever—have found the moment in which the pleasures of the oppressed are mobilized, socially, economically, psychologically, in ways that further empower the systems which subjugate them, be they capitalism, patriarchy, or any other hegemonic form of domination. As Scarry says of pain, pleasure is also inextricably bound with mechanisms of power. Pleasure functions as a sign in a system of psycho-corporeal inscriptions in which differences are socially and symbolically marked, organized, and evaluated. With pleasure arises questions of entitlement and desert, excess and absence, privilege and priority, authority and resistance. Pleasure is thereby already political and politicized. To think of pleasure politically means that we can no longer, as both Foucault and Cixous suggest, albeit for different reasons, think about pleasure within a binary opposition of yes or no, but instead must see how it is engaged by and within a nexus of power relations and systems of reproduction, which increase and circulate as well as regulate and restrict pleasure.[2] My aim in this chapter is to discuss one aspect of the politics of pleasure—namely, the contemporary strategy of disciplining pleasures.

The two disciplinary forms on which I will concentrate are those produced in the names of patriarchy and capitalism. I choose these as my focus because I believe they are two of the more comprehensive and persistent strategies for organizing and representing pleasure, especially in our age, and because they share common strategies and mechanisms which also have the effect of reinforcing and validating one another. Another way to put this, inspired by Foucault, is to say that both capitalism and patriarchy problematize pleasure in much the same way, or figure its instability in much the same language, and try to manage/discipline it with similar mechanisms.

One way of problematizing the instability of pleasure is by reference to the substitutability of objects, hence a problematic of proliferation and contagion. When that proliferative possibility is exploited by capitalism, it reemerges in the discourses of disciplines like advertising and marketing, as a series of strategic refinements designed to mobilize that potential for organized patterns of consumption for profit. Pleasure can be mobilized as both a lack and a potential that can be perpetually fulfilled by a never-ending chain of interchangeable commodities—a more pleasurable car to ride, or movie to see, or house to live in. The interchangeable objects of pleasure thus allow pleasure to be represented as malleable enough to be capable of flexible and highly mobile redirection in response to shifting social utilities. This tendency is also facilitated by advertising, marketing and other schemes designed to proliferate a discourse of strategically specific needs, desires and pleasures. These disciplines also work to produce subjects who come progressively to figure themselves as lacks which can be filled by gestures of consumption, which are by their very nature in perpetual need of repetition, and hence also have the effect of reproducing the hegemonic forms of control over the profit generated by such activity.

Such repetitions are further facilitated by a problematization and language of pleasure as episodic, momentary, and hence temporally and experientially unstable. Although there have been great debates within the history of Western philosophy about which pleasures are most enduring, all acknowledge that pleasure is a phenomenon of duration, and thus also of limits and lacks. In late capitalism, this eternal return is replicated and strategically mobilized as a promissory discourse about this year's model and the latest technological development. This strategy has the added advantage of being able to mobilize whatever gap exists between the promise and the object by projecting its fulfillment in the form of a commodity designed precisely to respond to and fulfill those previous lacks. (We have now come up with a dishwashing detergent that will relieve the unpleasure of unsightly spots, promised, but not delivered, by the earlier version.) Additionally, the episodic construction of pleasure in late capitalism allows episodes or moments to be commodified as such. ("Have the time of your life at Disney World." "Watch this TV program and it will bring your family closer together.") Far from seeking to eliminate lack, late capitalism seeks constantly to reconfigure it, so as to provide a perpetual motivation for socially coordinated patterns of production and consumption. The genius of commodity culture is that the subjects whose performance it produces and regulates come to take pleasure in its consistently mobile promises, and therefore in its lacks and gaps as well as its excesses. It is not only that we are controlled by incitement, but the control itself is pleasurable, and replicated not only in consistent consumption, but also through linguistic and imagistic representations. We can't wait to buy the newest issue of *Vogue* or *House and Garden* to tell us what clothes or home furnishings to buy next. The very notion that there is no limit to the logic of substitution of commodity culture, that there is no intrinsic limit to what we can consume, no end to the capitalist logic of production, has at this stage been ideologically represented as itself pleasurable, and therefore as a site for reinvesting social energies in the perpetuation of the economic and political system which makes all this possible, as well as the desires which sustain it. Capitalism helps discipline the instability of lack by reconfiguring it as a perpetual promise within a developmental logic of fulfillment figured as multiple occasions for repetition. Hence the lack associated with pleasure is retranslated as an occasion for fulfillment, the excess of which can then be mobilized in the forms of reinvestment of energies in perpetuating the very systems of disciplines themselves. The proliferative instability of pleasure is thus mobilized in favor of those institutions which are able to frame such fragilities in terms of a system of social utilities, like the differential distribution of profit.

As nineteenth-century theorists like Bentham and Mill already recognized, pleasure becomes a crucial currency for social control in a post-scarcity economy. Utilitarianism, in some sense, can be read as an effort at formulating a social calculus in terms of which pleasure can be distributed in a way that induces the population's reinvestment in the social order as the ground of the possibilities of its own satisfactions, even when those satisfactions are different and differentially distributed (an important consideration if the system to be sustained is capitalism, and the regulated production of economic and class stratification). Social utility in a post-scarcity economy depends precisely on representing pleasure as a perpetual promise or reward of membership in the social order, and of participation in its regulatory and distributive as well as productive mechanisms. Conversely, the challenge to the social order is to develop mechanisms by which not only the possibility but also the impossibility or scarcity of pleasure can be socially regulated as motivational and regulatory devices of incitement and pacification. The success of this strategy, as thinkers like Marcuse and Foucault have pointed out, depends precisely on how such limits and absences are socially constructed and represented. This demands a language of pleasure capable not only of distributing pleasure over an ever-increasing number of objects, but also of regulating or stabilizing the differences between them, and therefore a system of stabilized differences as such. This instability is reflected not only in the highly ambivalent language of pleasure, but also in the uses to which such language is put.

The proliferative instability of pleasure is, as is also especially evident in advertising and marketing discourse, reproduced, and further incited, by a highly variegated and complex language of pleasure. In this sense, the sign of pain works in the opposite way. If pain shatters language by exposing its lacks, pleasure pushes language in the direction of its disclosure as a system of ungrounded substitutable differences. Pleasure pushes language toward its proliferative limits. One might cite, as an example, the highly refined language of wine tasting designed to distinguish the particular pleasures of a good claret from those of a burgundy, or the language of fashion, which aims to distinguish the pleasures of a Dior and a Chanel. Such language takes on political and economic significance when it is also used both to represent and to incite a differential threshold of pleasure that is translatable as profit margin, i.e., to incite greater pleasure in consuming more rather than less expensive commodities.

But given the substitutability of objects, it is quite possible that this potential could be mobilized in the opposite direction, i.e., toward social dissolution and disruption. Hence there emerges a need for regulating or establishing ways of organizing and differentiating between substitutable objects. Pleasure must be socially condensed as well as proliferated. The strategy is to organize pleasure around some privileged object, some fetish. In capitalism the privileged fetish is the commodity, and the privileged pleasurable performance that of consumption and possession. This way of organizing pleasure is replicated through a language that uses the rhetoric of possession as a key term by which subjects and objects are pleasurably related. ("I had a good time." "We had great sex.")

The rhetoric of possession helps discipline pleasure in several respects. Most obviously, the language of possession helps sustain the privilege enjoyed by the commodity and the consequent activities of consumption in the very formation and expression of pleasure. But the language of possession also works to help privatize and individuate what might otherwise be seen as purely undifferentiated fields not only of substitutable objects, but of subjects or agents of pleasure as well. The discourse of commodity fetishism also produces, as part of its significatory surplus, a fetishism of difference, through which subjects are differentially produced and valued, at least in part through differential patterns of consumption. Through the discourses of taste and lifestyles, such differences themselves are fetishized as exercises of individuation and self-definition, even though, or maybe especially because, the objects of choice are precisely not individuated, but designed, marketed and produced and consumed en masse. ("You too can express your own domestic imaginary by purchasing one of Ralph Lauren's new modular design packages of coordinated interior accessories." "You too can commune with the Pepsi generation through ingestion of its sacred fluids.")

The discourses of style and taste, far from being extraneous, are in fact necessary for stabilizing the potentially unmanageable connections between pleasure and its objects, even though the stability such mechanisms provide is only temporary, as they are usually designed to last no more than one selling season. But because such discourse works not only to endow objects with promissory surplus but also to produce subjects in perpetual need of differentiation and identification, the forms of pleasure generated by these discourses can remain, even as the objects of satisfaction are continuously changed or recirculated. (Miniskirts and other retro garb are back.)

As any of a number of thinkers from Diana Vreeland to Michel Foucault have alerted us, style takes discipline. Because the discourses of style and taste depend upon fetishizing differences and investing even the most minute of them with intense significance (a heel too high or skirt too long can destroy the entire effect, marking one as dated rather than current, masochistic rather than self-affirming), the series of selections and practices out of which style emerges must be carefully regulated and designed, often with the help of experts or stylistic consultants of one kind or another. First and foremost, it is the body, its appearance, behaviors, and possibilities, which must be regulated by regimens of activity and aesthetics which differentiate between occasions and forms of fulfillment. A style establishes a significatory calculus which differentiates between possible objects and activities, what to eat (and not eat), how much to exercise, what to wear, what forms of experience to purchase, and so on. The discourse of style can be read as a strategic attempt by late capitalism to manage the anxiety of indeterminacy resulting from the very prolific character of the social production it encourages. So much to choose from—how to decide? The discourse of style provides one kind of answer, in which limits, of time, resources, and access, can be retranslated as personally imposed selectivity, discretion, a discipline of eye and mind that is itself a source of narcissistic self-fulfillment, the pleasures of autonomy figured as control over oneself and one's pleasures. Through the activities of stylizing one's body, one's environment, one's time, the subject can be sutured into the pleasures of self-production within a highly mediated scheme of identifications and differences. Style offers the promise of perpetual differentiation and individuation within a field that is designed for massive and coordinated gestures of social participation and consumption. Style allows for the creation of the individuals, whose behavior it then undertakes to coordinate through a mechanism of controlled or managed differences. That is why, in what is sometimes called the postmodern era, stylistic proliferation and transgression is rampant. Stylistic transgressions can be both tolerated and conspicuous because style is established as the most fragile and therefore revisable modality of the hegemonic organization of power. Style operates as the form in which power is present, in some sense, always and only to be transgressed. The disciplinary mechanism of style provides the ever-present possibility of liberation from what appears to be the force of mass-cultural inscription, through a private language of organized deviations.

Each of the forms of discipline instituted by capitalism upon pleasure—proliferation in the name of social utility and progress, management through condensation into a privileged fetish object, and discipline through stylization—is also operative and thereby reinforced in the organization of pleasures instituted by patriarchy. They depend upon mobilizing pleasure in ways which differentially mark bodies and thereby position subjects in a system of stratified power and privilege. For patriarchy, the key object of discipline is also the pleasures and behaviors of bodies, marked and thereby made subjects through the inscription of sexual differences, represented by the rhetoric of gender and preference. Considered from the perspective of the Western tradition, sexuality, even more than the commodity, is the culturally privileged exemplary case or form of pleasure. The language and theories of pleasure which emphasize its sensational presentation, in the language of tickles, and excitations, tingles, tension and release, clearly are modeled on the moments in which bodies are capable of producing in themselves and others affective possibilities through the exchange of flesh that allow not only for their affirmation, but also for their celebratory detachment and displacements onto other kinds of objects (like commodities and regimes). Sexuality is an optimum sphere for social regulation, because it constitutes a point of intersection between the individual and the social body which thereby also provides a site for the resolidification of individual and social investments, with the currency of pleasure as lubricant. Sexuality provides a medium in which social imperatives and utilities can be translated into a language of individuating styles of gratification.

Considered from a utilitarian perspective, sexuality has, even given its obvious instability, two powers so useful that it is worth attempting to manage, if not entire to regulate, them. Sexuality is useful to any hegemonic regime, reproducing a population of subjects, while at the same time functioning to gratify and hence pacify the existing population. Our culture in particular has figured its utility in terms of cost-effectiveness, hence a strategy that encourages an organization of pleasure such that the population is reproduced most efficiently, with the least amount of social investment for greatest return. This strategy has thus far entailed the development of mechanisms designed to encourage a division of bodies such that one segment of the population, the segment designated female, will be motivated to organize their lives so as to reproduce the population and the extant system of social relationship for free, i.e., without material compensation as a matter of choice. The disciplining of the substitutability of bodies accomplished by the imposition of the discipline of sexual difference not only allows for a division of social labor, but also guarantees that the bodies targeted for special services will not be those empowered by their value. French feminists have shown how sexual difference works to limit the substitutability of bodies to those which have at least the prospect of producing some social value, either in the form of biological reproduction, pleasure, or pacification, or represented as the perpetual promise of that social value. As soon as bodies are stylized by gender, regimentary organization of behavior can be imposed so that their regulatory function can be retranslated into the language of preference, and social utilities become inseparable from the codes which are supposed to oppose the social—the personal, the private, the individuated.

Any strategic effort to suture disruptive effects of the substitutability of bodies is not complete. There are categories of guilty pleasures and styles which transgress the hegemonic or socially privileged ones. To a certain extent, this proliferative possibility also has a certain utility. It serves to offer individuals a pacificatory imaginary populated by an endless stream of possibilities, as many of their other social options and points of access are radically diminished by the forces of international patriarchal capitalism. As Foucault points out, the figure of liberation from power through sex may very well turn out to be the governing fiction of our age. Capitalism is capable of marketing sexual pleasure, or at least the promise of it, in an increasingly refined and variegated sexual marketplace—of specially coded sexual practices, images, and tastes. The sex industry is very definitely in a period of growth. Sexuality is a relatively inexpensive way to pacify a population. Even in its most highly theatricalized and commodified forms, the commodification of sexuality through institutions like pornography, prostitution, and simulated sex requires rather minimal amounts of capital investment. These are labor-intensive forms of production which, in their very economics, already serve to subjugate and discipline those whose labor these institutions exploit, which is why the image, if not the reality, of prostitution assumes the prostitute to be female. The beauty of the sex industry as a strategic construction of patriarchal logic is that it serves to discipline and regulate sexuality in a form which can also be represented in the language of intensified access, transgressive gratification, and custom-tailored liberatory excursions. In sexual commodification, sexual pleasure is incited and controlled in a way such that the very mechanisms of regulation are experienced and represented as pleasurable. (The codes of femininity, and the restrictions they impose on the female body, are a very clear-cut example of this—what is more sexually incited than a woman's body cut by garter belts and *bustière*?).

The stylization of gender in terms of an oppositional and asymmetrical configuration of differences in a male-dominated culture works to manage the potentially disruptive consequences of the substitutability of bodies as objects and agents of pleasure by organizing surplus so that its benefits, for the most part, accrue to men whose imaginaries can be empowered by images like Don Juan, whose very immortality lies in his demonstration of the substitutability of one object of desire for another. Part of the disciplinary function of this mechanism lies in the absence of a female equivalent. (As we all know, the woman for whom men are substitutable is given another name, and occupies a very different zone in our social and political imaginaries.) As a consequence, not only are gendered bodies inscribed with differential prudential logics derived from their differential positions within this economy, but also with the very forms of pleasure which can work to mobilize and engage bodies in contact with one another. This differential, as Beauvoir pointed out almost forty years ago, has tremendous political implications. Not only does it result in serious misunderstandings and disappointment between men and women, but, as Cixous points out and Kristeva's work also suggests, the asymmetrical distribution of pleasure has been a primary mechanism for maintaining male dominance, both by establishing differential expectations of entitlement and visibility, and by alienating women from the forms of empowerment that come not only from being able to know and say what they want, but also from being able to see that expectation socially recognized and realized.

One disciplinary figure that works to reinscribe this differential is the privileging of the phallus as the singular sexual fetish object. Phallocentrism has the effect not only of organizing sexuality in terms of a practice and aesthetic of genital primacy, privileging some body part and forms of engagement over others. Phallocentrism also allows for an asymmetrical organization of sexual as well as gender differences, which can then be retranslated into a logic of mandatory heterosexism which imposes social utilities onto bodies whose identities are then taken as inseparable from this formative function. As a consequence, the language of sexual identity, preference or orientation would seem to imply an efficacy of human agency in the construction of sexualities each of which might, at least in principle, be asked on some occasion to give an account of itself and its genesis. But given that some preferences are also socially mandated, only those subjects whose preferences are readable as an unwillingness to fulfill those expectations are put in that position. (No heterosexual is ever, or perhaps only rarely, in circumstances designed specifically to make this point, asked why he or she is not gay. "When did you first know that you were hetero?")

The socially coordinative effects of the discipline of heterosexism and genital primacy are further supported and enhanced by the disciplinary mechanisms of the nuclear family. One important function of the family is certainly to manage the reproductive consequences of the substitutability of bodies, by establishing legally recognized structures of property relations designed to link offspring with their progenitors, thereby also ceding responsibility for the maintenance and development of those bodies to those responsible for having produced them, even if those responsibilities tend to be differentially distributed by gender. (At least that is the way it is supposed to work, according to the story.) The nuclear family is a socially cost-effective way to organize reproduction, since the economic and psychic costs of reproducing the population remain largely lodged in the private sphere, accruing to the producers themselves, rather than to those who benefit by the production.

More important, however, for my purposes is the role the family and the stylization of family relations in the form of the family romance play in the sexually differentiated constructions of pleasure. One reading of the family's strategic function in this regard has been provided by numerous feminist critiques of the nuclear family on the grounds that the family romance, with its images of the pleasures of maternity, has the effect of mobilizing women to seek gratification through the very forms of social organization that exploit and devalue them. In the family, women are supposed to be taught the pleasures of self-sacrifice, nurturance, and service, on the grounds that if women are psychically or otherwise gratified by performing such functions, they need not be compensated in any other way for them. The nuclear family allows for the institutionalization of domestic and reproductive slavery, i.e., unpaid work, under the guise of a self-imposed project of desire.

Because of the high degree of social utility attached to this form of pleasure, many social resources are devoted to maintaining conditions for its perpetual incitement. This is evident in the perpetual revision in the popular images of motherhood, and most especially in the ways maternity is being marketed to that sector of the population which is currently least likely to be reproducing on their own, i.e., white middle-class educated urban women professionals. (The new mother doesn't bake cookies, she wears Reeboks, carries a calculator, plays tennis.) The example of the new motherhood is intended to emphasize both the social forms of incitement to which such desires are subject and the cultural necessity to perpetually respecify such images, so that each generation can claim them as their own invention/discovery—an ultimate gesture of personalizing the most anonymous socio-biological function.

The logic of the feminist critique of the nuclear family and family romance would imply that women's refusal or release from the nuclear family should have the effect of liberating, empowering and empleasuring them. For some women, this probably has been the case. But as we are progressively coming to see, as the nuclear family continues to decline statistically, now constituting only a minority of the households in the U.S., for many women, especially poor women and women of color, the absence of a nuclear family signifies not empowerment but empoverishment. It is not the mothers in such situations who are liberated to maternity, but fathers who are liberated from any of the social and personal costs and responsibilities attached to paternity. Those of us who have long identified with this feminist position find ourselves in confrontation with another unhappy contradiction in its more typical middle-class formulation. In those situations, women who are likely, in the name of their own self-fulfillment and entitlement, to claim something better, are initiating the majority of divorces and insisting on retaining custody of their children, even though such action usually results in a radical diminishment of their economic position, and a correlative improvement in their former husbands' financial situation. It is in cases like these that the more optimistic orientation of the critical discourses which associated liberation with pleasure and promoted a politics of ecstasy becomes complicated by the contradictory relationships between the effects it might be said to produce. If one chooses to read the phenomenon of single-motherhood in urban inner cities as women's refusal of the institutional limitations of traditional nuclear families, or to read divorce as a choice to release oneself from an oppressive and restrictive institution, then one risks disregarding that too many women's experiences in these processes force the recognition that gestures carried out in the name of liberation are not always pleasurable; gestures made in the name of pleasure are not always liberating, even when those pleasures are not those already validated and recuperated by the social order. These questions should not be taken as a clandestine call for the resentimentalization of the nuclear family, nor a statement about its necessity or inevitability. Nor should they be read as indicating a fundamental flaw in the feminist critique. My point is rather that the relationship between pleasure and discipline is more complicated than the logic of liberation from repression would suggest. (Not that that process in and of itself is uncomplicated either.) It is also raises the question of whether or not there is anything like undisciplined sexuality, and what kind of politics can and should be mobilized/developed on its behalf.

Another symptomatic expression of the complexity of this relationship between pleasure and discipline can be read in the contemporary efforts to restylize pleasure, especially sexual pleasure, away from a romantic economy of spontaneity and abandon toward an aesthetic of prudential, carefully managed, safe sex. The imperatives for such reconfigurations are not entirely phantasmatic. Insofar as romance stylizes sexuality as a project undertaken in the name of a pleasure which can be satisfied by a series of objects or in a series of episodes, such discourse foregrounds the proliferative dynamic of pleasure, where pleasure is paradigmatically signified by sexuality. Insofar as romance encourages a proliferation of sexual episodes and objects, it also proliferates whatever risks and problematic consequences might emerge from such encounters. At this point in our history, we are being made acutely aware of many of those, including AIDS and other sexually transmitted diseases, unwanted pregnancies, instances of sexual abuse and violence—the list could be extended. One might think that the pain and suffering associated with such consequences might be appropriable for a project of socially reconfiguring sexuality. For some people, this probably has been the case, at least to some extent. But for the most part, such phenomena have been appropriated only in the name of a power that would seek more conspicuously and materially to regulate sexual exchanges socially. Figured in this way, such a project is most definitely to be resisted, especially to the extent that it can be translated into terms which legalize homophobia and the reproductive exploitation of women and children.

But what is ironic to me, and I suspect to others, about the contemporary situation in which the state apparatus is being mobilized in the promotion of what is being called "safe sex," are some of the forms of resistance, psychical as well as ideological, this campaign is encountering. In raising the following series of questions, I do not mean to imply that the current campaign to market safe sex— or what is being represented as safe sex practices—is unproblematic. This is far from the case, since much of the descriptive and prescriptive discourse on this issue operates within the disciplinary mechanisms of capitalism and patriarchy, and hence produces or assumes those asymmetrical configurations of power. The discourse of safe sex is sometimes phallocentrically constructed, classist, and probably racist. It figures power relationships through a medicalization of sexuality which justifies the production and circulation of technologies of interventions into the lives of bodies. Safe sex is already being commodified as series of devices and services which promise to provide or facilitate it. Its logic, which configures risk exclusively in terms of the communicability of diseases, erases or ignores the sexual risks that are specific to women, i.e., those arising from reproduction, and the attempts to regulate it, as well as the risks of violence and bodily harm women experience in the name or practice of sex.[3]

But as problematic as the current version of safe sex is, even more problematic are those forms of resistance to the very idea on the grounds of, or in the name of, an undisciplined, liberated sexuality. Whether that resistance operates through a romantic stylization, or through the aesthetics offered by a more self-conscious politics of ecstasy, both depend upon mobilizing the power attached to the idea of a sexuality, and a form of empowering pleasure accompanying it, that not only are separable from the disciplinary mechanisms, but can function as grounds for opposing them, as though that oppositional sexuality was not itself a product of a disciplinary production.

I think this moment of self-effacement, which is operative both in the discourses of romanticism and the politics of ecstasy, was intended to be somewhat tactical, i.e., empowering, mobilizing bodies on behalf of claiming or reclaiming that which the hegemonic forms of power denied or destroyed for women. The hope, I think, was to try to mobilize a population on the basis of what was taken away. But it is just such a nostalgic logic that constitutes the limits of this configuration of the dilemma. By figuring sexuality as that which was pleasurable, before the imposition of social relationships and therefore disciplines, sexuality is oddly depoliticized, i.e., as purest and more pleasurable outside the spheres of coordinated social activity, rather than as something yet to be, and therefore something that must be realized through coordinated gestures of social invention.

In terms of the contemporary situation, this configuration carries with it the rather killing contradiction of resistance to any concerted social effort to consider issues of sexual safety in the name of more pleasurable—i.e., less disciplined, spontaneous—sexuality, marked by the failure to consider or act in light of sexual risks, or, even more problematically, to eroticize them. What is worse, such logic tends to lull the population into a state of despair over having lost what was never really available as such in the first place. This does not create the best climate for invention, and invention is what is very definitely necessary, because the choice in the current situation is not between pleasure and power, disciplined and undisciplined sexuality, but rather a question of what forms of discipline are socially mobilized, and what the consequences are for empowering bodies, with respect to currencies of both pleasure and safety.

As Simon Watney suggests in his recent text *Policing Desire*, one of the challenges to the current ideological apparatus is to develop images and languages and practices which eroticize safe sex. This disciplinary intervention is not any more likely than its predecessors to completely suture the tension between pleasure and danger as figured in sexuality, but it does seem like an idea whose time has come. In order for such a conscious realignment to be possible, at least to some extent, we need to foreground in our thinking the productive relationships between discipline and pleasures, those moments when the discipline is not only pleasurable, but instrumental in the realization of that possibility, disciplines that not only regulate pleasures, but also incite, stylize, and circulate them. We need to reconfigure those stylistic possibilities as something other than loss, or as compensation for that which was never ours to begin with. In such a way of reinventing our collective erotic imaginaries and rhetoric may very well lie the possibility of producing forms of pleasure that empower us not by liberating sex from power and pleasure from social invention, but rather by facilitating forms of empowerment that resist and undermine the debilitating effects of the hegemonic forms of dominance. But to do this, we must think of ourselves as capable of recreating our pleasures, as well as the institutions that arouse or frustrate them. The hope is that we will be in a position both to recognize and take the pleasure produced from such an undertaking.

Notes

1. Sigmund Freud, *Civilization and its Discontents*.
2. See "Bodies—Pleasures—Powers," below, this volume.
3. It is unclear in what year the author wrote this sentence, and whether her estimation of safe-sex campaigns might have changed had she been aware of recent safe-sex campaigns by ACT UP, the National Gay and Lesbian Task Force, the Gay Men's Health Crisis Network and other efforts.—ed.

4

Regulating Women in the Age of Sexual Epidemic

The contemporary hegemony of sexual epidemic has ushered in new body techniques, aesthetics, and politics, among them "safe sex," "body management," and an "aesthetics of perpetual surveillance," as tactical responses to the anxiety induced by the destabilizing effects of a sexuality that is now linked with the forces of death and disease. Because epidemic conditions raise the social stakes attached to unregulated sexual exchanges, contagion becomes a major figure in social relationships and in social production. The population's panic in the face of contagion is often and differentially displaced and repeated in the form of a contagious proliferation of defensive strategies, aimed at combating this perceived threat to the health of the social body. Because the impetus for such strategies is defensive, the logic with which they operate tends to be conservative, i.e., aimed at preserving and protecting that which is seen as threatened by changes in the sexual political economy. Consequently, sexual epidemics provide occasions for the revivification of hegemonic forms of dominance, which now seem to have greater justification and utility, insofar as these can be mobilized in the name of health, safe sex, and the forces of life in a politics conceived as a struggle between life and death.

The earlier discussion focused on the way in which conditions of sexual epidemic have been exploited as an occasion for recirculating homophobic discourse which, in this case, especially targets gay men. But the centrality that the AIDS crisis now occupies in the public consciousness is an indication that gay men are no longer exclusively positioned as victims or pariahs, but have also come to occupy a central role in determining how the AIDS crisis is being represented, and what strategies are being proposed to cope with it. Safe sex techniques began as a local discourse within the gay community. Their current level of cultural circulation is testimony to the gay community's success in promoting a local product to the status of national prominence. This influence is also evident in the current literature on AIDS and the sexual epidemic. The effect of this gay male hegemony has been a figuration of the dimensions and issues considered under the rubric of epidemic in a way that, not surprisingly, reflects the positions that community occupies, namely, that of sufferers or advocates for the sufferers. One effect of this hegemony is that although increasing numbers of women are suffering from the disease, most of the literature tends to obscure or ignore this fact. The erasure of women as victims can be accounted for, in part, by the fact that most of these women belong to groups that are already marginalized. Most women victims at this point are black, Carribbean or Hispanic, poor, IV drug users or their lovers. The way the current discourse mobilizes sympathy which is focused on gay men is an indication of the influence the gay community has had in determining the ways the AIDS crisis is being represented and addressed.

Male hegemony has also functioned to structure the anxiety formation dominating the AIDS discourse as a crisis in phallocentrism, a fear that the phallus is also fatal, especially to and for men. Because the problem is largely represented as one of contagion, current discussion focuses on the political and ideological consequences arising from the construction and regulation of diseases in an economy dominated by death. Regulatory technology has thus far focused on the phallus as that which must be clothed in its circulation. Techniques of safe sex are aimed at minimizing the possibilities for contagion through the exchange of bodily fluids. In this economy of contagion, however, women's position is relatively marginalized and derivative, i.e., a consequence of their sexual contact with men. As long as the sexual epidemic is figured primarily as a problem of contagion, women's position can be overlooked or minimized by a prudential logic of relative risk.

Consequently, one of the underinterpreted consequences of the contemporary sexual epidemic, at least as far as most recent literature is concerned, is the ways in which women's bodies are being progressively retargeted as sites for intervention by the state, ideologically, and commodity systems. This consequence should not be surprising in light of the utility of sexual epidemics as occasions for reinscribing hegemonic relationships of dominance and prominence. Thus we can expect women's bodies to be the recipients of gender-specific forms of regulation. Given the oppositional organization of sexual difference in patriarchy, the phallocentric logic which identifies the male position with the force of death also produces an opposing position for women, who will come to be associated with the counterforce of life. When analyzed from the positions women occupy, the sexual epidemic changes shape and comes to encompass not only the regulatory mechanisms governing the control of disease, but also those technological and ideological tactics which socially organize the production of life through the reproduction of populations.

In this chapter I will examine some of the ways in which women are specifically positioned in the contemporary hegemony of sexual epidemic, and its subsidiary strategies of safe sex, body management, and surveillance. The expectation governing this discussion is that the sexual epidemic will look different when it is examined from the perspective of the multiple ways it addresses women's bodies, and addresses them differently by age, race, and class. Women can expect to find themselves differentially positioned, because different bodies and parts of bodies will be taken as targets for management. We can also expect that ideological productions will also address women differently and will produce different consequences, which in many cases are the polar opposites of those prescribed for men. Finally, we can expect that, in this case as in others, these differences will be represented and organized in a way that will systematically disadvantage or marginalize women and questions of their sexual safety.

This is because the risks for women who engage in sex with men far outstrip the risks of contracting a fatal disease. Women's sexual health and safety are intimately and directly tied to the ways in which reproduction is socially organized, i.e., how babies are made, under what conditions, at what price, and with what social rewards. How safe it is to be a heterosexual women and, correlatively, how safe it is to be a lesbian at any time, will be materially determined by such factors as the nature and availability of contraception, abortion, and fertility technology, as well as the repertoire of disciplinary responses to sexual violence, homophobia, and misogyny.

Women's sexual safety also depends on the social organization of the family, another hegemonic concept which is currently being repackaged for a new sexual era. As an accompaniment to the homophobic discourse, the family is currently the target of a promotional campaign. The advocacy of domesticated monogamous marital sexuality geared toward reproduction takes on special strategic value in an age concerned with the risks of multiple sexual contacts. As a consequence, the family has reemerged as a prominent figure not only in the discourse of the New Right, which appropriates such rhetoric as justification for a particularly authoritarian social agenda, but also in feminist discourse as well as the popular cultural imaginary. In an era of panic sexuality, the family is being repackaged as a prophylactic social device. In the age of sexual epidemics, the family can be marketed as a strategic and prudential safe sex practice.

Like the strategic marketing of condoms, the promotion of familial relations takes on special irony when examined in light of women's historical experiences within the family. That history reveals that the family has never been a particularly safe place for women and children. Most violence against women occurs within the family, as does the sexual abuse of children. In families, women have been simultaneously subject to an institution which exploits them economically, politically, and psychologically. When the rhetoric of family values is also used as a code word for a particular form of male control over the reproductive capacities of women, the prophylactic effect for women is questionable indeed. It may very well be that given the patriarchal organization of the family, women's sexual safety is substantially reduced by their participation in an institution structured to preserve male domination of women, and the products of their labor.

In light of these examples, it is really questionable whether the techniques being marketed under the rubric of "safe sex" actually make sex safer for women. In the following chapters, I will raise these questions with respect to the ways in which reproduction is technologically and ideologically regulated in the age of sexual epidemic. The aim of this analysis will be to provide justification for my suspicion that what is being offered as safe sex is likely, in most cases to have just the opposite consequence for women. At a time when sexual politics is being figured as a struggle between life and death, women's bodies are likely to be exploited for their life-producing capacities, especially if the crisis posed by sexual epidemic, and therefore the modes of responses to it, continues to be represented in exclusively phallocentric terms. In examining the social constructions surrounding reproduction, I want to consider their strategic value for the maintenance of male dominance, as well as entertaining the possibilities such developments provide for its rupture and reformulation.

Technologies of Reproduction

Contemporary innovations in technologies of reproduction produce contradictory social formations. On the one hand, there is some effort to produce technological advance in the development of contraceptive devices, and on the other hand, there is an increase in research and development in the field of fertility technology. Both moves seek to intensify the management of the reproductive process, to produce a well-managed body, and to insert technology into reproduction itself. Effects of this management can be found in a variety of techniques: ovulation prediction, donor insemination, in vitro fertilization, extra-uterine conception, fertility technology, fetal screening (amniocentesis as surveillance), techniques of sex selection, methods of donor and surrogate selection.

The major consequence of both kinds of technology is to increase men's control over reproduction while reducing their accountability. Men can fulfill their reproductive obligations, such as they are, without incurring corresponding social obligations of paternity and material support. The intensification of technological management over reproduction, then, works in the service of maintaining an already existing male prerogative.

Here the interests of male privilege work in concert with capitalist logic. The deployment of technology operates according to a logic of cost-effectiveness and efficiency. The goal is to make conception more malleable with respect to existing utilities, both demographically and individually. The technology subjects reproduction to an instrumental logic and plan; one can now wait for the right time and deliver on demand. It also provides for the elimination of cost-ineffective reproduction, i.e., "genetically deficient" children whose maintenance and care is expensive, children who will diminish a woman's earning potential. The institution of cost-effective reproduction relieves a woman from the necessity of being attached, however provisionally, to any man. Now she can acquire his semen without acquiring him. Such technology, however, will be purchased only by those in a position to avail themselves of capitally intensive technology. Here the question of racial demographics becomes pertinent: is such technology available on a differential basis that increases the fertility of white women and restricts that of women of color?

Reproduction thus becomes a site for capital investment and profit through the proliferation of commodified reproductive services and goods. Conception is for profit or, rather, is that which is made into yet another profitable enterprise. Technology also provides the occasion for the ideological updating of reproduction, putting it more in line with a postmodern technodynamic aesthetic. We are witnessing the proliferation of reproductive gadgets, and yuppies love gadgets.

Indeed, if Cuisinarts helped to make cooking sexy again, perhaps sonograms and sperm banks can have a similar effect, helping to market reproduction both to a generation who came of age during the era of sexual revolution and to those whose sexuality is being formed by the hegemony of epidemic. Technology is, after all, a way of disciplining and regulating the exchange of fluids—a prime concern in the age of sexual epidemic. Technology makes sure that these fluids are quite literally channeled in the appropriate—i.e., the most socially useful— and beneficial direction.

5

Reproductive Regulations in the Age of Sexual Epidemic

Developments in reproductive technology, and changes in the ways in which motherhood and family are represented, as well as demographic shifts in the nature of families, have forced existing regulatory institutions, including the judicial system, to reconsider, and in some cases revise, the operational definitions of parental and kinship relations. This process is complicated by the climate established by the hegemony of sexual epidemic, which has provided an occasion for justifying a return to "family values," i.e., to domesticated, reproductive, monogamous, heterosexual relationships, bound by the contractual stipulations of marriage, a common household and legally recognized paternity. This latest attempt to promote traditional domestic relationships comes at a time when the number of nuclear families is declining, and more children than ever are being raised by mothers who either never married or are no longer living with the child's father. Developments in fertility technology also offer new possibilities for accomplishing and organizing reproduction. Because there are now more ways than ever to produce babies, and because the conditions under which reproduction occurs vary significantly through the population, fewer children are born into the conditions assumed by the legal and policy systems, i.e., conceived and raised by coprogenitors who are married and share a common household. As these institutional representations are found to be more and more at odds with the situations they are intended to regulate, courts and legislatures will come to function as the forum for a societal reconsideration of the ways in which the reproduction of the population is socially organized.

One recent and very conspicuous instance of this kind of new age family melodrama was the case of the contested custody of a baby who was initially marked only as M, not only because her kinship and custodial relations were in question, but her name as well. Baby M was produced as a result of a contract signed by Mr. Stern and Mrs. Whitehead, the two eventual parties in the suit, which stipulated that, for a fee, Mrs. Whitehead would agree to be artificially inseminated with Mr. Stern's semen, would carry the fetus to term, and would then surrender the baby, and all claims to custody, to Mr. Stern after the baby was born. The legal problem arose when Mrs. Whitehead refused to surrender the child to the Sterns. As a consequence, the Sterns chose to file suit against Mrs. Whitehead, charging her with violation of the contract that ensured them custody and became the basis for their claim to infringement of Mr. Stern's rights as the child's father.

The resulting trial, as well as the main figures in the dispute, came to occupy a conspicuous place in the American public's imaginary, at least in part because this was not just any old custody hearing. What emerged from the news and other coverage was a kind of social theater in which not only questions of custody, but also cultural visions of motherhood, paternity, and the contradictory intersections of the technological, legal, and commodity systems all became condensed into the pathetic figure of a female infant with no name and no home. As a media event, the issues in the Baby M trial were subjected to the local codes and conventions of personality. This had the effect of foregrounding Mary Beth Whitehead as a figure for public scrutiny and commentary, casting her as a projective screen on which to focus culturally contradictory visions of mother-hood. The figure of the Sterns also helped provide a hook on which to hang the conflict of classes and lifestyles that were also being tried, at least in the public consciousness. What made the Baby M case even more compelling to the media was that, like many successful media events, it had a sequel. The initial ruling which granted custody to Mr. Stern was appealed. This provided the public another occasion for a glimpse of Baby M, and a reengagement in the issues raised by the case, in which there was by now clearly a much larger social investment.

The Baby M case was a trial about reproduction, but the event itself also became a site for reproductions, given Whitehead's sale of the rights to reproduce her story, recently aired by ABC. The trial provided an occasion for recirculating a hegemonic discourse of parental desire, as Mr. Stern repeated his desire to raise his biological offspring, and Mrs. Stern reiterated her wish to raise her husband's child even though she could not or would not produce it herself. This pathos was given a new twist, however, when juxtaposed to Whitehead's tearful expressions of maternal desire, a desire intensified, at least to the bourgeois mind, by the fact that Whitehead already had several children and clearly was not raising them in very affluent circumstances.

This trial caught on with the media, in part because there is utility in reproducing such images of parental pathos at a time when there is also perceived to be greater social urgency to mobilize sexuality into domesticated monogamous reproduction. Families are strategically important to the media because they are a very large segment of its advertisers' target market. Families are useful to advertisers, because they are sites for the consumption of commodities, many of which are designed and marketed especially for them. But the trial was also useful as a way of localizing or personalizing the conflict over changes in the way in which motherhood is practiced and concomitant shifts in the organization of families, and the positions women occupy in the family and outside it.

The Baby M case has become, and probably always was, more than a decision about what to do with one baby. As the language of both judicial decisions indicate, the decisions took into account the effect this case will have on larger policy and judicial determinations, helping to establish the mechanisms for deciding what to do about babies who are produced in other than the usual ways, and babies who will not be raised in what is assumed to be the optimal circumstances, namely, in a household with two married biological parents. Both decisions also acknowledge, although also ultimately deflect, the larger questions about social priorities and values that this case raises.

I will be reading the language, logic, and contagious effects of the Baby M decisions as strategic discourses, operating within the hegemony of sexual epidemic. The intent is to examine how women's bodies are managed in the legal discourse, to what forms of surveillance they are subjected, and how issues of sexual safety are figured and resolved, i.e., what kinds of safe sex are circulated in these decisions, and how their outcomes bear specifically on women's sexual safety. In analyzing the consequences of the original decision and appeal, there emerges a pattern consistent with the politics of sexual epidemic, namely, a tendency toward reinscription of traditional lines of privilege and authority.

In this case, this operates in the form of the priority given to Mr. Stern's parental desire which in both decisions also entitles him to custody. That Mr. Stern's position is the only one that remains fundamentally unchanged in both trials is significant as a marker of the privilege given to paternal desire, if and when it chooses to exercise itself. The initial ruling which granted legal custody as well as paternity is upheld on appeal. All other parties in the matter, however, find themselves in different positions. Mrs. Stern is no longer the child's legal mother. Mrs. Whitehead has now been designated as the child's mother. Baby M is the daughter of Mr. Stern and Mrs. Whitehead, but will live with, and be raised by, Mr. Stern and his wife.

The language and arguments operative in both decisions reproduce the contradictions that emerge from the effort to mediate and regulate conflicts of class-stratified interests, while at the same time denying or obscuring those conflicts. This strategy is operative in the terminology of "surrogate motherhood" introduced into popular parlance by the first trial, where the term was used to refer both to Mary Beth Whitehead, and to her position in the reproductive contractual exchange. A whole set of assumptions and values were condensed into this term and are also reflected in the logic governing the first decision, even though these assumptions are never themselves put, or acknowledged to be, on trial. These include assumptions about what kind of person a mother is supposed to be, and what kind of social situation is best for children. The most immediate effect of this terminology was to privilege Mr. Stern's position as the one in terms of which Mrs. Whitehead's position will be defined. For whom or what, after all, is Mary Beth Whitehead a surrogate? For Mr. Stern's legally designated coprogenitor, and his choice of coparent, Mrs. Stern. In what context is an uncontested coprogenitor designated as surrogate? Only in terms of a contract, initiated at Mr. Stern's request which so designates her. As soon as Whitehead is represented as surrogate, the issue has already been framed within an institutional and contractual logic in which Mr. Stern and the position he occupies are privileged. In this case it means that in addition to being able to claim his entitlement to custody of Baby M on the basis of his status as the child's biological father, and what the appeal court later acknowledges as "the natural rights" that follow from that position, he is also able to base his claim on the contractual and paternal kinship systems, both of which place him in an advantaged position, by comparison to Mrs. Whitehead. The language of "surrogate mother" also has the effect of obscuring Whitehead's position, and the one position she occupies comparably with Mr. Stern, namely, that of being the child's biological parent and genetic cocontributor. The attribution of surrogacy is designed to obscure the fact that she occupies this position regardless of her relationship, or lack of one, with the child's father.

That such language has had this effect is evidenced by the tactics operative in the first ruling, which displaced or decentered paternal privilege, reformulating the issue as a dispute between competing claims of maternity, the one legal and contractual, the other biological and genetic. The first ruling which granted custody of the baby to Mr. Stern, also resulted in the immediate processing of adoption papers which designated Mrs. Stern as the child's legal mother. What is significant about this aspect of the first decision, and the reversal on appeal, is the differing techniques working to circulate the strategic utility of extending as well as reinscribing paternal rights and prerogatives. In the first decision, Mr. Stern's desire to coparent with his wife becomes the ground of Mrs. Stern's entitlement to custodial rights of legal motherhood. But such claims were dependent, logically and legally, in this case, on her husband's expressed desire for custody. Had Mr. Stern chosen, for some reason, not to pursue his claims to the child, the question of Mrs. Stern's maternal status would never have come up. The logic of the first decision considered Mr. Stern's prerogative to be the definitive one in resolving the competing claims for motherhood, with the case being resolved in favor of the woman Mr. Stern wanted as the mother of his child. In the logic of this decision, Mrs. Stern's status is entirely a consequence of her relationship to the child's father, and his desire that she raise the child that is now legally recognized as his.

The dependence of Mrs. Stern's position in this case upon her husband's is refigured by the appeal proceedings in which she fares even less well. Since she has lost her legal status as Baby M's mother, her contact with the child will now be entirely contingent on her maintenance of a relationship with the child's father. Should Mr. Stern choose to divorce her and take the child with him, she has no legal basis on which to prevent this, nor to secure for herself any right to further contact with the child. Should he choose to leave without his child, Whitehead could either argue that custody reverts to her, or Mrs. Stern could be left materially responsible for a child to whom she has no legally recognized connection. As will be argued later, Whitehead also benefits little by Mrs. Stern's loss. It is Mr. Stern who is the sole beneficiary in the zero-sum game form assumed by both decisions.

The recognition of male desire for paternity in the Baby M case has definite strategic utility at a time when increasing numbers of men are either refusing to acknowledge paternity, or are deserting their children and failing to contribute to their support in larger and larger numbers. In response to this phenomenon, sectors of the culture are coming to recognize, albeit for differing and often conflicting reasons, the high cost, economically and otherwise, of socially indulging paternal prerogative. As the demographics of poverty become increasingly feminized, there is greater social impetus to encourage paternal desire and to socially reward it when it occurs, as a way of inducing more men to contribute to the support of the domestic economy. The logic and consequences of the court's first decision reflect the contradictory effects of attempting to regulate the socially undesirable consequences of de facto optional paternity, by reinstating as the central principle for determining kinship and property relations the very economy of privilege that it claims also to restrict. The odd thing about the larger symbolics generated by this decision, which also raises questions about the gender-invested conceptions of justice, is the negative correlation it establishes between maternal responsibility and entitlement, rights, and obligations. The larger sense of utilities seems to mandate a decision in which a man's desire to care for his biological offspring is given higher priority precisely because men are that much less likely to express such a desire than are women. Read in reverse, because women have taken so much more of the responsibility of caring for children, they are entitled to that much less social protection of their maternal prerogatives.

The initial judicial decision granting Mrs. Stern maternal status was reversed on appeal, when the court decided to "restore the 'surrogate' as the mother of the child," on the grounds that Mary Beth Whitehead (by then) Gould "is not only the natural mother, but also the legal mother and is not to be penalized one iota because of the surrogate contract." The language employed here is worth attending to, since it establishes the terms and oppositions of the claims which the decision undertakes to mediate, and because it marks a shift of thinking with respect to the first decision. First, the term "surrogate" is applied neither to Whitehead, nor to the role she has played in this exchange, but to the contract in terms of which her relationship to the child is one of surrogacy, given that it is there so stipulated. By invalidating the contract, therefore, the court was able to "restore" Whitehead to the position she would ordinarily occupy, namely, that of biological and—in their judgment, therefore—legal mother as well, reversing the decision of the first court, which distributed those positions differently.

The logic used by the appeals court to link what the first court had torn asunder, i.e., the correlation between biological and legal motherhood, operates within an economy of rights and with an ethic of equitable distribution. This decision, consistent with judicial techniques, works by producing and then distributing rights which function as socially protected entitlements in an economy of possession and exchange. The court's task therefore is to determine what rights each party may be said to possess, and to what possession of these rights entitle them, as well as to mediate between the disputed claims by establishing the scope and limits of their conflicting entitlements. The repertoire of rights that circulate through the decision include "the right to procreate," claimed by Mr. Stern, which the court separates or limits with respect to the rights of "custody, care, companionship and nurture," rights which the appeals court further separates by upholding the earlier decision to grant custody rights to Mr. Stern. But the court reverses that ruling by deciding to restore Whitehead's possession of the rights to "care, companionship and nurture." The basis for restoring these rights to Whitehead is that they are entitlements that follow from the rights she has as a "natural mother," rights which the court argues must, by statutory requirements, be distributed equally to both natural parents. On this basis the court is able to invalidate the Sterns' contract with Whitehead on the grounds that it discriminates against Whitehead, and because it "violates the policy of this State that the rights of natural parents are equal concerning their child, the father's no greater than the mother's." Later on, this same logic is used to separate the right to procreation from the right to custody, on the grounds that "[to] assert that Mr. Stern's right of procreation gives him the right to the custody of Baby M would be to assert that Mrs. Whitehead's right of procreation does *not* give her the right to the custody of Baby M." The court further separates the proprietal right to custody from rights to procreation and the position of natural parent by claiming that although Mr. Stern's custodial rights may also be constitutionally protected, the determination of the scope of those rights will also "involve many considerations other than the right to procreate."

In this case, the judges argue that such consideration is mandated by existing policy and statutes, that determination is to be made by consideration of the "best interests of the child," a consideration that is not quite a right but functions similarly, i.e., as a locus of entitlement to consideration, even though the decision leaves the terms of consideration completely unstipulated. On this basis, Mr. Stern's custodial rights are upheld, despite the court's acknowledgment that in surrogacy arrangements there is not the slightest suggestion that any inquiry will be made at any time to determine "the fitness of the Sterns as custodial parents, or Mrs. Stern as the adoptive mother, their superiority to Mrs. Whitehead, or the effect on the child of not living with her natural mother." The decision gives no explicit indication that such inquiry has since been made, at least with respect to the Sterns, although the decision does take great care to indicate that Mrs. Whitehead was "rather harshly judged—both by the trial court and by some of the experts" and that the portrait of Whitehead that has emerged in the media was a half-truth, and that its representations of her motives were "totally inaccurate." Furthermore, the decision represents Whitehead as a "perfectly fit mother" and then expresses outrage that she was not only expected to surrender her baby but "was then told that she was a bad mother when she did not."

Since Mrs. Whitehead is recognized both as the natural and legal mother, and to be perfectly fit, whence come the limits of her rights to custody or, conversely, from where does Mr. Stern derive his overriding rights to custody? In this case: from the interests of the infant, which, it is decided, are best served by its remaining with Mr. Stern. The effect of this aspect of the decision is to render moot, at least in this case, the earlier distinction between Mr. Stern's right to procreate and his custodial rights, even though the decision does leave room for another contested custody procedure, should Mrs. Whitehead elect to pursue the issue further. Given that the decision allows for and acknowledges Whitehead's claims for custody on the basis of fitness, from where does Mr. Stern derive his superior fitness to serve the child's best interests?

The factor that intercedes as the differential determinant in the face of equal and competing rights is privilege. In this case, Mr. Stern's privileges are those of gender and class. Even though the decision tends to minimize those differences, noting that "the Sterns are not rich and the Whiteheads are not poor," it is nonetheless clear that when considering the policy implications of their assumptions, class and property relationships are very much on the judges' minds. The decision acknowledges for example that "it is unlikely that surrogate mothers will be proportionately as numerous among those women in the top twenty percent income bracket as among those in the bottom twenty percent."

Insofar as the effect, even if not the explicit intent, of this decision is to conflate or equate best interests with superior class and social position, the judgment is both prescriptive and descriptive, and has strategic value with respect to protection of those systems of privilege. Since the court chooses to interpret the child's best interests to mean residence with the parent who is in the best position to assume custody, all other considerations like fitness being equal, it is not surprising that that person turns out to be Mr. Stern, the father, given the legal precedents and concomitant social and economic factors which already privilege that position. Legally, it is the father's desire to acknowledge paternity that renders his child legitimate, and hence advantaged relative to those who are not. Given the correlation between income and gender, it is also clear that in almost all cases the child will be economically advantaged as well by residing with the father. By ruling out of its sphere of consideration psychological factors like the effects on the child of not living with the natural mother, the court also eliminates any potential claim of special or competing fitness from the mother. Given the factors the court chose to take into account, therefore, it is not surprising that Mr. Stern was deemed to be the better parent, and residing with him to be in the child's best interests. In making this decision, the court in some sense simply recapitulates the obvious, namely, that it is better, at least within the existing legal and economic systems, to be male rather than female, more rather than less affluent. Given the logic and the social context in which the court was operating, this conclusion can be represented as the one "any rational man" would reach. Part of the surplus ideological and strategic value of these decisions is their reproduction and recirculation of this very form of rationality.

The language of equality and benevolence used in both decisions contributes to the production of these ideological effects. Because the appeal decision stipulates that all rights, save custody, are to be equally distributed between the parents, the decision is justified procedurally, i.e., on the ground that it was made fairly and in accord with existing statutory precedents. This emphasis on equality also helps conceal the differential factor of paternal privilege beneath a rationale that claims to speak on behalf of the child's best interests, with which the former, in this case, just happens to coincide. The utility of this argumentative and rhetorical strategy is that it produces privilege as an effect, while obscuring its function as a cause or reason that would then have to be explicitly justified. By separating paternal rights from custodial rights only in the end to reconflate them, both decisions have the effect of protecting male privilege and class privilege, while at the same time denying or concealing them as factors responsible for producing this effect. This case also sets a precedent for further cases. Given the class position of men likely to avail themselves of paid surrogacy arrangements, at least in states other than New Jersey where the trial took place, and the class position of the women to whom such a prospect will appear attractive, it is likely that if future cases are to be decided on the same basis as this one, the results will be the same, since it is also likely that the father will be deemed the parent better positioned to provide for the child's best interests. The ideological surplus produced by these decisions is that such a determination is also represented as rational.

Where does this surplus of rationality leave Mrs. Whitehead? She is left with the possession of her rights as natural and legal mother that the decision concerning custody then renders, absent further legal action, largely moot. The extent of her visitation rights has not been determined at the time of this writing. Whitehead also retains ground for further contesting custody, should she choose to initiate such action, although the precedent already established does not bode well in this regard. The consequences of this right to further contest custody, if any, are likely to be more substantive in this case than others, because in some sense, Whitehead is in a relatively privileged position by comparison with other future surrogate mothers. While Whitehead was uniquely scrutinized and likely victimized by the attention her case received, her visibility has also had exchange value. Because of it, she was able to sell the rights to her story, making funds available for further legal action. Few other women in this position are likely to have such options available to them. The effect of the distribution scheme operating in the Baby M case is to leave Whitehead with a collection of rights that entitle her to practically nothing (and will entitle future surrogate mothers, in the state of New Jersey at least, to even less), all packaged as an equitable resolution made with the best interests of the baby at heart.

The courts' decisions to withhold the baby from Mrs. Whitehead are also part of their larger strategic agendas, to limit surrogacy as a practice, and to eliminate monetary exchange from surrogacy arrangements. As these factors are positioned in the appeals court's decision, they are both reciprocally justified and justifying. The surrogacy contract is ruled invalid, because the judges find "the payment of money to a 'surrogate' mother illegal, perhaps criminal, and potentially degrading to women." Later the connection between withholding money and limiting surrogacy is acknowledged explicitly by the assertion that "it is unlikely that surrogacy will survive without money. Despite the alleged selfless motivation of selfless mothers, if there is no payment, there will be no surrogates or very few."

The justification for this ruling is cast in the longstanding rhetoric of judicial benevolence, which has historically been used as a ground for selectively limiting women's rights and privileges under the guise of paternalistic protectionism. By eliminating financial compensation as a factor in reproductive transactions, the court claims it is protecting women from the potential coercion or degradation such a factor might introduce. The court represents its role as protecting women from the risks accompanying the exchange of their reproductive services for money. They claim also to be protecting the child from the potential risks that might follow from being sold to the highest bidder. But because the appeal court decision limits only paid surrogacy, and cannot find basis for invalidating surrogacy as such, or what in its language is "voluntary" surrogacy (implying as well that paid surrogacy is somehow involuntary), it is fair to ask just exactly what risks are minimized by this ruling, and for whom surrogacy is being made safer.

Although the language of the decision targets women as the object protected, the key differential in legal terms is the exchange of money. The physical, psychological and social risks of producing a child for a man to whom one does not have any other connection are the same, regardless of whether or not one is also paid for this function. In making the financial benefit of women from these transactions the key differential, it seems clear that what the court is really protecting is the financial interests of the father, who is now protected in his right to expropriate the product of a woman's labor without financially compensating her for what she has produced.

The effect of this decision is therefore to make reproduction less safe for women, by providing legal justification and defense for the reproductive exploitation of women by men. Furthermore, such exploitation is deemed legal and undegraded, if and only if the reproductive services are also economically exploited. Men's entitlement to the use of women's bodies to serve their desire for paternity is further expanded by the court's decision, since such transactions need not be bound by the contractual stipulation of reciprocal marital rights, but can now be exercised by men without any corresponding obligations to the woman whatsoever.

The logic governing the political economy of surrogacy as regulated by this decision operates by exploiting a semantic slippage or equivocation between two different senses of freedom which are at stake in this decision, namely, the relationship between that which is done for free in the sense of being unpaid, and that which is done freely, in the sense of being uncoerced. In the strategic logic of this decision, there is a functional parallelism between them. Only that which is done for free is also done freely. Following from this, it is only reasonable to conclude that women are free only when they are also economically exploited.

The gender-specificity of this logic is clear when compared with the positive relationship usually assumed by legal discourse between freedom and economic benefit. One of the major functions of the legal system in a capitalist economy is to protect the rights of individuals to accumulate wealth, through the accretion of the surplus value of what others produce. What is said to justify the benefit of some by the efforts of others is that the transaction is freely engaged in, by both parties. The worker is said freely to choose to sell his labor power, and the owner is said to be exercising his right freely to pursue his economic self-interest. As long as the labor exchanged for financial compensation is male, such transactions are free, fair, and judicially protected. It is only when the labor is prototypically and exclusively female that economic benefit is something from which the laborer suddenly needs protection.

This feat of semantic and logical sleight of hand has had, and I suspect will continue to have, tremendous strategic value for the emerging politics of life. The logic is flexible, and allows for tactical responsiveness to shifting utilities. It allows for women's bodies to be progressively commodified, i.e., exploited for their use value, while withholding from women any material benefits that accrue from this value, maintaining their status as unpaid laborers whose value can be represented only in entirely mystical terms that carry no material entitlements. Under the logic offered by the Baby M decisions, men are free to expropriate the products of women's bodies. Women are free to be expropriated, and to surrender the products of their labor for free. Men are also free to make private financial arrangements with women who will no longer have any contractual protection if the father, for some reason, chooses either not to meet his financial commitment or elects not even to acknowledge paternity, once the child is born.

The larger consequence of the Baby M decision is to encourage the development and dispersement of reproductive technology in a way that will continue to systematically advantage men, even if such technology also produces beneficial consequences for some individual women. It allows men selective use of such technology, and selective use of the women on whose bodies this technology is applied, and discretionary prerogative with respect to the consequences and effects this technology produces. The latest decision expands the scope and entitlement of elective paternity, while in no way expanding the correlative sphere of social obligation. The effect of this decision is to preserve an enlarged, or potentially enlarged, reproductive brigade, without providing any form of compensatory benefit. In so doing, the decision helps perpetuate and respecify a central patriarchal utility, namely, normalizing the confluence between the economic and reproductive exploitation of women as the most cost-efficient way of socially organizing reproduction. From the point of view of the existing social logic, the best way to produce babies is to have women freely choose to do it for free.

By declaring that only unpaid reproduction is free, the circulatory logic of the Baby M decision comes full circle, suturing women into a contradictory logic which controls them precisely through the dispensation of freedom. Because women normally become pregnant without any stipulated financial exchange, it is assumed that they have freely chosen to do so, and are therefore also responsible for whatever victimization or exploitation they, or their children, may suffer as a consequence.

The assumption that unpaid reproduction is also uncoerced has particular utility insofar as it serves the function of mystifying and misrepresenting the conditions under which reproduction usually occurs, while absenting those conditions from recognition, and thereby also from legal protection within a system of reciprocal entitlements. Women usually are not financially compensated for their pregnancies. But that is in no way an indication that such pregnancies were freely undertaken. Women do not reproduce freely when their pregnancy is unintended, accidental, a result of faulty contraception, rape or incest, or when it is undertaken as part of an unofficial exchange for spousal support, familial recognition, or social viability. The effect of the Baby M decision is legally to acknowledge a form of reproductive freedom that women have never had and still do not have, while providing a justification for socially organizing reproduction in a way that increases the risks for women, while decreasing them for men. This is especially damaging in light of corresponding social movements to make reproduction even less safe, by limiting women's access to abortion and contraceptive technology, procedures that also place the bulk of the risk on women's bodies.

The Baby M decision therefore has particular utility at a time when sexuality is figured as an epidemic that is out of control, by authorizing ways of controlling sexual exchanges by subjecting women's bodies to gender-specific regulations, technologies and tactics. It also helps to extend male hegemony over reproduction to cover the consequences of the new fertility and social technology, while concomitantly increasing the risks accruing to women. The Baby M case also helps sustain a cost-benefit logic which regulates reproduction in a way that systematically supports and expands the sphere of male privilege. Reproduction will be neither free nor safe for women as long as men are in the position to regulate that interest on their own behalf, technologically, ideologically, economically, and legally. Women can be said to reproduce freely and in relative safety only when contraception and abortion are no longer stigmatized and are made widely available, when the risks entailed in contraception are more equitably distributed, when the ideology of mandatory motherhood is displaced, when paternal prerogatives are not institutionally privileged, and when women are no longer in the position of having to exchange their reproductive potency for their own economic support or their child's legitimacy.

Whether the Baby M case can also serve as a catalyst for mobilizing social resources in these directions remains to be seen. It seems clear that such possibilities will depend both on organized and concerted political struggle, and on introducing more factors into consideration of these issues than the New Jersey courts chose to acknowledge. With respect to the form such liberatory possibilities might take, at this stage the jury is still out.

6

Hospitalization and AIDS

. . . a form of power to which subjugated bodies give their informed consent, because they have no other choice.

Linda Singer

Hospitalization as a Structure of Epidemic Logic

The hospital is an institution already authorized to mark its own zone in our social thoroughfares with signs demanding quiet. This space of silence can then be filled with a certain reverential and deferential imaginary of the hospital as the socially privileged site for the production of life and the struggle against death. Because the hospital is the place where most American women will birth their babies while others are being sent there to die, its place in our social imaginaries is ambivalent, its signification a product of contradictory mechanisms of anxiety and desire. Under epidemic conditions, in which large numbers of people may well need some form of hospital treatment, the pressures and limits of its contradictory logic and rationale become intensified, stretched to the point of bursting, overflowing into a more diffuse hospital without walls. It is that movement, and its importance to the emergence of our current epidemic logic, that needs to be traced.

Under current epidemic conditions, the hospital and the institutional practices of hospitalization are the product of, and hence also subject to, duplicitous and contradictory desires and demands. As an alternative to, but also functionally allied with, other forms of incarceration—like prisons and asylums—the hospital is positioned as a threat, i.e., as yet another punitive apparatus. Beyond the hospital's function as a site of exile for the unmanageable or incorrigible, the prospect of hospitalization is always threatening because it is a sign that something is wrong. Although one might think of childbirth as the most notable exception, the prospect of birthing is still a source of anxiety—something might go wrong. The hospital is the place one goes—or is sent—when something is wrong with one's body. The threat of hospitalization is the threat of not being all right and not being all right in a way that is all too socially visible and, hence, presents an all too unavoidable encounter with that visibility for the person so marked. When one is not all right, one must leave the habitual world and enter another which is mysterious because its workings go on in a silent zone. The hospital and its workings are kept quiet, but this is largely done quietly.

Hospital windows provide a one-way gaze. They do not provide access to passersby. The hospital zone from which the healers and the sick look out is inaccessible to an outside from which those inside remain effectively invisible.

One enters this mysterious zone differently, however, than the prisoner enters jail—and with a different set of expectations. Specifically, one undergoes hospitalization with the hope that what is not all right will somehow be made right. We enter the hospital in the belief in its essentially benevolent motives and effects. We hope that as a consequence of hospitalization we will be cured, healed, cared for, made all right again, or in some cases (like plastic or corrective surgery) made better than we were before. This promise of beneficent remediation is the hospital's siren call. (In cities like Cincinnati, where hospitals can advertise, competing claims are made in the language of superior care, sympathetic as well as effective treatment.)

Although hospitalization represents a kind of threat, it also represents the possibility of removing or countering the threat to our well-being that motivates our entrance. The hospital promises release from the threat of disease, corporeal deterioration, and, in some ultimate sense, death. The hospital is thus positioned as a site of extraordinary care, where one goes for forms of remediation and salvation that are not available elsewhere. It is, in part, this very singularity, the apparent non-replaceability of the hospital's functions and forms of competence that helps to account for the authoritative place it occupies in our current institutional semiotic. The hospital calls up some of our deepest anxieties—about pain, decay, and death—in the promissory rhetoric of the remedial. The hospital is thus typical (or perhaps paradigmatic) of the kind of power (institutional power) that calls not only in the punitive language of the threat, but also in the mode that aims to seduce the desire to struggle against, overcome, be freed of death and pain.

Under epidemic conditions, the struggle between the hospital's functions as the institutional manager of both life and death becomes more highly charged—stretched to its limit. The hospital, and the medicinal and surgical apparatus to which it gives a home, is also that which is said to be threatened. The threat to hospitals is figured as an epidemic health crisis with which existing levels of facilities, material and human, will be unable to cope. The threat is one of both quantitative overload and contamination. Too many patients will have to remain too long, and in many cases will also be unable to pay. The hospital is also threatened with loss of one of its capital reserves, an untainted blood supply, as well as with a compromise of its integrity, its cleanliness as an institution capable of dispensing a range of services and functions that can be represented as "adequate health care." The hospital cannot escape from the constantly circulating stories of the indignities to which it subjects many of its clients, especially those suffering from AIDS. To read or hear these narratives is to be thrust into an elaborate gothic zone which horrifies in a way that is awful, violating a social imaginary which invests faith in hospitals as sites of remediation, amelioration, and care.

The public enters the hospital through doors marked "in-" and "out-patient," consents to the transformation such entrance entails. To be in the hospital, even as an out-patient, entails a ritual inscription, a documentary signing, in which one is obliged to write down one's name. To be a patient, one must also be patient. To be in the hospital is to wait under the hopeful rubric of anticipatory remediation, expecting cures, restoration of one's health or well-being, or, at the very least, an amelioration of pain. The articulatory apparatus of medical practitioners works to frustrate this phantasmatic project, as well as to protect itself from the threat of its own malpractice, by representing its functions within a rhetorical framework of procedures, regimen, orders, and recuperations. This is language which carefully avoids referencing the sphere of cure and care. The terms of exchange relieve the institution of the burden of false promises, as well as ameliorating responsibility for consequences to which the patient has already signed off on in a documentary inscription of "informed consent."

The ambivalent status of informed consent that is the first stage of the process of hospitalization provides a point of entry into how power is organized and circulated within an epidemic logic. The kind of "informed consent" testified to in the signing of the document which certifies it, is neither informed nor consensual in the ordinary senses. It is not really informed, insofar as the prospective patient (and particularly the first-time patient) is told little about what will actually occur—beyond some narrative, usually provided by the admitting physician, which is largely functional—a nominal account of the procedure to be performed and the reasons it is necessary. Patients are not told that they are also consenting to an erasure of privacy, as staff doctors and nurses enter their rooms unannounced at any hour of the day or night to perform procedures and surveillances without explanation or rationale. They are also not told how completely their schedule and body will be disciplined by the institution's schedule and organization, and that the significant points of temporal punctuation are provided not by the rhythms of one's body and its needs, but by the organizational demands of the particular institution. (If the shift changes at 6 a.m., one will be awakened by the new team of staff doctors, even if one has been given a sleeping pill only hours before. If the preceding shift has failed to sign the order papers, the procedures will be performed again. If the consulting physician's secretary has failed to make proper arrangements, one lies naked on the gurney for hours until one can be located.) To be a patient is to have to be patient with the institution and with one's body. That is probably why there are no clocks on patient and procedure floors in hospitals. Or maybe there is an absence of marked time for the same reasons that there are no clocks in gambling casinos—as a way of severing patrons from their pre-established habitual temporalities so that they become more malleable to reconfiguration in the face of a particular form of institutionalization. To be in a hospital is to lose time; the time of pleasure and work, sociality, and intimacy. It is to lose the time of productivity and activity in a waiting game where one is cast as receptacle and consumer of whatever is being dished out. In the hospital one's time, like one's sentence, is determined by the institution and its power to extend an eternal present in a way that obscures any agency with respect to the future. In signing, one informs the institution of one's consent to become one who can no longer consent, or whose consent carries no weight, authority, or power. Hospitalization is the process by which subjugation to an institution is represented as that to which we knowingly agree, and freely consent.

One does not have to be a devout postmodernist to see how hospitalization dismembers the subject, and with it any connection with the liberal contractual model of power relations as exchanges of rational self-interest. Any notion of informed consent that might be evoked as a limit or resistance to institutional latitude is undone in the very recognition that informed consent, in institutional terms, is obligatory, i.e., one will not be admitted to the hospital without it. One is not free to give one's consent. This dissimulating encounter with unfreedom is redoubled in the ironic moment in which one is forced to recognize that within a certain existential calculus in which life is valued, perhaps without sufficient reason, over death, one has no choice but to enter the hospital. If one is in need of its technological equipment, expertise, or other remedial regimens, the decision to subject oneself to the institutional mechanisms and indignities of hospitalization acquires a certain existential necessity, independent of any particular form of knowledge of what will happen there, or its consequences for one's body. The power relations and forms of subjugation typified but not limited to hospitalization are organized around a certain ironic construction—that of a form of power to which subjugated bodies give their informed consent, because they have no other choice.

Hospitalization, with or without walls, constructs a temporal zone and social imaginary in which regimentary repetitions produce the effect of normalization. The hospitalized subject comes to expect resubjection by an apparently endless series of questioners to a repetitive series of interrogations: name, Social Security number, health insurance company, blood type, credit card number, address, phone, place of employment. In the process the interrogated become accustomed to a kind of authority which exercises its force in the form of an insistence on disclosure—the production and repetition of certain forms of knowledge on demand. The hospital is but one of a network of institutions that people come to recognize as entitled to pursue such interrogations and exact particular forms of discourse. We get used to spilling our guts to the Department of Motor Vehicles, the Internal Revenue Service, and other organs of the state, as well as to the credit card company, our employers, and the local video store.

This aspect of the hospital-without-walls situates us in a repetitive network of informational systems and transfers which erode or otherwise compromise that space which was socially inscribed as a protective sphere of privacy. In the hospital-without-walls we are subject to perpetual surveillance (the gaze substitutes for the wall, is the invisible architecture of incarceration). Our phones can be tapped, as well as our spines. We can be scanned by a CTV machine or by hidden cameras. Our relationships to these mechanisms of surveillance and invasion are invariable. Some operate without our knowledge, other are submitted to willingly—if one is employed or wishes to drive a car or get a credit card or rent a video. This seemingly consensual dimension helps to acculturate us to an interventionist logic of power whose latitudinal reach can also be read as protective or benevolent. We willingly expose ourselves to attain the imagined benefits of power.

When subjected to hospitalization, one occupies the paradoxical position of losing one's usual site of validation in a system of gazes and regards. One is outside one's world and, hence, invisible in one's world, while also remaining perpetually on display. This duplicitous mode of being present comes to characterize the citizen's relations with the state and other hegemonic institutions in which one feels alienated through one's anonymity (as just a number), while also feeling vulnerable to the risk of exposure (as a private individual). Such mechanisms help to produce and circulate a kind of paranoia in the realization that we can be controlled by what others know about us, without our knowing what or that they know. This scene is often enacted quite specifically in hospitals as doctors, nurses, and technicians exchange information about the patient's condition in terms that the one spoken of cannot decode or understand. This drama can be restaged and revived when one's credit is being checked or when one applies for a job that demands "security clearance." It is the ubiquity of this dramatic form that helps provide justification for mandatory AIDS and drug testing—as well as being that which mobilizes the resistance to them.

For the public that lives in the hospital-without-walls, invasive interrogations into the life of one's body, and the body of one's life, come to seem normal, legitimate, and protective. But they are also subject to paranoid projections and schizoid episodes, which often emerge in correlation with one's own legitimacy or marginality and one's degree of identification with or alienation from hegemonic institutional formations.[1] Within the paranoic space of the hospital-without-walls, certain power dynamics and positions become ambiguous, especially when it is a question of just who is at risk, who or what is a threat to whom or what. It is, therefore, not all that surprising that those people who fancy themselves as members of some moral majority can feel threatened by the existence of gays, intravenous drug users, and other local subcultures which they will never see and with whom, knowingly, they will likely have little or no contact. At the same time, those who are targeted will feel at risk as that policy agenda, in all its hegemonic varieties, encroaches progressively upon their world, directly and at a distance.

At present, the hospital-without-walls has been mobilized around and by the figure(s) of AIDS, and a series of socio-political interrogations of who or what is at risk, who is a threat to whom. These interrogations destabilize and problematize our overdetermined erotic imaginaries (in their similarities and their differences). The problematic of making such determinations is complicated by the hermeneutic circularity that tends to structure discussions of these questions. Just who is at risk will be determined in part by what the risk is, and the nature and location of risk will also mediate the constructions of the strategic responses it receives from the medical establishment, the state, and other sectors of the political economy. These strategic considerations help to explain the centrality of the question of just how much of a risk AIDS poses for non-drug-using heterosexuals.[2] And how this question is answered bears directly on the determination of whether AIDS is over- or underfunded.

AIDS enters social policy discourse as one of many competing needs and urgencies which must ultimately be subjected, under the conditions of a controlled scarcity of resources, to a decision-making framework similar in structure to the kind of lifeboat ethics which frames questions of resource allocation in hospitals. Concretely, the questions of allocation emerge in the following kinds of questions: Who gets to use the dialysis machine? Who will be given organs for transplantation? Should existing resources be focused on gerontological syndromes or on those medical conditions affecting fetuses in utero? Should biotechnical research be devoted to fertility or contraceptive technology? At this point, under a regime of scarce resources, the politics of difference becomes truly difficult, especially with respect to supplying ethical justifications for the choices one makes.

AIDS: Politics, Patienthood, and the Medical Apparatus

One consequence of the AIDS epidemic is that the situation of being a medical patient is being significantly reconstituted. This is the reconstitution of the patient from his/her status as victim to that of an activist. The contemporary politicization of patienthood has constituted the patient's position as one of making demands for participation in the organization of remediation. ACT UP and other activist groups demand that people with AIDS (PWAs) and their advocates be involved as integral participants not only in helping to establish the development and course of medical research and treatment, but in deciding on the distribution of funds, the development of drugs, and other therapies. This demand effectively reconstitutes the patient as an interested party whose vested interest and expertise are invaluable resources in the decision-making process.

The contemporary politicization of patienthood by AIDS activists and others has also produced an important resistance to the isolation imposed by illness, an insistence on maintaining some sense of community and constituency with other PWAs and with advocacy groups within and outside the gay community. In this sense, the AIDS epidemic has politicized patienthood in a way that cancer has not. The situation is different with cancer, where there is a lack of organized patient advocacy, where technocracy and desperation dominate.

The gay community's response to AIDS has effectively organized large patient populations to extend and expand their own political networks. The identification with the oppression conferred by AIDS is linked with an identification as a population already subjugated (by homophobia), which has facilitated political mobilization in a way that is not usually the case with other diseases, such as cancer, where patients cannot easily identify others in the same situation. And even when that identification is possible, there is not likely to be anything else politically significant in common besides the disease.

The capacity of AIDS to politicize those who suffer from the disease and their potential advocates is perhaps enhanced by the way that AIDS has been fetishized and stigmatized by a variety of social forces. AIDS activists and advocates are not usually members of the medical community, but political activists as well as those who may very well be new to organized political movements, but who are motivated by the existential urgencies of their personal situations, i.e., having lost many friends or loved ones.

The political resistance that has emerged around AIDS, a political resistance in the name of AIDS, has many targets: the National Institutes of Health, the Catholic church, various drug companies, hospitals, civic and national politicians. The demands formulated within this resistance have been not only for a wider and more integral participation of AIDS activists in developing treatment and urging development of drugs and other therapies, but also for a new language, a new rhetoric, as in the humanizing nomenclature "PWAs," people with AIDS. AIDS rhetoric and politics acknowledge, in a way that usual medical and public health discourse does not, the anger and frustration of contracting a disease for which there is no existing cure, and where medical knowledge and practice are inconclusive and indecisive. Throughout the rhetoric of AIDS politics, there is an important rejection of religious logic and a religious imaginary, the hope for salvation or apocalyptic reprieve. There is a rejection as well of the posture of placing faith in doctors, searching for another Lourdes, "being a good patient" or pious recipient who accepts whatever is offered gratefully and without question.

The tragedy of AIDS has given way to a resistance that does not cast itself within the imaginary of faith, optimism, and hope—it is a resistance cast in the language of *the demand*.

AIDS is a disease that has emerged within a social imaginary of punishment and stigmatization (those who contract AIDS have been figured as deserving the punishment they get by virtue of engaging in certain acts or practices: sex, drugs, etc.). Despite resistance to these constructions, this social imaginary has not by any means been transcended. And yet the rearticulation of this social imaginary has resulted in a more explicit discourse of resistance to these cruel fictions.

Notes

1. Gilles Deleuze and Felix Guattari, *Anti-Oedipus: Capitalism and Schizophrenia*, trans. Robert Hurley, Mark Seem, and Helen R. Lane (Minneapolis: University of Minnesota Press, 1983).

2. Michael Fumento, *The Myth of Heterosexual AIDS* (New York: Basic Books, 1990).

II
Selected Writings

Editor's Introduction

We decided early on that we would publish a selection of Linda Singer's essays along with the *Erotic Welfare* manuscript. The manuscript remained incomplete at Singer's death, but during the period she was working on it she finished several essays closely related to the book in subject matter. The essays would give a sense of Singer's project as a whole and fill gaps as best they could be filled.

But it was not only or even mainly as supplementary sources that we wanted to reprint the essays. They deserve a place here in their own right. Singer was a complex thinker, and she had a unique writing style. A distinctive style can, of course, best be seen in a work completed for publication. And in the case of Linda Singer, thought and language seemed especially closely connected, a fact about her that many people noticed and no doubt a sign of the seriousness of her voice.

We also thought of the opportunity a group of essays could provide of showing the range and character of Linda Singer's thought. What follows is not a systematic selection, but the essays provide a good sample of Singer's later work. All were written in the mid- to late eighties and published or prepared for publication before her death in 1990.

The first essay, "Bodies—Pleasures—Powers," can be read in close conjunction with *Erotic Welfare* and is, indeed, a kind of synopsis of the book. It introduces a number of its central concepts—sexual epidemic, for example—and describes the historical situation that Singer saw unfolding in the late eighties.

The next three essays are important in seeing how the various dimensions of Singer's thinking came together. Linda Singer situated herself at the intersection of Continental philosophy, feminist theory, and cultural studies. Very much alive to her time—its politics and cultural currents—Singer often found surprising connections among forces others saw as disparate. Similarly, Singer's intensely contemporary focus involved a continuing reflection on the past. Well read in the history of philosophy, Singer remained concerned about the role of the tradition for the feminist philosopher.

Linda Singer's own practice in reading the tradition is represented here by two papers. In "Interpretation and Retrieval: Rereading Beauvoir," Linda Singer addresses Beauvoir's absence from the philosophical canon and presents an original reading of Beauvoir's concept of freedom and its place in ethical discourse. She points forward to a feminist reading of ethics, at the same time providing a feminist perspective on Sartre and the existentialist tradition.

In "True Confessions," Foucault and Cixous are read for the light they shed on a future feminist discourse on sex. Singer examines their seemingly contradictory views on sexual discourse, their differential treatments of sexual difference, their textual strategies. Looking forward, Singer points to our need to talk about sex in a way that will transform our relations to our bodies and our pleasures.

A more discursive essay, "Defusing the Canon," is a wide-ranging reflection on the relations of feminist philosophers to the tradition. Remarking that feminist philosophers read many of the same books as their colleagues but definitely not in the same way, Singer examines various feminist readings of the canon and points forward to an increasingly autonomous feminist agenda.

Linda Singer's work in cultural studies is represented here by the essay "Just Say No: Repression, Anti-Sex, and the New Film." In this reading of a number of recent films, notably *Fatal Attraction*, Singer looks at sexual representation—the discourse of sex and anti-sex—in ways related to the major themes of *Erotic Welfare*.

The last essay, "Feminism and Postmodernism," written for the recently published collection *Feminists Theorize the Political*, addresses this conjunction of "isms" as a proposal. Singer looks at how Continental philosophy and feminist theory are conjoined in the proposed union "Feminism and Postmodernism." Suggesting that we see "the libidinal formation at work," she examines the conjunction as an expression of the long-standing desire to unify knowledge through methodological prescriptions.

A bibliography of Singer's work, based on the last vita she prepared, is provided at the end of this book. I would like to thank Peg Simons for her timely recommendation to reprint the essay on Beauvoir.

Maureen MacGrogan
1992

1

Bodies–Pleasures–Powers

Although the 1960s are the decade usually credited with making sex a political issue and the subject of popular and scholarly discourse, the 1980s have been a time when sexual political issues have become both targets of major social agenda, and ubiquitous elements of popular culture. It is also a time when sexual politics is not very sexy.

We have become accustomed to daily news reports on the AIDS crisis. The recent past has been dominated by sexual political dramas such as the Baby M case, the Vatican's latest document on reproductive technology, the bombing of another abortion clinic, the debate on sex education, the rise in teenage pregnancies. Sexual paraphernalia and technology are enjoying wider circulation and distribution. Erotica is marketed to women in their homes like Tupperware, or through cable channels and video cassettes. Such marketing strategies have not only expanded the range of potential consumers, but have also resulted in some new sexual services, like phone sex and party lines, and new genres of erotica (Ehrenreich et al. 103–60). Fertility technology is more affordable and widely available, and the business of adoptions and surrogate mothering is said to be booming while rights to legalized abortions have been reopened for debate. Television promotes the prophylactic use of condoms and advertises home pregnancy tests and ovulation detectors with names like "First Alert," while devoting more programming time to subjects like teenage prostitution, transsexuality, domestic violence, rape, homosexuality, incest, and AIDS.

Despite this proliferation of sexual commodities and systems for their distribution, most contemporary sexual discourse is not very sexy, because it operates within a logic and language of "sexual epidemic." Central to the emergence of epidemic as a historically specific hegemony[1] has been a concern with the rise in sexually transmitted diseases, most notably AIDS, but also the herpes virus

---

From *Differences*, vol. 1 (April 1989). Reprinted with permission.

which, though not fatal like AIDS, is a chronic condition which has been in wide circulation for some time. According to epidemiologists and public health officials, both diseases are expected to increase in incidence, not only because they are transmitted through intimate contact which is difficult to regulate, but also because the viruses can be carried and spread by infected individuals who are and may remain asymptomatic, or who continue to engage in sexual activity after having been diagnosed. The relative unreliability of the AIDS tests and the chronic nature of herpes further complicate the conditions of contagion, and attempts to control these diseases have been difficult to coordinate.

The threat and fear of contagion have transformed the economy of sexual exchange, reconfiguring the relationship between prospective profit and loss, benefit and risk, for both individuals and the so-called "social body." When one of the possible consequences of sexual activity is the contraction of a debilitating fatal disease or one which is likely to remain and recur, the logic and strategies of judgment and decision are irrevocably altered, even for those who try to avoid such considerations.

Hence it is neither deniable nor surprising that the emergence of the hegemony of epidemic is affecting personal sexual practice, a change with existential and political implications. The anxieties unleashed by the current epidemic are not limited to concerns about disease transmission. The recognition of this unhappy connection between sex and death has also prompted renewed concern about the production of life itself, about reproduction, fertility, and the family, which are also seen as threatened by current conditions. At a time when so-called sexual adventurism is under attack as unsafe, there is a felt need to construct a new, more prudential sexual aesthetic, in terms of which desires and behaviors are stylized, valorized, and eroticized. As a result, there is renewed emphasis on domestication and on the kind of restraint emblematized by the recent "Just Say No" campaign. While gay men find their situation made problematic by a revived and newly legitimated climate of homophobia, women are also being subjected to a new set of gender-specific regulatory strategies designed to maximize their social utility as breeders while minimizing the social costs attached to sexual exchanges. Such strategies include, but are not limited to, rapid developments in fertility technology which allow, in surrogacy situations, reproduction without exposing men to the risks entailed in the exchange of bodily fluids. It is not surprising that, at a time when there is a need to reinvent sexuality or reorganize the erotic economy, a disproportionate weight is falling on the bodies of women. It is hard to disconnect recent campaigns to limit abortions, for example, from a strategy aimed at restricting sexual encounters by raising the risks of such encounters for women. This punitive logic is also responsible for helping shift the terms of sexual exchange, and the climate in which they occur.

The mentality of epidemic has many important symptomatic consequences for policy and ideological debate in explicitly public spheres, consequences that necessitate further reflection. This shift can be summarily described as a move from an inflationary economy of optimism toward an economy of erotic recession or stagflation. Nowhere are the consequences of this shift more poignantly evident than in the gay male community (Shilts), both because it has been the sector of the population hit hardest by the disease so far, and because so much of the ideology of "gay pride" and of the social codes that defined gay life were predicated on the prospect of open-ended sexual proliferation, a prospect fostered by the growth of specialized zones like Christopher and Castro Streets which provided the gay community with relatively protected and defensible sites for such activity. The discourse of gay pride and its proliferative imperatives emerged within and was supported by the larger hegemony of "sexual revolution," which engaged the imaginations and energies of segments of the feminist, lesbian, and heterosexual communities as well.

Sexual revolution, as it was conceived, was centered around a "politics of ecstasy" which sought liberation in the form of release from an apparatus of repression. Liberation, according to the politics of ecstasy, necessitated a revaluation of sex apart from reproductive utilities, as well as resistance to organizations of sexual energies according to aims other than human fulfillment. The policies of ecstasy sought to mobilize the population in a revolutionary transformation of sexual theory, practice, and politics that would make sex better, or make better sex. Better sex, closely connected but not identical with ecstasy, operated with a certain semantic fluidity, given the multiplicity of subjects and articulatory positions from which such discourses arose and to which they were addressed. Differences in gender, sexual orientation, race, and class, amongst other factors, help account for the diversity of visions animating this collective (if uncoordinated) effort to dramatically restructure existing sexual hegemonies.

Included as elements in the referential network of "better sex": more sex, with more partners, in more ways, with greater orgasmic potency, intensity, emotional satisfaction, and intimacy, at a lower cost economically, socially, biologically, and psychologically. Sexual proliferation made sense as a strategy, since what was understood to stand in the way of better sex was a regime of repression and an economy of self-denial, which was circulated in a variety of currencies. The substantive analysis of the regime of repression was extensive and varied in its targetings of the nature and operation of the repressive apparatus. The discourse of sexual revolution also produced critiques of specific sexual institutions such as mandatory heterosexism, phallocentrism, male dominance, monogamy, and the nuclear family, all of which were identified as culprits contributing to a climate of surplus repression that was costly in psychic, social, and political terms (Weeks). Common to all discussions of sexual liberation was an awareness of the political dynamics of dominance and hierarchy that structured and were reproduced in sexual exchange. Under attack was a hegemonic formation that privileged heterosexism over homosexuality and lesbian experience, phallocentricity over gynocentricity, reproductive over non-reproductive sex. Following this logic, the regime of repression could be challenged on political grounds, namely, that its operations constituted unauthorized, arbitrary, or unjustified restrictions on the lives of bodies and the forms of exchange in which they privately chose to engage. Hence sexual revolution necessitated confrontation with and transgression of forms of sexual authority which constituted barriers to better sex. Conspicuous proliferative sexuality, which violated and exposed the repressive regime, consequently took on the value of liberatory strategies of subversion, critique, and rebellion, especially for those groups which had been most disadvantaged or marginalized by the operative sexual economy. For many women and members of the gay community, a climate of proliferative sexuality offered occasions both for self-affirmation and for enfranchising their needs and desires in a way that connected them with larger movements of resistance to these same systems of privilege.

In this sense, sexual political struggles over the past two decades have not just been struggles over sexual activities as such, but have also been concerned with contesting the order of privilege and visibility defined by the operative political organization of sexual differences. For gays, especially gay men, the urgency to make those differences visible by getting out of the closet and into the street was compatible with and facilitated by a proliferative aesthetic which functioned as a promissory alternative. For many heterosexual women, a proliferative sexuality provided a potent weapon against the double standard, while allowing them to explore a gynocentric economy that had been marginalized by the phallocentrism that dominated social life. For groups whose desires had been ignored, or worse, targeted (i.e., marked as sites for regulatory surveillance or judgment), the claim of entitlement to pleasure was a gesture of political assertion which carried over into other social arenas as well (Altman 146–71).

Epidemics and Sexual Politics

With the rise of the hegemony of sexual epidemic, the optimism implied by this proliferative logic reaches a certain kind of dead end. Consequently, a variety of strategic and tactical shifts have emerged which contribute to what I have earlier in this text described as a "recessionary erotic economy." The ethos of an ecstatic carnival is progressively being displaced by a more sober and reserved aesthetic of "sexual prudence" and "body management." The language of "better sex" is being replaced by that of "safe sex" and the promotion of a "new sobriety." These historically specific changes are most visible and pressing at this point for gay men[2] but will not remain so for long as the AIDS virus spreads to other segments of the population. Given the current state of medical research, epidemic conditions are likely to persist for some time and hence continue to structure the context for sexual-political discourse, particularly in the absence of some counter-hegemonic discourse of resistance.

The age of sexual epidemic demands a new sexual politics, and therefore, a rethinking of the relationship between bodies, pleasures, and powers beyond the call for liberation from repression. That is because, as Michel Foucault pointed out with a certain prescience, the power deployed in the construction and circulation of an epidemic, especially a sexual epidemic, functions primarily as a force of production and proliferation rather than as a movement of repression. The determination that a situation is epidemic is always, according to Foucault, a political determination (*Birth* 15). Epidemics differ from diseases not in kind but in quantity. Hence the epidemic determination is in part a mathematical one, made by those with access to information and the authority to make and circulate such determinations. An epidemic emerges as a product of a socially authoritative discourse in light of which bodies will be mobilized, resources will be dispensed, and tactics of surveillance and regulation will appear to be justified. Foucault argues that a medicine of epidemic could only exist with supplementation by the police (*Birth* 15). In this view, the construction of an epidemic situation has a strategic value in determining the configurations of what Foucault calls "bio-power," since the epidemic provides an occasion and a rationale for multiplying points of intervention into the lives of bodies and populations. For this reason, epidemics are always historically specific in a way that diseases are not, since the strategic imperatives motivating particular ways of coping with an epidemic always emerge as tactical responses to local utilities and circumstances. The construction of a sexual epidemic, as Foucault argues, provides an optimum site of intersection between individual bodies and populations. Hence sexual epidemic provides access to bodies and a series of codes for inscribing them, as well as providing a discourse of justification. When any phenomenon is represented as "epidemic," it has, by definition, reached a threshold that is quantitatively unacceptable. It is the capacity to make and circulate this determination, and to mobilize people in light of it, that constitutes the real political force of the discourse of sexual epidemic (Patton 51-66). With respect to our current situation, it is important to emphasize that the response to AIDS has been quite different from that given to other sexually transmitted diseases before remedies for them were found. This is not because venereal diseases did not have dire consequences for those who contracted them. Rather, the differences can be attributed, at least in part, to the belief that Victorian social structures could limit transmission by restricting the access of bodies to one another, especially given the dominance of particular institutions and ideologies. The AIDS epidemic is different, in part, because it comes on the heels of a period of explicit advocacy for proliferative sexuality, and because this epidemic first surfaced in a community that was already regarded as marginal, and to some, as morally suspect.

The history of the institutional responses to AIDS reveals how the politics of epidemics can work to solidify hegemonies. For years, gay activists and supporters lobbied for better funding for AIDS treatment and research, as the impact of the disease on their community increased. Such efforts went largely unrecognized and received little support from elected officials and health care professionals (Shilts). It was not until the disease spread to other segments of the population and taxed health care resources that medical professionals began to speak of an epidemic. This indicates not only how power is operative in constructing epidemics but also how that construction can be used to organize attention, energy, and material support. In light of the strategic value of epidemics, it is also important to point out that in a contemporary context, the primary medium for circulating the hegemony of epidemic has not been a medical discourse, but an explicitly political and ideological one. The forces most responsible for intensifying the political stakes entailed in sexual epidemic have been a collection of conservative groups from La Roucheans to Christian fundamentalists which have been able to exploit concern about AIDS to solicit support for their rather specific and rigid social agendas. The politics of epidemic is conducive to the New Right because an epidemic situation justifies, and is in fact constructed so as to necessitate, a complex system of surveillance and intervention. The New Right is willing to provide it in the form of a constitutional ban on abortion, restrictions on the distribution of contraception and sexual information, and on the production and distribution of sexual representations (i.e., pornography, erotica), as well as mandatory drug and AIDS testing. Conservative forces have also been able to exploit the anxiety operative in plague conditions to launch a revisionist critique of the sexual revolution and a defense of "family values" which demand a particular absolutist political program.

The conservative argument begins with an acceptable premise, namely, that the unbridled proliferation of sexually transmitted diseases is unacceptable. The emergence of these conditions is taken to be a consequence of a climate of permissiveness which multiplied sexual contacts and helped contribute to the erosion of authority, i.e., absolute paternalistic religious authority, which was better able to organize sexual energies for socially useful purposes like reproduction and consumption. It was the failure to heed that authority, it is argued, that has produced the crisis in which we now find ourselves. In the absolute logic of this position, the epidemic is interpreted either as a retributive consequence of past transgressions, or as a call to revivify and intensify that authority. These larger concerns both motivate and justify an expansion of the language and logic of epidemic, since it is argued that what is at stake in this plague is not only a threat to our physical well-being, but to our spiritual and social health as well.

The establishment of a connection between epidemic and transgression has allowed for the rapid transmission of the former to phenomena that are outside the sphere of disease. We are thus warned of the "epidemics" of teenage pregnancies, child molestation, abortion, pornography, and divorce. The use of this language marks all of these phenomena as targets for intervention because they have been designated as unacceptable, while at the same time reproducing the power that authorizes and justifies their deployment. According to this discourse, it is existing authority that is to be protected from the plague of transgressions.

Part of what is useful about the conservative polemic is that it provides some insight into the anxiety and malaise that permeate sexual discourse, even amongst those populations, like monogamous heterosexual Christians, who are least at risk of contracting a sexually transmitted disease. By using the occasion of a health crisis to revivify authority, the New Right makes clear that, as another theorist of plague, Albert Camus, points out, plagues are never just medical problematics. They are also world-transforming moments of ontological crisis which pervade the entire logic and fabric of a community's existence by calling it into question in a fundamental way, i.e., within the currency of life and death (Foucault, *History* 145). A plague, according to Camus, always marks a radically anxious point of rupture with respect to the economy of the everyday and its system of stabilized and sedimented significations. A plague is always "unusual, out of place" (Camus 3). One can no longer simply go on with business as usual. One is forced to call one's habits, values, and pleasures into question, precisely because the world in which they have a place is in the process of slipping away. Just what one calls into question and just what is lost will depend on one's position within the operative configuration of differences. For the Christian Right, what is lost is a world of stable systems of values and hierarchies of authority, and with them the confluences and coordinations of behavior they produce. What is lost for those who identified with the movement for sexual revolution is the promise of sexual future without threat, guilt, and suffering. The development of contraceptive technologies and remedies for venereal disease seemed to offer the prospect of organizing sexuality around the pursuit of pleasure. Now that prospect has been deferred by new diseases which present other kinds of risks.

Part of what makes a plague so oppressive is that it presents the individual with a situation that forces reflection and decision at the same time that the random and impersonal movement of contagion limits choice and truncates the sphere under her or his control. Because a plague is always a rupture both in the order of things and in the operative hegemony, it marks the limits of a prudential logic of calculation, either because possibilities are radically reduced, or because they are diminished in their differences. The plague ruptures rationality in the direction of the absurd demand that the unjustifiable be somehow justified. This is the obvious appeal, at least for some people, of the conservative position which offers a radical form of explanatory closure. Because plagues confront us with the limits of our assumptions and fictions, they also call for the generation of new assumptions, new fictions. What is being called into question in current circumstances is the whole way our culture has constructed and valued sex, and with that, all the other deployments of bio- and economic power with which it is connected. Plague conditions force one to ask the question of whether sex is worth dying for.

Camus's analysis helps to explain the malaise and despair that seems to have permeated much of the sexual political arena, a mood that marks a radical break with the optimism induced by the politics of ecstasy. The threat posed by the new sexual epidemic is the problematization of sexual hegemonies in a direction of diminishing returns and reduced expectations, especially for those who came of age during the sexual revolution. But the sexual epidemic has also helped to induce a reversal in the direction of social policy. In the 1960s and 1970s, legislative and policy initiatives reflected traditional liberal concerns for civil rights, individual freedom, right to privacy, and the principles of equality and equity. The liberal initiative helped establish legalized abortion and civil rights for homosexuals, enfranchise the principles of affirmative action and compensatory legislation, as well as contributed a climate of tolerance for sexual pluralism. What is disturbing about the current state of sexual political debate, particularly in the sphere of social policy, is the apparent failure of traditional liberalism to provide an adequate alternative to a conservative authoritarian social logic which advocates increased surveillance and regulation of bodies in ways that support and reproduce hegemonic relationships of dominance.

Traditional liberalism proves inadequate to an epidemic situation which lacks the fundamentally rational teleology that liberalism assumes to characterize most social phenomena. The utilitarian logic of maximizing social utilities while leaving individuals free to pursue their private pleasures in a climate of tolerance does not, and cannot, provide a strategy applicable to an economy of diminishing returns, both because the possibility of maximizing happiness under such conditions is radically suspect, and because epidemics, insofar as they are epidemic, cannot simply be tolerated. Yet such systematic and authorized intervention into the populace's lives and bodies is incompatible with the liberal principles of privacy and respect for the integrity of persons. Hence the liberal repertoire will be limited often to contesting such initiatives as they arise. Because the dynamic of contagion raises the social consequences of individual choices, the liberal model of freely chosen self-regulation is also inadequate as a response to epidemic conditions precisely because epidemics radically alter the context for such decisions in ways that are not and cannot be chosen.

Liberalism also finds itself without a sufficiently mobilizing rhetoric, especially since much of its language has been appropriated by the forces of opposition. For example, the concept of "respect for persons," central to liberal humanism, has been incorporated into the Vatican's rhetoric as grounds for denying women access to abortion and fertility technology, claiming that such procedures do not respect the fetus's personhood.

What is even more interesting is that such "humanist" language is used extensively in the Church's polemic against secular humanism. This language was also employed as part of the Supreme Court's decision to limit affirmative action suits to those filed by individuals, on the grounds that only individual persons can be victims of discriminatory practices. The rhetoric of "tolerance" and "pluralism" has been used as grounds for including representations of conservative positions like "creation science" in textbooks and popular media.

The limits of existing political discourse, as well as the urgency of the current situation, call for new forms of sexual political discourse, currency, and struggle. In this context, Foucault's work is especially helpful since his analysis of the proliferative operation of power supplements the limits of the repressive hypothesis, and offers the option of a strategic analysis which allows us to consider not only what is lost but also what is produced by the current organization of the sexual field which is itself a product of previous power deployments. This means that, counter to a logic which opposes erotic urgency and social utility or ghettoizes the sexual as some stable and invariable set of imperatives, Foucault's analysis demonstrates how the construction of each is dependent upon and made in light of the others, often, as in our age, with dire results which place our existence as a species in question. Part of the agenda for a sexual politics of epidemic will have to be a reconsideration of this "Faustian bargain," along with the generation of alternatives capable of mobilizing bodies sufficiently so as not to paralyze them in an economy of deprivation (Watney 123-35).

With respect to the techniques of embodiment operative in this particular sexual epidemic, we should expect to find that these techniques will reflect and inscribe a system of utilities and pleasures compatible with other demands made on bodies in late patriarchal capitalism. Foucault's insights provide conceptual machinery for making sense of some of what is at stake in the new sexual technology, which operates not through threat of death and pain, but instead establishes dominion over life through a currency of historically specific pleasures and powers. According to Foucault, the consequence of much of contemporary body techniques is that modern man has become "an animal whose politics places his existence as a living being in question" (Foucault, *History* 141). The implication of Foucault's analysis is the need to reconsider strategies in light of historical specificities.

Epidemic Strategies

In an effort to concretize and extend Foucault's analysis, which in some sense was cut short by the sexual epidemic, I will examine some of the modes of embodiment that have emerged as responses to current conditions. I will begin by discussing the discourses of "safe sex" and "the new sobriety" as two tactical responses to the hegemony of epidemic. I will then focus on some contemporary techniques of "body management" and will conclude with a discussion of some contemporary technologies aimed at intervening in human reproduction as strategies for exercising power over the lives of bodies and populations.

Part of the proliferative surplus produced by the hegemony of sexual epidemic are the discourses and techniques known as "safe sex" and "the new sobriety." Both represent exercises in theory and practice which emerged from discussions within the gay community, at once the initial source and the audience for them. But as AIDS begins to infect other segments of the population, these techniques are being far more widely promulgated and circulated through mainstream channels of communication and the voice of authority figures like the Surgeon General. As opposed to the absolutist logic employed by the New Right, these secular strategies employ a cost-benefit logic drawn from the discourses of finance, management, and to some extent, preventive medicine. Both strategies assume that sexual proliferation, like nuclear proliferation and the national debt, is not something one can hope to eliminate. The goal instead is to try to manage it strategically so as to minimize the risks of sexual contact without resorting to abstinence, which for many is clearly an untenable option.

In "safe sex," one minimizes the risks of sexual contact by developing an erotics which privileges prudential judgment over spontaneity, and prioritizes selectivity over variety. Minimally, safe sex entails the prophylactic use of condoms and avoidance of what are termed "high risk activities," like anal sex, and "high risk groups," like IV users. Making this prudential logic operational will demand changes in the economy of genital gestures and erotic choreography. It will also necessitate a reorganization of pleasure, a reconstruction of the erotic body, and an alteration in the terms and expectations of sexual exchanges.

Part of the change proffered by epidemic conditions is a shift in the relationship between knowledge and desire as they function in erotic situations. Specifically, knowledge of one's partners' physical condition and sexual history now becomes a prime object of concern. The erotic gaze is thus infected to some degree by the medical gaze which must learn to see sickness. The prudential aesthetic which characterizes the new sobriety creates specific forms of desire, like dating agencies which promise matches with prescreened AIDS-free partners.

Failing such elaborate screening procedures, and given the limits of their reliability, the ideology of safe sex encourages a reorganization of the body away from the erotic priorities with which it has already been inscribed. Specifically, safe sex advocates indulgence in numerous forms of non-genital contact and the reengagement of parts of the body marginalized by an economy of genital primacy. It also entails a reconfiguration of bodies and their pleasures away from an ejaculatory teleology toward a more polymorphous decentered exchange, reviving and concretizing the critique of genital condensation begun over twenty years ago by sexual theorists like Marcuse and Firestone.

The underlying assumptions about the relationships among bodies, pleasures, and powers which make safe sex possible depend, at least indirectly, on Foucault's analysis and its destabilizing consequences. Safe sex presumes that pleasure and practice can be reorganized in response to overriding utilities and presumes, as well, the capacity of regimentary procedures to construct a body capable of taking pleasure in this new form of discipline. Unless bodies and pleasures are politically determined, they can not be redetermined, even in cases where that is what rational prudence would demand. The success of this strategy will thus depend not only on promulgating these techniques, but also on circulating a discourse that allows individuals to reconsider their bodies in a more liberatory and strategic way.[3] What is new about the new sobriety is that its aesthetic of restraint is not represented in terms of a monastic economy of self-denial or obedience to some authoritative imperative, but is instead presented as a gesture of primary narcissism, a way of caring for and about oneself. Liberation, in this context, is relocated in an economy of intensification of control over one's body and one's position in sexual exchanges.

The new sobriety constructs a body well designed for the complexities of life in late capitalism, which requires a worker's body and a body of workers that are well managed in the way a portfolio is well managed, i.e., a body with flexible and diverse investments which maximize accumulated surplus as negotiable profits. The body constructed in the discourse of the new sobriety is inscribed with a discipline that is supposed to allow for more efficient functioning and control in both sex and work, in part because this bodily regimen has been represented as an exercise in self-fulfillment and development which should be part of the well-managed enlightened life.

The connection of the discourse of "body management" with primary narcissism creates a complex of strategies and disciplines which extend beyond the sphere of sexual practices to include other bodily techniques like nutrition, fitness, hygiene, cosmetics, diets, and what is referred to as "body building." I want to focus on the phenomenon of body building, partly because it is undergoing an historically unprecedented popularity, especially among women, and partly because body building, as both theory and practice, reveals how bodies are constructed within the new disciplinary regime, and what utilities, pleasures, and powers are being pursued in this reconstruction.

The very language of "body building" already targets a body that is assumed to be rebuildable. The disciplinary regimen, and its accompanying aesthetic, mobilizes the body as a divisible collection of parts which can be individually fine-tuned or standardized according either to some aesthetic ideal, or to the demands of the labor process. Such a regimen often involves the use of mechanical apparatuses like the Nautilus machine which isolate, target, and differentially work specific muscle groups. The fine-tuning of the body is often supplemented by far more interventionist procedures like plastic surgery, skin grafting, hair coloring and transplants, and the tanning booth to further control and refine the finished product, which is regarded as in need of perpetual maintenance and surveillance. The popularity of these techniques can be attributed to the proliferative effects of the slippage between energies organized according to a predetermined pattern of behavior, and the mobilizations of those energies as activities of self-love and personal development. Rather than depending on a regime of repression, the new discipline operates through a strategy of control by stimulation, which mobilizes energies through anonymous channels of regulation which can also be represented as activities of individuation.

When reproductive imperatives are added to the utilities to be mobilized by the discourse of body management, women's bodies become targets for gender-specific strategies and tactics. If, as Foucault suggests, the deployments of modern power seek to intervene at a place where individual bodies intersect with the body of the social, it is not surprising that reproduction is being restructured by a series of technologies designed to make that process, and the bodies who accomplish it, more malleable and responsive to fluctuations in demographic utilities.

Given women's subordinate position within a patriarchal social order, discipline has always been a technique used to marshall women's energies and bodies in pursuit of utilities not of their own making. Given that women's place is often constructed as one of self-effacing service, it is not surprising that female disciplinary strategies often take the form of radical self-denial, as in the case of body practices such as anorexia and bulimia. But the well-managed female body of the '80s is constructed so as to be even more multifunctional than its predecessors. It is a body that can be used for wage labor, sex, reproduction, mothering, spectacle, exercise, or even invisibility, as the situation demands. It is also a body that is constructed to accommodate the variable whims of fashion, and a postmodern aesthetic which demands the capacity to project a multiplicity of looks and attitudes with apparent effortlessness.

Most important, however, and what is historically specific about this construct is that this body's reproductive potential is managed and disciplined so as to be capable of conceiving and producing children on demand, as well as deferring that process until the time is right. Most of the innovations in reproductive ideology and technology have sought to render women's bodies more easily mobilizable in response to shifting utilities, most notably the production and coordination of populations. In order to address the different sorts of intervention that produce the contemporary ideologies of motherhood, I will begin by examining the differential strategies by which motherhood is being marketed to particular segments of the female population. I will then analyze the strategic value of the new reproductive technology and will conclude with a discussion of one recent and conspicuous case of fallout from this technology, the Baby M case.

The differential strategies by which women are addressed by these ideological discourses borrow their tactics and logic from advertising and market research, two disciplines which have devised elaborate mechanisms for segmenting the prospective market and for designing highly specific occasions of incitement which can be tailor-made to appeal to particular predetermined segments of the population. The necessity to market motherhood appears to have been motivated, at least in part, by the development of contraceptive technologies which give women some measure of control over their fertility and its consequences. Current marketing strategies have also emerged as responses to what can be read as a demographic gap in the birth rate amongst white middle-class educated women who, beginning in the early '70s, began in larger numbers to defer motherhood or to avoid it altogether. This mobilization of women's energies was facilitated by a feminist discourse which explicitly challenged the reproductive imperative (Allen 91–101) and in some cases made women's liberation dependent upon refusing such imperatives. During approximately the same period of time, however, there was also a statistically significant rise in pregnancies amongst teenagers, especially poor women of color, who were more likely than their older counterparts to have their babies delivered, and in some cases supported, at state expense. In a white-male-dominated culture this was perceived as a situation that called for adjustment.

Hence we start to find images of attractive successful women like Christie Brinkley, Patti Hanson, Shelley Long, as well as media feminists like Erica Jong, proudly posing on magazine covers and bus shelters advocating the pleasures of motherhood. Never mind that these women mother under conditions that are likely to be radically different from those of the women addressed in the ads. The strategy of these campaigns was to inscribe motherhood within a series of elements the sum of which was represented as "having it all" in the proper sequence, which is the mark of any "superwoman." There is some evidence that this strategy worked, helping to contribute to what *Time* magazine has dubbed "the mini baby boom," a discourse circulated without irony, and without ever raising the question of "boom" for whom or what.

Contemporaneous with these images is an ad campaign in which Planned Parenthood addresses potential teenage mothers. The poster series consists of several versions of the same basic format varied by racial type, in which a young woman holding a baby stares dead-pan at the viewer in what is clearly depicted as dismal surroundings. The accompanying boldface copy reads, "It's like being grounded for eighteen years."[4]

The tactics employed in these cases are obvious at the first and are intended to work in precisely opposite ways, discouraging younger women of color from reproducing by emphasizing the burdens of motherhood, while effacing those burdens when addressing women whose reproductive services are regarded as useful, either from the standpoint of maintaining race and class dominance, or as a strategy for inducing women's voluntary defection from more competitive segments of the labor market. Certainly, if motherhood demobilizes women, it does so regardless of the mother's age, though class, race, and educational differences determine the forms such demobilization will take. But for a variety of reasons it is strategically desirable to circulate a discourse of differences, and to abridge recognition of the continuities in women's experience that emerge as a consequence of the gender caste system, which links all women by their subordination to phallocentric utilities. In any case, given the complexities of race and class differences, along with the degree of specificity attempted, we should not be surprised when some of these messages get crossed in transmission and arrive at destinations for which they were not intended, since within any dominant strategic deployments sites of opposition and resistance are also created. The political challenge is to develop strategies for organizing and coordinating those positions in a way that mobilizes their counter-hegemonic potential.

At the level of reproductive technology and technique, the radical disparity between the development rates of fertility, as opposed to contraceptive, technology in the last twenty years helps mark both a strategy and a dominant set of utilities. While fertility technology becomes more sophisticated and widely available, contraceptive technology and distribution, along with public debate, seem in many respects to be moving in the opposite direction. New fertility clinics and surrogate mothering agencies open while abortion clinics are being bombed.

The current fertility technology has been strategically designed for maximum flexibility in its capabilities for deployment. It can be used, or has the potential to be used, either to intervene so as to enlist more women in the reproductive brigades, or to render women biologically extraneous. Developments in fetal medicine and eugenics offer the prospects of regulating the product as well as the process of reproduction and normalizing intervention into the lives of persons by beginning even before they have that status. Each of these techniques touches the core of the bio-power system, the control over production of life, in a way that thus far has worked primarily to solidify and support a hegemony of white male heterosexist dominance. The question remains as to whether such techniques also offer more liberatory possibilities. Any response to this challenge will be dependent upon recognizing the complex intersections between bio-power and other systems of deployment which produce both the discourse and the terms of sexual struggle.

Nowhere do the complexities of this multi-layered apparatus become more visible in their contradictions than in what has probably been the hottest and most widely circulated sexual political issue of the '80s, save AIDS, namely the Baby M case. Its import is immediately felt at the level of language, where it introduced the neologism "surrogate motherhood" into popular parlance. But as one might expect, it also began a new logic and politics of parental privilege.

The use of the term "surrogate mother" to apply to Mary Beth Whitehead already reflects a bias in favor of paternal prerogative and a privileging of contractual relations regulating commodities over issues of biology and maternal desire. Given the way the issues were framed, i.e., as a choice between legally authorized paternity and biological maternity, and the context presumed by legal discourse, i.e., a class-stratified male-dominated hegemony, it is not surprising that the ruling granted custody of the child to the more affluent father. But what is really at stake in this case is less a contest between paternal and maternal claims than a question of maternal prerogative. The strategic value of the Baby M case, and its resolution, lies more with the way it manages the contest between two competing claims of motherhood, the one legal and contractual, the other biological and genetic, which in this case was resolved in terms of a legal discourse structured by and facilitating class stratification and male dominance. The consequence in this case was the determination of Whitehead as the surrogate mother, and most significantly, the granting of immediate legal motherhood to Mrs. Stern.[5] But apart from a contractual discourse which defines Whitehead as surrogate, Whitehead is in every other sense the mother of the child. She is the female progenitor, and genetic contributor, and hence, at the very least the child's birth mother. She has the connection with the child regardless of her relationship to the male progenitor. In the context of the case, Mrs. Stern's claim to maternity is entirely dependent upon and has status only in terms of her husband's desire to claim paternity. Had Mr. Stern for some reason chosen not to exercise his paternal claim, the question of Mrs. Stern's maternity would never have come up.

But the claims made on behalf of Mrs. Whitehead and the language of organized feminist support which focused on Whitehead's rights as a "natural mother" are equally problematic, and in some sense they reproduce the ideological framework in terms of which Mr. Stern's claim proved to be more legally persuasive. Specifically, the appeals to "natural motherhood" overlook an extensive feminist discourse which documents how the discourse of motherhood has been strategically deployed historically to exert control over women's bodies while devaluing and effacing maternal labor, effort, and commitment which are therein reduced to the status of a natural aptitude. These contradictions point toward the strategic value of the discourse of surrogate motherhood, part of which is to pit women against women, largely on the basis of class, and then to reinstitute male prerogative and class privilege[6] as the legal basis for resolving competing claims.

The arguments made on behalf of Mr. Stern's property rights reveal the intersections between the sexual reproduction system and the logic regulating the commodity market. Mr. Stern's attorney argued that he was entitled to the child not because he had paid for her as such, but because he had paid for the use of Whitehead's body for breeding purposes. Retreating to a neo-Aristotelian biology, Stern's attorney redescribed Mary Beth Whitehead as a vessel rented by the client for the express purpose of gestating and delivering the product of his seed. As such, it is argued, he is entitled to get what he paid for, while Whitehead's consent to the contract invalidates any of her further claims.

These arguments clearly place surrogate motherhood on a continuum with other institutional forms of commodifying women's bodies, including prostitution and "mail-order brides." Surrogate motherhood is a technological extension of the wet-nurse, where some women are in the position of using their bodies to support other more privileged women's offspring. In some sense, the decision in this case is compatible with the logic which produces laws that protect the consumers rather than the providers of women's sexual services and that use women's position as sellers to limit their rights and prerogatives. In the case of prostitution, the woman's position as seller of sexual service is regarded as making her unfit for inclusion under laws that protect providers in most other industries. In the case of surrogate motherhood, the judge determined that Whitehead's decision to sell her body for breeding purposes is an indication of her unfitness to mother.[7]

The figuring of the issue of maternal fitness in the Baby M case also reveals the strategic considerations already invested in the discourse of surrogate motherhood. In this case, the question of Whitehead's fitness to mother emerged only as a consequence of Mr. Stern's desire for custody. In cases where paternity is unacknowledged or refused, custody falls *de facto* to the mother, independent of any discourse of maternal fitness. Under ordinary circumstances, questions of parental fitness are displaced to the private sphere of familial autonomy. They arise in this case only as a consequence of paternal and class prerogatives. In this case "fitness" is determined to mean fitness to produce potential consumers rather than potential providers of surrogate services. Hence not only custody but also contractual prerogatives are distributed along hegemonic lines of class and gender privilege.

The way the Baby M case both raises and settles questions about the social and political organization of parenthood and about the meaning and power attached to the positions of paternity and maternity is part of its historically specific strategic value. What makes the Baby M case possible is a confluence of social forces which divide the body and body functions into separable units, linking them with a commodity system that proliferates sites and forms for these exchanges, a legal system that regulates and authorizes such transactions, and a system of sexual and class differences according to which functions and prerogatives are differentially distributed. It was against this background that a drama represented in the language of desire was played out, pitting Mr. Stern's desire to father a child to which he had a genetic connection against Mrs. Whitehead's desire to remain in touch with the child which had emerged from her body. What was being asked of the court in this case, and what is likely to be demanded in the future, was the production of a discursive grid in terms of which the claims established within different disciplinary codes could be mapped, ordered, and ultimately resolved. The Baby M case is the beginning of the attempt to construct the differential calculus. But because the resolution is likely to be challenged, and because this case raises as many questions as it answers, maximum flexibility in deployment is maintained which in turn allows for adjustments in the organization of reproduction according and in relation to other variable utilities and imperatives.

I have chosen to conclude my discussion of sexual politics in the age of epidemic with a discussion of the Baby M case because I think it points toward the kind of sexual political issues that are likely to confront us in the future, and because it functions as the opposing pole to those issues emerging from the logic of sexual disease. Given the proliferative possibilities of both reproductive technology and commodity culture, it is likely that more cases of contested parenthood will arise. It is clear that in the case of surrogate mothering, as in the case of prostitution, a regime of repression, even if one could find grounds for endorsing it, would prove inadequate as a response. In instances of surrogacy, perhaps the best solution will be to treat problems as cases of breached contract, and to let prospective fathers know that there are risks in making such an arrangement.

In a larger context, issues surrounding reproductive technology and organization constitute another series of challenges that confront us in the age of sexual epidemic. Conflicts which entail bodies, pleasures, and the production of life will continue to play out against the background of the struggle against death. Both kinds of struggle will be transacted, at least in part, at the level of cultural currency identified as sexuality, in forms that are likely to reflect and reproduce sexuality's proliferative dynamics, and with an intensity which speaks to the levels of cultural investment in this discourse.

If sexuality, now more than ever, constitutes the turf and terms in which struggles of life and death will be transacted, questions of sexual politics, i.e., of the construction and distribution of bodies, pleasures, and powers, will no longer simply be sites of elective engagement. Because sexuality functions as a force of production and proliferation as well as a currency of valuation, conflicts, as they arise, will continue to force reconsideration of our assumptions about and investment in these hegemonic formations, with the recognition of how much is at stake in the decisions we make. One way to begin is to relocate the sexual not outside but at the intersection of the multiplicity of discourses by which bodies, pleasures, and powers are circulated and exchanged. We ought to do so strategically with attention paid to the specificity of local conditions. We must also remember that in saying yes to sex we are not saying no to power. If sexuality in our age has become, at least for some people, worth the exchange of life itself, it behooves us to reconsider the situation in which we find and risk losing ourselves. The real sexual epidemic may very well turn out to be a politics which places our very existence in question. We therefore need to ask ourselves, with renewed urgency, whether sex is worth dying for, how it is we got to this place, and where we can go from here.

Notes

1. The term "hegemony" is used frequently in the text, and therefore bears some clarification. As I am using the term, "hegemony" refers to any social construction which has sufficient currency or legitimacy to operate as a naturalized point of orientation for social discourse. Hegemony is not false consciousness, because its organizing and explanatory functions have not been cast in the currency of truth. Rather, the hegemonic apparatus works to provide a context for social struggle by condensing a shared set of assumptions and symbols that set the terms for discursive struggles and for their resolution. I am using the term in this context because I think the language of "sexual epidemic" does not just name an existing state of epidemiological affairs, but it also is a condensation point for a whole set of assumptions about sexuality in terms of which the contours of new sexual-political issues are being framed. By treating the sexual epidemic as a hegemonic construct, I want to emphasize the social labor entailed in its elaboration and circulation, as well as call attention to its strategic function, without denying that the spread of AIDS has reached quantitatively unacceptable proportions, i.e., is epidemic. For a recent discussion of hegemony which has informed my usage, see Laclau and Mouffe.

2. For a discussion of contemporary strategies for re-eroticizing safe sex within the gay community, see Watney, 1–38.

3. For a range of attempts in this direction, see Kroker.
4. This ad campaign was placed in subway stations in New York during the summer of 1987.
5. The initial ruling was subsequently reversed on appeal, restoring Mrs. Whitehead's status as the legal mother. Consequently, she has been granted rights to regular visitation, though the baby will continue to reside with the Sterns.
6. This argument has prompted legislation in several states to outlaw paid surrogacy contracts.
7. This judgment was also reversed on appeal.

Works Cited

Allen, Jeffner. "Motherhood: The Annihilation of Women." *Women Values: Readings in Recent Feminist Philosophy*. Ed. Marilyn Pearsall. New York: Wadsworth, 1985. 91–101.

Altman, Dennis. *The Homosexualization of America, The Americanization of the Homosexual*. New York: St. Martin's, 1982.

Camus, Albert. *The Plague*. Trans. Stuart Gilbert. New York: Vintage-Random, 1972.

Ehrenreich, Barbara, et al. *Remaking Love: The Feminization of Sex*. Garden City: Anchor-Doubleday, 1986. 103–60.

Firestone, Shulamith. *The Dialectic of Sex: The Case for Feminist Revolution*. New York: Morrow, 1970.

Foucault, Michel. *The Birth of the Clinic: An Archaeology of Medical Perception*. Trans. A. M. Sheridan Smith. New York: Pantheon, 1973.

————.*The History of Sexuality*. Trans. Robert Hurley. Vol. 1. New York: Vintage, 1980.

Kroker, Arthur, and Marilouise Kroker, eds. *Panic Sex in America*. New York: St. Martin's, 1987.

Laclau, Ernesto, and Chantal Mouffe. *Hegemony and Socialist Strategy*. Trans. Winston Moore and Paul Cammack, London: Verso, 1985.

Marcuse, Herbert. *Eros and Civilization: A Philosophical Inquiry into Freud*. Boston: Beacon, 1955.

Patton, Cindy. *Sex and Germs: The Politics of AIDS*. Boston: South End, 1985.

Shilts, Randy. *And the Band Played On*. New York: St. Martin's, 1987.

Watney, Simon. *Policing Desire: Pornography, AIDS & the Media*. Minneapolis: University of Minnesota Press, 1987.

Weeks, Jeffrey. *Sexuality and Its Discontents: Meanings, Myths and Modern Sexualities*. London: Routledge, 1985.

2

Interpretation and Retrieval: Rereading Beauvoir

This paper is written in response to a problem of intertextuality which is not best represented through an examination of texts because it is a problem of absence, the erasure of writing, and as such resists documentation. The problem is the erasure or absence of Beauvoir's work from the philosophical canon, and the resulting marginalization of her discourse within the conversation which constitutes professional philosophy. As a consequence, Beauvoir's work receives little space in the social network of journals, conferences and classrooms through which philosophical practice is concretized.

In the light of the extra-textual dimensions of the problem, it is with some irony that I propose a rereading of Beauvoir's theoretical texts in light of the philosophical contexts and conversations from which her work has been absented, and in which the professional devaluation of her work becomes justification for the community's failure to read it in the first place. My proposed reading will thus proceed by a paradoxical strategy which aims to retrieve the significance of Beauvoir's work in light of the contradictions of historical forces which have produced its peripheral position. This contradiction consists in the conjunction of reasoning according to which Beauvoir is not worth reading because she is either too far removed from the standard terrain of philosophy, i.e., too identified with the extra-philosophical turf of the feminine, or, on the other hand, because she is too closely identified with that tradition as a "pseudo-Sartrean." Both of these ways of not reading Beauvoir are misguided in my view, and certainly make any genuine appreciation of her work impossible.[1] My reading aims to dislodge these readings by offering an interpretation of Beauvoir as a female-identified voice who addresses the discourse of philosophy from that standpoint.

My intention is to provide a selective reading of *The Second Sex* (1952) and

From *Women's Studies Int. Forum*, vol. 8, no. 3 (1985), pp. 231–38. Reprinted with permission.

Ethics of Ambiguity (1948) (Beauvoir's major theoretical texts) which retrieves their import in the context of the ethical discourse and theory of value promised, but not delivered, by Sartre and Heidegger. In this sense, Beauvoir can be understood as directing her discourse toward the historical tradition of ethics, and the language of freedom and responsibility privileged by existentialists, most especially Sartre. But Beauvoir's work does not stand contained or restricted to the Sartrean discourse, despite her occasional demure protestations to the contrary, because as I read her work, Beauvoir's discussion, unlike Sartre's, is identified with and emerges from the situation of femininity. Her position with respect to Sartre's work is therefore, on my reading, not complementary or supplementary, but rather oppositional and subversive, especially with respect to the concept of freedom and its position in the ethical discourse.

Beauvoir marks the site of her opposition in *The Second Sex* when she names the character of cultural representation in writing, as phallocentric.

> Representation of the world, like the world itself is the work of men;
> they describe it from their point of view which they confuse with the
> absolute truth. (p. 161)

This recognition marks Beauvoir's discourse as a discourse of otherness and of difference.[2] I will be concentrating in my text on the concept of freedom as the marker of this difference. Far from being contained as a supplement within the frame established by Sartrean language and the larger conversation in which his work participates, Beauvoir's writing ruptures or disrupts the structure of the very phallocentric language and speech which claims to speak for and include the position marked as "other." By naming sex or sexual difference as a repressed structure of philosophical discourse, Beauvoir recasts the nature and scope of philosophy's assumptions. Specifically, Beauvoir's recognition that the sites and positions from which women and men converse are different, and not only different but opposed in a way that privileges the masculine standpoint and its standards of representation, decenters the practice of philosophical signification by which some are entitled to speak for all, and where femininity comes to signify a marker created in and aimed at a position coded as alien or other.

Taking the insights of existentialism seriously with respect to its denial of a supervening perspective and its affirmation of the situational character of discourse, Beauvoir begins the project of writing the other side, giving voice to the discourse of otherness. Part of the purpose of the existential analytic of feminine development in *The Second Sex* is to give social and historical sense to this sign of otherness, thus reconstituting femininity as an existential project with an integrity, and not just an empty sign for deferred male desire. With the elaboration of woman as other comes the discourse of difference, the writing of female signification in its difference. Beauvoir speaks to the traditional discourse of philosophy, and to its sense of problems and issues, but she speaks to it from the other side, or the side it has positioned as other.

My efforts in this paper will focus on Beauvoir's rewriting of the discourse of freedom from the position of the oppressed feminine. The discourse of freedom has been privileged in ethical writing, but on Beauvoir's analysis, it is also revealed as a discourse of privilege. Borrowing from Elizabeth Janeway's discussion of power (1981), freedom, like power, has been written, historically, from the standpoint of those who have it, and thus has been treated as a quality or attribute of persons, rather than relationships. This has resulted in a reification in theory and practice, the effect of which has been to support and perpetuate an arbitrary system of privilege. Beauvoir broaches the question of freedom from the position of the second, i.e., from the standpoint of women whose containment is secured by the traditional discourse. She engages in this discourse for the purpose of liberating those so contained. Her rewriting has the effect of shifting the locus of freedom from that of isolated autonomous individuals to freedom emergent from a situation of relatedness and affinity. This sense of a freedom which realizes itself in engagement with and for others provides Beauvoir with the basis for the morality of commitment and concern described in *The Ethics of Ambiguity,* which I read as an oppositional text with respect to the history of ethics. It is my intention to show that it is only with this reconstitution of freedom that an ethics of liberation in light of human finitude is possible.

My rereading attempts to situate Beauvoir's work within the context of the ethical discourse as the voice of the ethics of otherness, i.e., the sense and practice of value which emerges from the feminine situation. While most ethical theory presents its position as gender neutral or transsexual, recent research by Carol Gilligan (1982) provides good reason to believe that gender is a marker of difference in ethical decision making, and that men and women do in fact arrive at moral decisions differently, by privileging alternate aspects of the problematic situation. The difference, Gilligan notes, is often belied by a phallocentric bias which tends to view the feminine simply as an underdeveloped mode of the masculine. Based on her research, which included extensive interviews with women, Gilligan distinguishes between two moral models which can be correlated with gender difference. The first is the masculinist model, which privileges the concept of a morality of rights predicated on equality and centered on the matter of fairness (p. 164). The feminine model, by contrast, privileges an ethic of responsibility predicated on equity and recognition of difference in need (p. 160).

While Gilligan's analysis does not address the origins or reasons for this difference *per se,* there is no reason to assume an essentialist or deterministic explanation. Read in light of Beauvoir's analysis of femininity, it is reasonable to interpret these differences in judgmental strategies as deriving from the opposed roles and situations women and men occupy in patriarchy. Those most likely to be given the power to legislate and judge will also be those most likely to privilege these functions, while women, to whom falls the burden of care and nurture, are likely to privilege these aspects in their judgmental activities.

I will be reading the relationship between Beauvoir's and Sartre's discourses on freedom as emblematic of the opposition between these two standpoints. Considered in this light, Beauvoir is not a "pseudo-Sartrean." Hers is a voice of discord and resistance to the sense of freedom in isolation. Since such a view provides insufficient basis for moral responsibility, Beauvoir maps an alternative conception of freedom identified as an agency of commitment and concern. To support this reading, I will try to tie the Sartrean discourse to its displaced origins in a masculine position of privilege and then show how Beauvoir's rewriting of the feminine provides the basis for a revivified concept of freedom and responsibility and ultimately of morality itself.

To understand the relationship between these two ideas of freedom and relatedness, it will be necessary to give a brief account of Sartre's model of consciousness which is the locus for the exercise of freedom. Sartre's model of consciousness extends a philosophical tradition of dualism which positions subjects, who are conscious, and objects, which are not, in an oppositional relationship. This rift in being creates two regions which Sartre identified as regions of positivity and negativity "without communication." Consciousness is identified with the region of negativity since "it is nothingness which is at the very heart of transcendence and which conditions it." Negativity is the central structure of consciousness since positional awareness of something is only possible by virtue of a prepositional act of nihilation, a recognition that consciousness is not that of which it is conscious. Consciousness of objects is possible on this view only on the basis of the fundamental separation or difference between consciousness and its objects, which Sartre describes as an abyss of nothing. Consciousness, in Sartre's words is a "total emptiness since the whole world is outside it." The emptiness of consciousness is a phenomenon of absence, and it is from this sense of absence, of determination, motives or causes, that Sartre derives the view of the consciousness as radically free. Because consciousness is nothing, not a thing, it cannot be eclipsed or compromised except by being reduced to a thing in the midst of the world by another consciousness. Because consciousness is empty of objects as the condition by virtue of which there are objects for us, consciousness retains its power of transcendence, with respect to the choice of positions toward that which it positions, and thus maintains a radical sense of self-sufficiency, which marks its privilege with respect to objects. Consciousness is privileged, on Sartre's view, because the subject is free to determine or constitute objects while being free from being determined or constituted by them. The absence of content or determinations for consciousness means that consciousness lacks origins or foundations, and thus is thrown back on itself as the site of its unconditioned choices.

It is the recognition of the groundlessness of our choices which is the source of the anxiety for a radically free consciousness. This anxiety in turn motivates the flight from freedom in an act of bad faith, by which the subject endeavors to escape from the necessity and responsibility for essentially spontaneous or groundless choices. The movement of bad faith, which attempts to decenter freedom in objects, amounts to a denial of the radical autonomy of consciousness, and a refusal to acknowledge its sovereignty over all which it is not. A consciousness defined in terms of its separation from all that is, in the Sartrean view, betrays itself in this moment of displacement. Consciousness is thus compromised by its commitments, its attachments and relationships, since such attachments serve to mask the essentially nihilating activity of consciousness from itself. A consciousness moved or motivated by its attachments is interpreted by Sartre as being in flight from recognizing its complicity with them, and its freedom to do otherwise. In allowing oneself anything other than commitments treated as groundless or arbitrary, consciousness displaces its freedom onto objects, and so itself becomes objectified.

This brief account was designed to show that Sartre's concept of freedom is such as to construe that term in a sense that is primarily solipsistic and negative. Sartre's freedom shows itself as a self-sufficient power of nihilation posed over and against a world of positivity from a position of privilege. The consequence of this conception of freedom is to compromise the prospect of freedom establishing and realizing itself in any other than solipsistic and isolated modes. The limits of this view are apparent in Sartre's discussion of interpersonal relationships, which produces rather fatalistic conclusions about the possibility of establishing affinities and identifications between freedoms.

Because the free exercise of subjectivity is always manifest, on Sartre's view, as objectification, relations with others degenerate into circular and unresolvable sado-masochistic conflicts, in which freedom seeks supremacy in the face of otherness. From Sartre's perspective, I am conscious of the presence of the other as another subject only by virtue of that subject's capacity to objectify me with the look. In the eyes of the other, I am aware of myself as a transcendence-transcended. I have been reduced to a standpoint eclipsed by the constitutive activities of a freedom which functions and is known only as a threat to my own, since its operations decenter or compromise the scope of my constitutive powers. The look of the other is a source of anxiety because it alerts me to my own lack, specifically the limits of my otherness to myself, and hence my being without foundations. In this sense, Sartre says, the other holds the secret of my being, since he is the possessor of that which I need to be my own foundation and that which I will always lack. The motive force for my relationships with others on this view is the ultimately narcissistic goal of self-completion by attempting to possess or appropriate the freedom of the other in its otherness. Such efforts, however, are ultimately futile because I can appeal to the other only by making myself an object of constitutive activity, denying my own subjectivity in the process. My efforts to capture the other's freedom through the exercise of my own also fail, since such activity reduces the other to the position of an object and hence fails to deliver the freedom I seek as freedom.

On Sartre's view, the co-presence or mutual recognition of freedoms is therefore impossible since two consciousnesses that aim for totality with respect to their constitutive objects cannot co-exist and so must move between the equally untenable positions of sadism and masochism. Because other people function in Sartre's model as objects for consciousness, in a relationship of opposition to it, interpersonal relationships will be structured by categories of reification, displacement and deferral. Because freedom is identified with a position of solipsistic self-sufficiency without foundation in the world, freedom precludes the formation of genuine attachments with others, except as the abstract recognition of the other's constitutive powers being like my own—an ultimately empty analogy.

Given this view of interpersonal relationships, it is not hard to understand why the discussion of *mitsein* receives so little attention from Sartre in his discussion of "Concrete Relations with Others" in *Being and Nothingness* (1953). It is also easier to understand why the ethical theory Sartre promises at the end of this text is never delivered. If freedom and relatedness are essentially opposed, one cannot construct an ethics capable of accommodating them both. Either freedom is radically unconditioned and ethical choice is indistinguishable from pure spontaneity and thus is completely arbitrary, or consciousness is motivated in the ethical moment and thus is not radically free. Given this configuration, at best this problem could be resolved by the judicial model of liberalism with its contractual models of consent and self-regulation. But it should be clear, given Sartre's position, why he found such an alternative unacceptable, as a denial of the radical freedom he took such care to elaborate. As a result, Sartre has had little to say by way of constituting an alternative discourse founded upon this view of freedom and finitude.

The task that now remains is to show how Beauvoir's discourse on freedom subverts the Sartrean conception and with it, its impasses. The core of Beauvoir's insight lies in her decision to return freedom to its roots in the patriarchal configuration of masculinity, and then to oppose to this the repressed discourse of the feminine marked by the sign of a different sense of freedom. This allows for an alternative conception of moral agency marked by a privileging of affinity and care in a way which contributes to, rather than compromises, the integrity of moral agents or the world they constitute in common.

What is most subversive about Beauvoir's approach to freedom is her efforts to find origins, in human experience, for the very sense of freedom which is described by Sartre as anxious by virtue of its lack of origins. Sartre considers freedom from the perspective of a human subject thrown into the world with a consciousness already other than and free from the situations in which it is developed, disclosed and discovered. Even for the finite subject who exists in time, freedom is not a developmental phenomenon, on Sartre's account. It is a preestablished structure of potentiality indifferent to the occasions of its irruptions and irrevocably separate from them, hence without attachments.

Beauvoir traces the development of freedom through its embodied, social and temporal phrases, beginning with its origins in infantile vulnerability. Both male and female begin existence dependent upon and contained by mother's body. From the time of weaning, however, male and female children will be positioned differently toward the mother, the body, and the question of origins. In childhood, Beauvoir says, the young girl seems to be favored, since she is allowed to remain longer within the protective and supportive sphere of the maternal. Young girls can be kept with mother because motherhood is their future. To remain bonded to mother is also to be bonded to a future, a future of transformation and care-taking through the medium of the body, which her patterns of play will also aim to re-identify as pleasure. The girl's sense of freedom is forged in a context of mirroring, and so her identity will come to be established for her through the refractions of approval, recognition and affinity with others.

The young boy, by contrast, is removed sooner from the maternal sphere because, as Beauvoir puts it, "great things are in store for him," and those great things lie outside and separate from the world of the mother. To enter the world of the fathers which operates by principles of competition and conflict rather than care, he must overcome his attachment to mother as the site of his vulnerability and original dependence. In the context of male development, transcendence is attached to this overcoming of origins, in the body, and in women, while the pursuit of foundations comes to be associated with a form of regression. His development will be marked by his movement away from protection toward self-sufficiency, or at least, the symbols of same. What will buttress this effort will be his emergence in a system of sexual difference in which he is positioned as other than and privileged with respect to the world of the mother. The young girl, who will herself be an originating body, will not seek freedom in nihilation but productivity. Her understanding of the significance of origins, connections and attachments will thus be opposed to that of the boys. This is not accidental but overdetermined since her survival and recognition will depend upon occupying this opposite pole.

It is with respect to the question of origins that Beauvoir's discussion of sexual difference in discourse takes on import with respect to the concept of freedom. In light of the difference Beauvoir names, the Sartrean idea of a freedom without foundation is recast within the frame of the distinctly masculine frame of reference which emphasizes the project of separation begun by distinguishing oneself from the mother and the socially deprivileged maternal sphere she comes to embody and represent. The male figure of freedom thus becomes associated with distance, separation and the nihilation of origins. Such distance is possible, for men, because the world of the father is a world at great remove from the world he inhabits as a child, a distance greater than that between the girl's domestic games and actual domesticity. The young man, confronted with an open future, experiences anxiety in the face of his range of possibilities. The more open the field, the more likely he is to recognize the non-necessity of any particular path, as well as to identify with his own powers of choice with respect to that situation. As a consequence he can come to feel himself to be the source of his own choices. This configuration of freedom as an autonomous choice among possibilities bespeaks a position of male privilege, since arriving at the idea of self as an agency of choice depends upon being in a situation open to such possibilities. In patriarchy, this pluralization of possibilities is a dimension of male privilege, and thus Sartre's so-called foundationless freedom is in fact tied to conditions of sociality and embodiment which make such recognitions possible. The significance of Beauvoir's analysis of childhood can thus be read as an interpretation of the discourse of freedom without origins, which can now be understood as a discourse of male privilege. On this reading, the female strategy of pursuing freedom and identity in the context of relations with others is only coded as dependent or regressive if one chooses to normatively privilege male experience. But as feminist theory has shown, years later, there are alternative ways to construe this difference.[3]

Beauvoir continues her analysis of female development by pursuing the configurations of sexual difference throughout the life stages of individuals. During adolescence, for example, the course of differentiation begun in childhood takes on particularly dramatic import with the emergence of the sexual body. For the boy, the appearance of the markers of manhood are permeated by the sense of entitlement he knows they confer upon him. For the girl, however, with the emergence of her womanly attributes, the future seems to take up residence in her body. These changes in her mode of embodiment which occur beyond her will or complicity seem to seal her fate, throwing her into a world of glances, expectations and desires not yet her own. Even more intensely than in childhood, the adolescent female will come to identify herself with her image as it is mirrored and refracted through the eyes and attitude of others toward her. Adolescence is the phase in which the confluence of pleasure and power with the state of being looked at will take hold of the female consciousness. She will come to associate her efficacy with the power to fascinate those who are essential. For the adolescent girl, as Beauvoir describes her, the pleasure others take in looking at her will become inseparable and indistinguishable from her own pleasure.

Differing from the patterns of male narcissism which aim at self-completion through appropriation, the adolescent girl will pursue the pleasure of refracted narcissism, which depends upon the other's glance remaining other as a source of validation. As a consequence, her being for others will not seem to compromise her freedom, but will rather be construed as providing the most fertile field for its exercise. Far from being an empty consciousness seeking to incorporate the other's freedom as fulfillment, the adolescent girl waits for the man who is ready to receive and appropriate her plentitude and through this to give meaning to her facticity. With the emergence of her sexual body, woman is constituted in patriarchy as a locus of abundance and generosity opposed to the emptiness and neediness of men.

> Appearing as the other, woman appears at the same time as an abundance of being, in contrast to that existence the nothingness of which man senses in himself. In woman is incarnated in positive form the look that the existent carries in his heart. . . . (p. 160)

Already marked with the look of the man who at this point has come to signify for woman the essential dimension to which she is opposed, female freedom already receives a trajectory which ties her fate to those of others. While male maturation pursues a course of separation, connection, with man becomes the marker of recognition and value for women. While being seen or desired functions in the masculine discourse as a site of compromise and ambivalence, a threat to their sense of autonomy and integrity, the threat for women is the opposite, the fear of being unseen and invisible. In a world which constitutes her as other, connection becomes essential for women. The woman who is not recognized by others begins not to recognize herself. Rather than identifying with their own lack and freely seeking its fulfillment, women identify with their ability to anticipate and fulfill the needs of others. The negativities which structure her world are not gaps or separations between isolated subjects, but rather come to be seen as absences of concern, care and response. The disappointment she may experience in her relationships stems from her expectations that the other with whom she engages is as prepared to see these omissions as well as seeing her plentitude.

It is this difference in expectations that grounds the conflictual structure of interpersonal relationships, a difference which places men and women in dominant and submissive positions with respect to the larger social and historical context which forms the background for such engagements. The failure of interpersonal relationships, on Beauvoir's view, need not be understood as structurally endemic to our being for others, as Sartre seems to suggest. Rather than immersing subjects in a circular movement between the equally untenable poles of sadism and masochism, each of which necessitates the move to the opposing pole, social relationships operate in a context which already situates subjects differently by gender with respect to these positions. It is therefore not the fluid exchange of positions that compromises genuine contacts between people, on Beauvoir's view, but a social organization of sexual difference which institutionalizes and ossifies this difference as an asymmetrical opposition of supremacy and inferiority. In a patriarchal context which privileges men at women's expense, interpersonal relationships (particularly of the heterosexist variety) will always be characterized by rupture, refusal, conflict and disappointment. But in Beauvoir's analysis, as distinct from Sartre's, such conflicts are amenable to human freedom and transcendence. Rather than containing our freedom in a discourse of alienation and exile, being-for-others calls to human freedom as the agency of transformation, such that genuine human contact will be possible but only through the concerted efforts we make with others to transform the conditions which bring them about.

Beauvoir's conception of freedom which emerges from the discussion of female development qualifies as gynocentric or female-identified in a descriptive rather than normative sense. I think it is a confusion between these two senses which has led many to read and dismiss Beauvoir as male-identified and implicitly misogynist.[4] This I believe is a serious misreading, which discounts the substantial contributions Beauvoir has made to the now thriving discourse of feminism and femininity. Beauvoir, when writing of women, is describing the situation of women in patriarchy, which is that of being the second sex, where femininity is a situation constituted by a patriarchal system of representation to devalue and contain it. But the naming of the moment of devaluation is also a naming of the site of opposition to that devaluation which also offers the promise of a transvaluation of value. While Beauvoir does not yet occupy the position of the valorized feminine, operative in the discourse of contemporary feminism, her writing of the oppressed feminine makes the emergence of such a position possible. By naming the freedom that emerges from the feminine situation Beauvoir articulates the very sense of freedom capable of accomplishing this movement of liberating transcendence. In this sense, Beauvoir is identified with femininity as situation, and not with the pseudo-Sartrean conflict of pure structural opposition.

The discourse which Beauvoir seems more explicitly to address in her theoretical texts, however, is that of traditional philosophy with its set of problems and issues, which is why I think it is important to read her work in that context as well. In this light, Beauvoir's developmental account of freedom can best be appreciated as providing the foundations for an ethics and politics not possible on Sartre's account, because freedom is taken to exist separate and apart from its social, historical and material origins. By articulating a freedom which arises in response to a progressively emergent body in situation, Beauvoir gives freedom what it had lacked in the traditional existentialist account, which is to say that Beauvoir gives freedom a foundation, a context, a history, and something to do. A freedom which nihilates its own past as Sartre's does, will be a freedom with only an impoverished or imaginary sense of future. A freedom that finds in connections with others only its own bad faith and flight from itself will be incapable of engaging with others to produce a situation which better facilitates its exercise. Besides, it is just this kind of faith which Sartre calls bad faith which is necessary for ethical and political change.

Beauvoir's retrieval of freedom as a developmental aspect of human existence marks a path for its engagement in a socio-historical world amenable to its efficacy while avoiding the Sartrean *cul de sac* of bad faith. Because freedom for Beauvoir is positioned on the side of the plentitude of being both imply bonds with others. Freedom, on this view, finds in others not only obstacles, but also its sites of realization and recognition. Far from perpetuating the masculinist romanticism of the isolated individual, the higher particular, Beauvoir's free ethical agent recognizes the absurdity of a freedom which is inefficacious because it is in perennial flight from others when it is not seeking to dominate them. The freedom of the ethical agent, in Beauvoir's discourse, is not exercised primarily in the interests of judgment as prescribed by a morality of rights. The ethical agent is not so much free from as free for responsiveness and care in the face of the recognition of the freedom of others.

> . . . no existence can be validly fulfilled if it is limited to itself. It appeals to the existence of others. (p. 67)

> I concern others and others concern me. There we have an irreducible truth. The me-other relationship is as indissoluble as the subject–object relation. (p. 72)

The ethical moment Beauvoir marks in *Ethics of Ambiguity* is the moment where each subject is free to recognize the responsibility that exists toward others in non-codified form. With respect to the Sartrean discourse, which also names a moment of responsibility, Beauvoir's sense of that term takes on a radically different signification. For Sartre, responsibility involves the absurd recognition of accountability for the fate of others. Its refractions end up ultimately with the subject himself, who is thrown back on his own groundlessness and powerless with respect to the freedom of others. Because Sartre construes the scope of responsibility so widely and at the same time so abstractly, it is ultimately inefficacious as a guide for action or choice of commitments. Beauvoir's concept of responsibility, which already has as its locus the needs and concerns of others, functions by contrast as a force of positivity acting in opposition to failures of concern and indifference.

> Contrary to the formal strictness of Kantianism, for whom the more abstract the act the more virtuous it is, generosity seems to us to be better grounded therefore more valid the less distinction there is between the other and ourself and the more we fulfill ourself in taking the other as end. This is what happens if I am engaged in relation to others. (p. 144)

What becomes clear in this passage is the origins of Beauvoir's ethic of concern in the feminine situation where caretaking and taking responsibility for caring is uniquely privileged. The sense of what happens when engaged with others is a reference to the distinctly female role in patriarchy. But in the context of Beauvoir's discourse, where freedom is marked by difference, female facticity is transcended without nihilation, transformed from an imposed destiny and mode of containment into an ethical appeal to the freedom and recognition of others. In this sense, female existence has itself become a normative foundation which is to say it has become ethical because, to use Beauvoir's words, ethics is this very "triumph of freedom over facticity" (p. 44).

The significance of Beauvoir's work, marked as it is by difference, can now be appreciated as a calling to awareness of the limits and one-sidedness of the ethical problematic as it has been traditionally configured. Given a conception of freedom the integrity of which consists in its autonomy and self-sufficiency, the dilemma of freedom becomes centered on the moments in which freedoms conflict and threaten one another with annihilation or debasement. It is the privileging of conflict which engenders the judicial model of morality as an effort to garner the complicity of freedoms necessary for resolution in the form of minimization of differences. It is also clear, given their privileging of differences, why existentialists like Sartre (but also Nietzsche, Kirkegaard and Heidegger) would resist this mode of resolution. It also helps explain why existentialism was loath to construct an ethics conceived as a general set of prescriptions for social behavior.

Beauvoir's work offers an alternative way of configuring the ethical dilemma, in part because her discourse emerges from the standpoint of other where integrity is a function of interpersonal recognition and the preservation of relationships through conflict. Choice is demanded in situations which thrust upon the individual the necessity to act in light of needs of others as opposed to the abstract imperatives of autonomy which privilege the individual relative to the circumstances that call for action. Beauvoir's ethics of ambiguity constitutes a challenge to the assumption upon which the masculinist model rests, i.e., that human situations can be codified sufficiently so as to be amenable to a system of juristic prescriptions conceived independently of them. The foundation of her challenge rests with her having enfranchised freedom as a developmental potency with the power not only to transcend its situation so as to judge it, but also, and perhaps more importantly, to create and change the very social and interpersonal situations which call for its exercise. Because freedom is efficacious in the face of the world, one cannot absent oneself from complicity with the circumstance one presumes to judge, nor can one construct a position from which the force of this attachment can be neutralized. From Beauvoir's point of view, it is not clear that such a position of neutrality would be desirable, since ethical activity is conceived as motivated by care and concern, rather than by obligation and obedience to law.

Because Beauvoir writes from the standpoint of the oppressed other, she is situated so as to recognize the limits of an ethics which assumes human freedom as a birthright which need only be protected from unjustified intrusion or debasement. For those whose freedom is denied social recognition and import, an attitude of responsibility expressed through indifference and distance is insufficient. It both presumes too much (the need to maintain the freedom which is already there for the subject), and not enough (because it fails to commit to creating the conditions for enfranchising that freedom.

As a consequence of her developmental model of freedom tied to material conditions, Beauvoir recommends an ethic of commitment geared toward a situation in which freedom ought be mobilized in concert with others for the purpose of creating the conditions for its further development by engaging others in the recognition and exercise of their freedom. The significance of this difference lies in the fact that freedom exists primarily as a progressive force, identified with rather than opposed to the concerns of those whose freedom is similarly directed. As opposed to an ethics of autonomy in which freedom wills the limits of its obligations to others, an ethics of ambiguity construes freedom as a will to action and commitment, where its presence to the recognition and judgment of others is endemic rather than antithetical to its integrity and power. Because she construes ethical activity as the exercise of freedom in affinity, Beauvoir can proffer a theory of value which gives freedom more than the paternal prerogative of judgment, moving freedom toward the maternal discourse of liberation aimed at freeing others toward their own possibilities through commitment and concerns for them.

Far from being male-identified, Beauvoir begins the process of writing "the different voice" both by marking the situation from which that voice speaks, and by naming its integrity as an activity of commitment and care. In Beauvoir's work, female existence, and the values emergent from it, no longer remain contained within a discourse of domination but are freed for the purpose of becoming ethical, and thus changing the world, and the lives of human subjects who must make their ways there. In Beauvoir's discourse female existence triumphs in its freedom over facticity, and in so doing, marks a new path and a new future. The world Beauvoir names is our own. Her promise and vision deserve a place in it as well.

Notes

1. For a broader discussion of the relationship between Beauvoir and Sartre which argues against reading Beauvoir as a "pseudo-Sartrean," see Margaret A. Simons (1981).

2. Beauvoir's discourse of "difference" is not yet the "*différence*" of deconstruction, although I believe Beauvoir's texts have served as an unacknowledged source of that discourse. The difference which grounds signification is founded upon a preconstituted sphere of social relations, most notably that of gender caste privilege. As such the ground of signification is ruptured so that the prospect of common meaning for terms like love is impossible. Love cannot mean the same thing to both sexes, because it is positioned differently in the life worlds of men and women. See *The Second Sex*, Chap. 23.

3. Gillligan's (1982) approach is a supplementary conjunction of sexual difference by which we arrive at "a more complex rendition of human experience" (p. 174). Mary Daly (1982) interprets sexual difference as a principle of radical separatism, and the possibility of gynocentric values.

4. Beauvoir's "descriptive" identification with femininity consists in the recognition of writing of woman as woman. But because the situation Beauvoir describes is that of the debased feminine, i.e., femininity as represented within the frame of male privilege, much of Beauvoir's writing repeats the alienation attached to that position, and the masculinist modes of representing it. Given the absence of an intertextual support system, it is not surprising that Beauvoir speaks from a position that can now read as isolationist, or as a discourse of the "queen bee." But to read this textual slippage as an indication of moral ambivalence is unfair and misleading: unfair because it reduces Beauvoir too narrowly to her circumstances; and misleading, given the history of the fate of *The Second Sex*. If that text were male-identified, men would have appropriated the text for their discourse. As Simons (1981) suggests, if *The Second Sex* were male-identified, men would identify with it.

Works Cited

Beauvoir, Simone de. 1948. *The Ethics of Ambiguity*. Translated by Bernard Frechtman. Citadel Press, New York.

Beauvoir, Simone de. 1952. *The Second Sex*. Translated by H. M. Parshley. Random House, New York.

Daly, Mary. 1978. *Gynecology: The Metaethics of Radical Feminism*. Beacon Press, Boston.

Gilligan, Carol. 1982. *In a Different Voice*. Harvard University Press, Boston.

Janeway, Elizabeth. 1981. *Powers of the Weak*. Morrow Quill, New York.

Sartre, Jean Paul. 1953. *Being and Nothingness*. Translated by Hazel Barnes. Washington Square Press, New York.

Simons, Margaret A. 1981. Beauvoir and Sartre: The question of influence. *Eros* 8(1): 25–42.

3

True Confessions: Cixous and Foucault on Sexuality and Power

Almost everything is yet to be written by women about feminity: about their sexuality, that is, its infinite and mobile complexity, about their eroticization, sudden turn-ons of a certain miniscule-immense area of their bodies; not about destiny, but about the adventure of such and such a drive, about trips, crossings, trudges, abrupt and gradual awakening, discoveries of a zone, at once timorous and soon to be forthright. A woman's body, with its thousand and one thresholds of ardor—once by smashing yokes and censors, she lets it articulate the profusion of meanings that run through in every direction—will make the old single-grooved mother tongue reverberate with more than one language.

—Hélène Cixous[1]

It may well be that we talk about sex more than anything else; we set our minds to the task; we convince ourselves that we have never said enough on the subject, that, through inertia or submissiveness, we conceal from ourselves the blinding evidence, and that what is essential always eludes us—so that we must start out again in search of it. It is possible that where sex is concerned, the most long-winded, the most impatient of societies is our own.

—Michel Foucault[2]

These excerpts from the work of Hélène Cixous and Michel Foucault mark a site of difference in contemporary sexual politics. The question is whether the discursive representation of woman's sexuality is, as Cixous asserts, still a vital liberatory practice or whether, as Foucault implies, such discourse is compatible with and contributory to the proliferation of operative hegemonies. One of the ironies of our age, according to Foucault, is our investment in the production of sexual discourse in the belief that "our 'liberation' is in the balance."[3] If liberation is not at stake in proliferating sexual discourse, what is?

These questions become all the more pressing in light of the contemporary AIDS epidemic which dramatically alters the stakes attached to sexual proliferation and circulation. When one of the possible consequences of sexuality is contracting a fatal, debilitating disease, we are all forced to question our investments in sexuality, to ask not only whether we can be liberated through and for sex, but also whether sex is worth dying for. Foucault notes, with an ironic and

The Thinking Muse: Feminism and Modern French Philosophy, Jeffner Allen and Iris Marion Young, eds. (Bloomington and Indianapolis: Indiana University Press, 1989). Reprinted with permission.

eerie prescience, that the dominant sexual politic of our age predisposes us to answer in the affirmative.

Foucault is not the only voice to raise questions about the state of contemporary sexual discourse. American feminists have raised questions about the ideological surplus produced by a representational apparatus which identifies women as the emblem of sex and uses that identification to market commodities and marginalize women. Debates continue in the public sphere around issues of access to sexual material including pornography, paraphernalia and information about contraception, abortion, and sexually transmitted diseases. The anxiety emerging from epidemic conditions, not only with respect to sexually transmitted diseases but also with respect to phenomena like the rising rate of teenage pregnancy and divorce, has also provided occasion for a revisionist critique of sexual discourse, and a revivification of a traditional rhetoric of repression.

Given Foucault's insight into the self-perpetuating character of sexual discourse, the question cannot be resolved within a logic of prohibition and permission. If Cixous is right about the absence of a sexual discourse adequate to women's libidinal economy, feminists and others critical of existing sexual arrangements will need to investigate the conditions responsible for producing this absence. As a culture we may be talking extensively about sex, but given the limits of our representational repertoire, we feminists may still need to find new ways to speak about sex. For as Cixous would argue, the contemporary state of affairs provides ample evidence that it is not yet being done right. Give Foucault's insights into the potentially fatal consequences of our contemporary sexual logic, the need to generate new sexual scripts and stories becomes all the more urgent.

Here I intend to read some of Foucault's and Cixous's texts as strategic responses to the problem of sexual discourse in the age of epidemic. In doing so, and this is my first confession, I subject them to my own purposes. Even though these texts do not address one another directly, both writers situate their work in what may fairly be described as a common turf. Both address the relationship between sex and power and the constitutive effects of discourse on these dynamics. Although neither can or should be read as pamphleteers or advocates in the conventional sense, both writers do engage in prescriptive rhetoric which attempts to address historical specificities from a position of resistance or opposition to the operative sexual hegemony. Both would agree on the need to reconstitute the terms and language of sexual interaction. Though their positions do not oppose one another, the differences point to the limits of their respective analyses. Foucault's reconsideration of the way sexual discourse functions to circulate and intensify the effects of sexual hegemony, raises questions with respect to Cixous's optimism about the transformative effects of women's writing of the body. But more significantly, from the standpoint of feminist concerns, Cixous's emphasis on the role of the asymmetrical configuration of sexual difference in maintaining male hegemony over the construction of sexuality and sexual desire, points to a blind spot in Foucault's analysis of how the sex-power system operates. Foucault's failure to consider male dominance as one of the effects produced by the circulation of sexual discourse results in a series of strategic recommendations that circumvent the issues of greatest concern to feminists. Feminists, therefore, ought to reconsider the merits of Foucault's prescriptions lest our efforts only end up contributing to the maintenance of a system that has historically circumscribed our powers and possibilities. While much of what Foucault writes is useful for developing liberatory strategies for addressing the political paradoxes that accompany the hegemony of sexual epidemic, we must also avoid identifying ourselves with what, in some sense, is yet another paternal discourse of instruction which claims preemptive entitlement to speak to and for women in their absence.

Sexual Discourse and Its Discontents

Part of the difference in strategic emphasis can be attributed to the different ways in which Foucault and Cixous conceptualize the operations of the sex-power apparatus and its consequences. While both understand sexuality to be correlated with political formations, they differ in their assessments of how power has worked to produce sexuality and about the consequences of these historically specific constructions. As a result, their analyses operate with different strategic priorities that are worth considering for their differences.

Cixous's advocacy of women's writing proceeds from her analysis of the construction of sexuality in patriarchy as an asymmetrical opposition between "masculine" and "feminine" which functions as a mechanism for maintaining male privilege. Male dominance is maintained by a phallocentric organization, founded on a masculine economy which distributes pleasure and entitlement differentially according to gender in a way that disadvantages women, and which inscribes bodies of both genders with a logic of male dominance. This differential economy affects not only sexual practices but also sexual discourse which, Cixous argues, is organized by a structuring absence, an absence of a discourse of "feminine jouissance."[4] This absence serves and extends the logic of phallocentric sexuality. Women who do not know or are incapable of representing what they want are that much less likely to demand or pursue it. The absence of a female-identified discourse adequate to representing women's sexuality in its difference is both a symptom of and instrumental to the continued subjugation of women within the patriarchal order.

In patriarchy, male privilege is both marked and exercised, at least in part, by control over the production, circulation, and representation of pleasure. Such control is operative both at the level of the erotic choreography which structures heterosexual encounters, and at the level of cultural representations, which are designed to accommodate and normalize masculine preferences and patterns of gratification. Because pleasure is one currency in which differences are marked in a phallocentric economy, women's pleasures, insofar as they differ from men's, are relegated to a marginal position as that which cannot or may not be represented or circulated, and thereby enfranchised. Phallocentric hegemony is thereby maintained by an absence of cultural forms which allow women to represent ourselves to ourselves and others as agents, rather than as mere objects of desire.

The absence of discursive forms capable of representing women's pleasures in their differences has obvious benefits for a patriarchal social order. Since differences in erotic economies and desires are primary markers of sexual difference, failure to represent women's desire amounts to an annihilation of difference. In the absence of a female-identified voice, or for that matter the recognition by women of this absence and the conditions that produce and normalize it, self-interested male dominated discourse is free to construct women's desires in their absence, and to construct us in ways which both mark our subjugation and reproduce it, by investing us with forms of desire that facilitate their domination, like the pleasures of surrender, self-sacrifice, and service to others. More useful still to existing social arrangements are women who do not know what they want, since we will thereby be incapable of demanding it or acting to secure it. As long as men are the only ones providing answers to the question of what women want, the answers offered will continue to reflect and solidify male interests and male privilege. Because the silencing of women has been a tactic used to keep women in their place, Cixous believes that women's breaking silence by writing can work to disrupt and subvert the existing order.

> (W)riting has been run by a libidinal and cultural—hence political, typically masculine—economy, that this is a locus where the repression of women has been perpetuated, over and over more or less consciously, and in a manner that's frightening since it's often hidden or adorned with the mystifying charms of fiction; that this locus has grossly exaggerated all the signs of sexual opposition (and not sexual difference), where woman has never *her* turn to speak—this being all the more serious and unpardonable in that writing is precisely *the very possibility of change*.[5]

In this passage, Cixous shows what is at stake for women in writing their bodies. Given the relatively monolithic history of masculine hegemony over the sexual, despite variations in the apparatus which secure it, woman's sexuality has been represented either as lack, or as a series of self-interested masculine projections. This has allowed men to construct women in their absence, constructing and re-constructing sexual difference in a way that perpetuates men's position of dominance. By resisting this repressive dynamic through writing, women's discourse can disrupt or subvert a sexual order that has historically depended on our silence.

When as women we articulate what we want and what gives us pleasure, such writing carries with it the force both of a demand that these desires be fulfilled, and a self-validating statement of entitlement to gratification and satisfaction. Insofar as such demands are formulated in heterosexual terms, men can now be held accountable for refusing to cooperate, since they can no longer appeal to the traditional excuse that they do not know what it is that women want from them. To the extent that women's desires are addressed to other women, men are displaced from their position of centrality, and heterosexist hegemony, and all that follows from it, is subjected to challenge, critique, and ultimately denial. But beyond the effects such discourse will have in forcing a reconsideration of male-dominated assumptions about sexuality and desire, such discourse is also empowering to women, both because it legitimates our needs by making them public, and because expression allows for a contagious expansion of women's sphere of entitlement. Rather than having to settle for the options available through phallocentric discourse, women are also authorized to construct, elaborate, and celebrate differences, as well as having the occasion to have our desires recognized and validated by other women who read the work, and are prompted to contribute to an intertextual fabric by producing texts which support and proliferate a female-identified system of pleasure and desire.

In contrast to Cixous's analysis which stresses the stability and centrality of sexual difference as a constitutive principle, Foucault's analysis emphasizes the flexibility and diversity of power deployments with respect to constructing sexuality as a site for intervention into the lives of bodies and populations. Because power deployments always aim to organize social energies in the name of some contextually specific goal or utility, power is neither unitary nor uniform in its character or in its operations. It is certainly not limited to a dynamic of repression.

Foucault engages in an extended questioning of "the repressive hypothesis" which, he says, has been the dominant way of conceptualizing the relationship between sex and power. The repressive hypothesis assumes a negative relationship between sex and power, deployed as a dynamic of repression, control, and the demand for the conformity of sex to law. Foucault challenges this "juridical model" of power, which represents power as a figure of absolute authority. The figure of power is the figure of the King. What this repressive model of power with its emphasis on negative operations fails to capture, according to Foucault, is the proliferative dimension of power, which operates through a network of variable and context-specific social relations, each of which results in the creation of local authorities and points of resistance to them. Since "power is everywhere,"[6] there is no possibility of getting outside of power or of occupying a position untainted by its operations. There is also no discourse which cannot be contained by existing political deployments.

> (W)e must not imagine a world of discourse divided between accepted discourse and excluded discourse, or between the dominant discourse and the dominated one—but as a multiplicity of discursive elements

that can come into play in various strategies. . . . Discourses are not once and for all subservient to power or raised up against it any more than silences are.[7]

Because power does not operate on the basis of some uniform repressive apparatus, one can no longer speak of some "liberatory discourse" opposed, through its productivity, to the negative operations of power. One can also no longer assume that by rallying energies in the name of "sex," one occupies a position from which the deployment of power can be resisted. Consequently, the assumption that sexual discourse will function as a liberatory movement which counters the repressive function of power becomes problematic. Sexuality is not so much opposed to power as it is a product of a power deployment. "We must not think that by saying yes to sex, one says no to power; on the contrary, one tracks along the course laid out by the general deployment of sexuality."[8]

Foucault's reservations about the liberating potential of sexual discourse stem from his analysis of sexuality as a political construction, rather than as some natural or instinctual zone that can be isolated independently of the mechanisms by which it is aroused and regulated. Power in the modern era has functioned to circulate the demand for sexual discourse in the form of confessions which position subjects as sites for disclosure of truth and knowledge of sex. Foucault traces the proliferation of confessional discourse from its origins in a religious context to its further manifestations in medical, literary, and psychoanalytic discourse, each of which contributed specific mechanisms for facilitating the transformation of sex into discourse. The discursive structure of the confessional apparatus is revealing of how modern power deployments achieve their effects. First, the proliferation of confessional discourse results in a proliferation of local authorities who are empowered to hear, analyze, and judge the discourses of others and to act, therapeutically, punitively, managerially, on the basis of the discourse produced. It also produces specific subjects for these discourses, individuals whose bodies become subject to the rulings produced by these disciplinary discourses. As a consequence, power produces multiple points of access to the body, access gained through the discursive participation of its potential targets. Participation is not usually elicited through force, but through the production of context specific pleasures, pleasures attached to the production of sex as disclosive discourse. We have become a "singularly confessing society," according to Foucault, because our erotic economies have been inscribed by the politics of the confession. We take pleasure in reproducing ourselves as sexual subjects, and in sustaining the demand for the production of sexual discourse. As a consequence of its alliance with and construction of the sexual as that which must be represented and repeated, modern power works primarily through an apparatus of incitement rather than through the threat of repression. "Pleasure and power do not cancel or turn back against one another; they seek out, overlap, and reinforce one another. They are linked together by complex mechanisms of excitation and incitement."[9]

The privileging of sex as a theme of confessional discourse is therefore not a consequence of some instinctual impetus, but must rather be understood as the result of its strategic utility. Because sexuality serves as a link between individuals and the social body, power gained access to the body by being "organized around the management of life rather than the menace of death." In a post-scarcity economy, power intervenes in the lives of socially individuated and differentiated bodies not through an economy of deprivation but by organizing energies through the force of what it produces. As a society becomes more modern, i.e., more complex and functionally differentiated, the need for coordinating the activities of bodies becomes more necessary and harder to achieve. Thus sexuality, far from being censored, must be relentlessly circulated and reproduced. Sex is fundamentally allied with, rather than opposed by, modern methods of deploying power. Foucault challenges the idea of a struggle for sexual liberation through the production of sexual discourse, because he believes that the demand for such production is entirely compatible with the logic of hegemonic formations. If power does not operate primarily as repression, liberation of sex can no longer be conceived of as the disclosure of sex through discourse.

The connection between liberation and sexual disclosure is based on the assumption that sexuality has been concealed, a position Foucault refers to as "the repressive hypothesis." This hypothesis, which has dominated discussions of sexuality, needs to be challenged because it misrepresents the relationship between sex and discourse, and because it results in a series of erroneous expectations about the possibilities of liberation through the disclosure of sex. The repressive hypothesis assumes that power operates on sexuality in an essentially negative way, as a force which denies, conceals, or otherwise suppresses or limits sexual energies and expressions of sexual interest. According to Foucault, this hypothesis overlooks the ways in which power, far from working to restrict or limit the effects of a sexuality that exists separate and apart from it, actually serves to produce and intensify sexuality as a way of focusing and mobilizing bodies and populations. The function of power is not to limit or repress sexuality, but is rather to produce and proliferate sexuality and the demand for its disclosure through discourse.

By displacing the repressive hypothesis with a proliferative model of power, Foucault effects a *gestalt* shift which alters the way we think about power and the tactical and strategic options available for resisting it. Foucault is concerned that our concepts of power absolutize its operations, investing authority with force produced by the subjects constituted and ordered by it. Our concepts have not kept pace with historical transformations in the way power is deployed. The symbols and mechanisms of power have changed, but our concepts and language for representing it have not. Although we have abandoned the institutions and practices of monarchy, our understanding of power is still lodged in that anachronistic form. "In political thought and analysis we have not yet cut off the head of the king."[10]

Much of what Foucault writes about sex and power can be read as a challenge to the basis upon which a feminist like Cixous identifies the political problems and the strategies for addressing them. Most specifically, Foucault challenges the claims for the historical stability of sexual difference as the fundamental structure linking patriarchal deployments which differ in tactics, but not in their intent. If deployments of power are always local, variable, and unstable, as Foucault argues, we can no longer conduct political analysis in terms of an oppositional logic between classes, genders, and included and excluded groups. Following Foucault, strategic analysis must remain local and resist reifying the terms of its own discourse by investing them with a discursive stability. Foucault instead recommends that we attend to the historically specific mechanisms through which power is capable of transforming its operations so as to appear capable of satisfying the needs of the subjects it generates.

> We must not look for who has the power in the order of sexuality (men, adults, parents, doctors) and who is deprived of it (women, adolescents, children, patients); nor who has the right to know and who is forced to remain ignorant. We must seek rather the pattern of the modifications which the relationships of force imply by the very nature of their process. . . . Relations of power-knowledge are not static forms of distribution, they are "matrices of transformations."[11]

This strategic recommendation has potentially serious consequences for the course assumed by feminist theory. Following this line of reasoning, it becomes problematic to talk, as Cixous does, of "feminine writing" as such or to advocate its proliferation on the basis of its having been repressed or excluded. Cixous's claim that feminine writing would function counter-hegemonically is also questionable from the point of view of Foucault, because feminine writing would be as subject to conditions of overdetermination and hence differentiation as is masculine writing. If the repressive hypothesis is displaced, feminist discourse can no longer mobilize women's energies in the name of retrieving a sexuality that was never ours to begin with.

If Cixous is right about the centrality of sexual difference, however, then Foucault's position can be read less as a contestation than as a prolongation of a patriarchal logic which constructs sexual difference and then selectively ignores it in a way that allows men to take control over the meanings attached to each of the poles of the sexual difference system. Considered within Cixous's context, Foucault can be regarded as extending "the chain of fathers" which has historically deployed sexual difference tactically, attenuating or intensifying differences as circumstances demanded. Because Cixous writes from a position explicitly identified with the feminine, she is more sensitive to the repressive dynamics of power, and better positioned to recognize that the elasticity of power has operated to advantage the masculine position which retains control over how and when the feminine is spoken. Cixous might very well argue that Foucault finds himself in a position where he can afford to displace the repressive dimension of sexual difference in a way that those identified as women cannot. In a phallocentric economy which has persisted by using sexual difference to deny or displace the feminine, women cannot afford to ignore the structures that have produced the feminine position, or the conditions that mandate writing. Rather than effacing the conditions of their own productions, Cixous urges women to seize them as the conditions and motive for writing, precisely because they are not essential but political, and hence subject to reconstitution.

> If woman has always functioned "within" the discourse of man, a signifier that always referred back to its opposite signifier which annihilates its specific energy and diminishes or stifles its very different sound, it is time for her to dislocate this "within," to explode it and turn it around and seize it and make it hers.[12]

From the language of this passage, it is clear that when Cixous speaks in terms of "man" and "woman," "masculine" and "feminine," she is referring to signs situated in a symbolic system of sexual difference which are opposed not on the basis of biology or for some other essential reason, but for purposes of maintaining male dominance. Because there are no essential invariable features in which to ground this difference, "man works very actively to produce 'his woman.' "[13] Woman must be continually reinvented both for reasons of maximum deployment capability, and because these projective fictions cannot be sustained without the continuing demand for their actualization.

Because sexual difference is a product of a political deployment, woman's silence must be regarded as a tactical construction, and not as some case of collective congenital aphasia. Because women's silence has been produced politically, it can also be contested, most forcefully by women's refusal of that position in writing. Writing is a particularly forceful gesture because it is public and because it has the potential to incite and provoke more writing. Unlike speaking, which is restricted in its effects to the situation that occasions it, writing allows for a wider sphere of circulation, and thus offers the potential for a far broader, and more enduring sphere of influence. In addition, writing is a cultural practice already invested with a certain authority, the authority to elicit a readership and hence establish and mobilize a community. For women whose field of expression has largely been restricted to the private domestic sphere, writing offers a way to take up a position in the public sphere of social constructions, as well as to reappropriate what has largely been a male-dominated space. Such writing also works to subvert the language which has stabilized sexual difference as an

asymmetrical opposition, by giving voice to the feminine pole, which has historically been relegated to silence.

Cixous is decidedly non-utopian in her recognition of the obstacles women
will have to confront in engaging the representational apparatus. The first is a
condition of self-censorship, which allows power to efface its operations by
enlisting women as self-stifling agents. Closely allied to this is a system of
language and thought inadequate to the representation of a woman's economy,
i.e., the system which produces, circulates, and reproduces the currency of
women's desires and the modes by which they are satisfied.

> This opposition to woman cuts endlessly across all the oppositions that
> order culture. It's the classic opposition, dualist and hierarchical man/
> woman automatically means great/small, superior/inferior . . . means
> high or low, means nature/history, means transformation/inertia. In
> fact, every theory of culture, every theory of society, the whole con-
> glomeration of symbolic systems—everything, that is, that's spoken,
> that's organized as discourse, art, religion, the family, language, every-
> thing that acts upon us—it is all ordered around hierarchical oppositions
> that come back to the man/woman opposition, an opposition that can
> only be sustained by means of a difference posed by cultural discourse
> as "natural," the difference between activity and passivity.[14]

Because language and discursive practices are structured by a hierarchical
arrangement of sexual difference, women writers will be faced with contradictions
when trying to articulate their power in the language that has thus far produced
a repertoire of self-interested masculine constructions of femininity. That is why
women cannot resort to the utopian move of writing as though women have
always written, denying the very denials that have historically defined their
position. As a strategy, Cixous recommends that women writers engage these
male constructions with the intent of reappropriating and ultimately subverting
that history. "In telling it, in developing it, even in plotting it, I seek to undo it,
to overturn it, to reveal it, to expose it."[15]

Much of Cixous's work is devoted to examining the proliferation and circulation of feminine types. She analyzes classic narratives and symbols of femininity
which have constructed women variously as Sleeping Beauty, Little Red Riding
Hood, sphinx, vamp, and hysteric, and traces their circulation through the discourses of literature, philosophy, and psychoanalysis. In many respects the tactics
operating in these re-readings are the opposite of what Foucault would recommend. Rather than focusing on their specificities, Cixous's analysis aims to show
that although its forms and fashions may change, male dominance of the processes
by which feminity is constructed and exchanged have not. The effect of this
sustained strategy is not what Foucault's analysis would lead us to expect, because
feminine writing is not simply a consequence of the existing power deployment,

but is precisely that which cannot be anticipated or realized within its operative logic.[16] Rather than further empowering these constructions, the effect of women's writing is to demystify these images, empowering women in relation to them. But such empowerment depends on our recognizing that we are differentially placed in a way that disadvantages us. Because feminine writing is differentially positioned it must also avail itself of different strategies and ought not subject itself to the conventions of legitimation that dominate phallocentric discourse and which have been responsible for stifling the articulation of the feminine in its difference.

Given that sexual difference is always a political determination, and not a biological one, feminine writing differs not by virtue of the gender of the author, but on the basis of the textual strategies it employs, strategies that reconstitute the relationship between reader and writer, this text and others. Because feminine texts differ in the ways that they construct and circulate authority, they also work to reconfigure the patriarchal power-knowledge alliance, calling attention to its operations by subverting them. The subversive power of feminine writing is thus not a function of its occupying an ahistorical position of opposition, but is rather a function of a strategic determination, i.e., a context-specific judgment about how the power that comes from our writing may be maximized in its impact and effect. Feminine writing is therefore always already political.

Comparative Textual Politics

Now I will return to the questions Foucault raises about sexual discourse and address them, as he would recommend, strategically. I will compare Cixous's and Foucault's respective textual strategies to indicate how they produce and circulate authority, who they empower and how. The crucial factor will be the differential treatment given to sexual difference as it affects writing. Analysis of this difference shows that Foucault's textual strategies often appear to be at odds with his stated purpose, recirculating the very forms of authority he aims to displace. Because he does not adequately thematize the effects of sexual difference as it operates in reading and writing, Foucault's analysis remains unhappily complicitous with the self-effacing dynamics of phallocentrism. Conversely, if the task is to decapitate the king, Cixous's strategies seem far more promising as a means of undetermining the self-concealing operations of power, because they articulate and authorize a power economy that does not enact domination. If as feminists we want to behead the king, we cannot forget, as Foucault sometimes seems to, that the king is also a man.

Faced with the prospect of defining a "feminist text" in a way that is not simply reducible to biological or sexual difference, Cixous focuses on two textual strategies that, to use Foucault's language, function as "matrices of transformation" which establish a different relationship between reader and text, this text and others. The first is a strategy she calls the "affirmation of difference."[17] This strategy, which parallels and complements the rereadings of feminine tropes, works to transform the meaning of the feminine, from a site of subjugation to a source of power. By playing with the dominant constructions of sexual differences in a way that problematizes contempt for the feminine, Cixous's texts produce a space and rhetoric for revaluing the feminine, while inciting women readers to do the same. Where women have been debased by their association with the body, Cixous valorizes that connection. Against a background which has exploited maternity and used it as a ground for radically circumscribing women's sphere, Cixous reinterprets pregnancy as a metaphor for women's boundless life-giving capacities. Although women's alienation from a phallocentric economy has been used to discredit their discursive practices, this alienation reemerges in Cixous's texts as an emblem of their strength and subversive potency.

This strategy is directed toward women readers whom Cixous addresses frequently in her texts, with the hope that "in writing from woman and toward woman . . . woman will affirm woman somewhere other than in silence."[18] This tactic has the effect of calling attention to the male readership assumed by most texts, while displacing its centrality. Such a transgression of usual textual etiquette induces a kind of reversal which allows women readers a moment of identification with a rarely held position of primacy. Although Cixous is aware that women cannot simply rewrite the history of subjugation, her invocation of women as readers is intended to incite us to write so as to continue the process by which we will come to recognize and exercise our powers. As a polemical moment of the discourse, the affirmation of difference begins with constructions of the hegemonic feminine in order to begin the process of exploding it from within. Although it is offered to women readers in a rhetoric which elicits recognition and identification, it is not a discourse that demands or seeks agreement or allegiance. Because she considers essentialism to be a male construct, Cixous recognizes that affirmation of difference applies to her chosen readership, i.e., women, as well. Affirming women somewhere other than in silence means affirming the voicing of differences, including differences with the discourse offered by the author for recognition.

Foucault, by contrast, presumes rather than produces a position of identification with the readership, addressing them with a rather unselfconscious use of the royal and sexually undifferentiated "we" as when he speaks of "we other Victorians."[19] Because Foucault does not examine the operations of sexual difference in reconstructing the Victorian sexual economy, his analysis leaves the reader with the impression that men and women occupied comparable positions within the Victorian family, i.e., both were comparably victimized and gratified by it, and both were comparably culpable for its perpetuation. At the very least Foucault leaves women readers with the sense that differences in gender roles are not relevant to understanding how this particular deployment of power operated. Foucault's discussion of Victorian hypocrisy also suffers from the failure to make such distinctions between the positions women and men occupied in the illicit sexualities, like rape, prostitution, and adultery, that were also produced by the Victorian organization of sex.

Foucault's rhetorical strategy parallels the analytic one, with the combined effect of displacing women readers, while claiming to speak for and to them. In so doing, Foucault assumes a traditional discursive prerogative of failing to address women directly, rhetorically, or substantively, while assuming a right to position them in a place comparable to that of a male reader. By failing to leave a place for a discourse of women's difference, the effect of Foucault's textual strategies is to reconstitute self-effacing masculinity as a unitary voice of authority. If part of Foucault's intention is to articulate a decentralized and proliferative model of power, his textual strategies work against this by consolidating authority in a form that denies difference and impedes access and authorization for women readers. This displacement is particularly problematic in the context of a genetic analysis of sexual power and is disappointing in a theorist as attuned to specificities as is Foucault. From the standpoint of his own project, if the point is to displace a repressive model of power with a proliferative one, a strategy which suppresses recognition of difference is not the most appropriate.

Foucault's textual strategies work to sustain a traditional economy associated with masculine texts which, to use Cixous's expression are "closed" by contrast with feminine texts which are "open."[20] The difference between open and closed texts is not primarily a difference of form or style. Certainly no text, masculine or feminine can be closed in the sense of being self-suturing, immune to polyvalence and intervention. The "open-closed" metaphor can best be understood as describing the text's relationship to authority, its readership, and other texts. Masculine texts are closed to the extent that their textual strategies limit access and intervention from readers and other texts by consolidating authority in the form of authorial privilege. They establish privilege at the expense, in part, of other texts which the masculine textual economy seeks to eliminate through mechanisms of subsumption, consumption, or conscription. Cixous attributes such strategies to the death wish that underlies phallocentrism.[21] As a consequence, discourse is organized on a model of combat which seeks to eliminate texts and positions by "herding contradictions into a single battlefield."[22] By marshalling evidence and accumulating knowledge that can be exchanged for authority, the masculine textual economy proceeds with a strategy of bibliocide geared toward eliminating other texts on the basis of their lack. In a death-ridden economy it is more important to know which texts to close than which to open.

Foucault is not above employing such combative tactics with respect to the other theories he addresses, most notably the repressive hypothesis which he seeks to replace. He is also not above appealing to a legalistic language of "rules" in articulating his meta-theory of power,[23] a strategy that is ironic in light of his critique of the juridical model. Foucault attempts to establish his authority with respect to these issues in fairly traditional ways, most notably on the basis of an accumulation of knowledge, in the form of readings of historical texts which are intended to certify the writer's expertise. The effect of this is to consolidate knowledge and hence authority in the voice of a unitary author who stands in a privileged relationship to the evidence presented, because Foucault is often reading documents to which he has relatively privileged access by comparison with his readers. His tactics reflect allegiance to and complicity with traditional codes of legitimation and authority.

Ironically, these tactics of condensation work against the direction mapped out by the language of proliferation. The relatively closed character of Foucault's text emerges more clearly in comparison with the way Cixous's texts work. To establish her differences from hegemonic forms of authority, Cixous dispenses with or conspicuously transgresses much of the textual etiquette and many of the conventions of academic discourse. Her texts are constructed eclectically, juxtaposing a discussion of Freud with a Chinese fable, the history of philosophy with fairy tales. By transgressing disciplinary and paradigmatic boundaries, Cixous positions her work within a different economy of legitimation. Dispensing with conventional footnotes and attributions, she constructs her authority as separate and apart from validation through the chain of fathers. This latter tactic also helps to minimize the distance between author and reader that is usually established on the basis of privileged access and expertise. When Cixous re-reads texts, she almost always chooses examples that are part of a general cultural repertoire with which her readers are likely to be familiar. Rather than attempting to establish her authority on the basis of superiority to her readers, Cixous seeks the identification and recognition of women readers as the source of an authority that is always mobile, moving in an open-ended circuitry between reader and text.

Cixous's texts resist closure through a strategy of multiplying voices and positions in ways which circumvent hegemonic exclusivities and oppositions, even as it invokes them. Rejecting a linear logic that culminates in some definitive position, Cixous's texts work against the reader's tendencies to stabilize meanings and consolidate textual power in the figure of a knowing author. This practice has two kinds of strategic value. On the one hand, this tactic results in texts that cannot be fully contained by a patriarchal logic because these movements confound its ossifications. Like a loop which ties up a computer in an endless but circular repetition of its own logic, Cixous texts move cyclically in a way that resists a phallocentric logic of closure. The other merit of this tactic is to transfer authority to women readers who are moved not to repeat a linear narrative of explanation, but rather to produce texts, and texts which are different.

With respect to the project of decapitation, the affirmation of difference and transvaluation of the feminine allows Cixous to operate from a relatively privileged position, since decapitation has traditionally been the fate of women in an economy dominated by masculine anxiety. "If man operates under the threat of castration, if masculinity is culturally ordered by the castration complex, it might be said that the backlash, the return of this castration anxiety is its displacement as decapitation, execution of woman as loss of her head."[24] Cixous's juxtaposition of these mutilatory practices is both ironic and ambiguous in its demonstration of the perverse oppositions produced from a hierarchical logic of sexual difference. The choices and contradictions generated by this opposition cannot be resolved or closed, nor, if these are the only choices, should they be.

Writing New Sexual Stories

To reopen the discourse of decapitation, Cixous retells "a little Chinese story" which provides a lesson in the strategies of decapitation. It is also a "perfect example of a particular relationship between two economies, a masculine economy and a feminine economy."[25] Because Cixous says "(e)very detail of this story counts," I include the entire tale.

> The king commanded General Sun Tse: "You who are a great strategist and claim to be able to train anybody in the arts of war . . . take my wives (all 180 of them!) and make soldiers out of them." We don't know why the king conceived this desire—it's the one thing we don't know . . . it remains pre-wish after all. So Sun Tse had the women arranged in two rows each headed by one of the two favorite wives, and then taught them the language of the drumbeat. It was very simple: two beats—right, three beats—left, four beats—turn or backward march. But instead of learning the code very quickly, the ladies started laughing, chattering and paying no attention to the lesson, and Sun Tse, the master, repeated the lesson several times over. But the more he spoke, the more the women fell about laughing, upon which Sun Tse put his code to the test. It is said in the code that should women fall about laughing, instead of becoming soldiers, their actions might be deemed mutinous and the code has ordained that cases of mutiny call for the death penalty. So the women were condemned to death. This bothered the king somewhat: a hundred and eighty wives are a lot to lose: He didn't want his wives put to death. But Sun Tse replied that since he was put in charge of making soldiers out of the women, he would carry out the order. Sun Tse was a man of absolute principle. And in any case there's an order even more "royal" than of the king himself: the Absolute Law. . . . One does not go back on an order. He therefore acted according to the code and with his saber, beheaded the women commanders. They were replaced and the exercise started again; and as if they had never done anything except practice the art of war, the women turned right, left and about in silence and with never a single mistake.

One could read this as a cautionary tale about the price women have to pay when we step out of line. Read this way, the connection between silence and survival for women is but a part of the fallout of a system whose absolute law is death. What remains unaccountable, however, is the desire which sets this system in motion and sustains it, because it is a king's desire after all. Remaining unaccountable, it offers no account of itself beyond demonstrating its proliferative capabilities on the women who will continue to swell the ranks. Remaining within this unrecountable logic, there is no way to valorize women's position. But Cixous offers the prospect of rewriting that story in ways where women are not forced to repeat old endings. It also makes it possible to tell stories about how to decapitate the king. Spurred by Cixous's invitation to produce new texts from reading hers, I offer the following as one possibility.

> The King wants an army and has enlisted the master of discipline Sun Tse to whip his wives into shape. Luckily the king has been prolific enough in dispensing his phallus to have collected sufficient female capital for such a project. But women being women, they do not respond as the disciplinary logic would dictate. They still walk like women and not like soldiers. They talk during drills, often so loudly that Sun Tse can barely make himself heard. Frustrated, he goes to the king seeking reinforcements. Rather than appear himself, the king sends Sun Tse back to the training ground armed with the royal sword and permission to use it. As Sun Tse enters, the women rapidly break rank, deploying themselves in different positions, surrounding and confounding him. Startled, his hands sweat, loosening his grip on the sword. He is disarmed. Swallowing up the master in the network of their bodies, the women fill the corridors of power with the echo of their footsteps as they approach the king's quarters carrying the sword above their heads. They each know the way. They have been this route before, at least once, but each one alone. The road feels different when it is walked with other women. Entering the king's chambers uninvited, they give back the king his henchman. The silence is broken by a woman at the back of the room, "What made you think to send a man to do a king's job?" whereupon the women begin to laugh. The laughter builds, vibrating with such force that it shatters the sword, splintering it into a thousand pieces at the sovereign's feet. In the face of such occurrences, the king, stunned, loses his voice, and begins to whimper like the child he has been. Having lost his sword, he has also lost his head.

What place do stories and laughter have in a sexual economy progressively dominated by the anxiety of epidemic? If as feminists we no longer ought to invest ourselves in the belief that liberating sex will set us free, especially in an erotic economy of diminishing returns, what can or should we expect from the process which transforms sex into discourse, and from a society committed to proliferating this talking sex? Are we condemned to continue to produce confessions even without the barest prospect of salvation through them?

Although their tactics and strategies differ, Foucault and Cixous have each devoted considerable effort to alerting us to the need to generate some new stories, stories that do not mourn an irretrievable sexuality but that begin the process of formulating feminist images and symbols, so as to be able to invest our power and energies in an eroticism no longer ruled by a royal triumvirate of death, domination, and desire. At the conclusion of the first volume of *The History of Sexuality,* Foucault offers the following provocative suggestion. "The rallying point for the counterattack against the deployment of sexuality ought not be sex-desire, but bodies and pleasures."[26]

Cixous, in another ironic twist on the tactics of castration urges women to take up the task of subverting the masculine economy through insistence on a different *jouissance.* "(D)ephallocentrize the body, relieve man of his phallus, return him to an erogenous field and a libido that isn't stupidly organized around that monument, but appears shifting, diffused, taking on all the others of oneself."[27] In one of her more visionary moments, Cixous imagines the outcome of such a process not as some new self-stabilizing script, but as an emerging narrative which would allow for "a transformation of each one's relationship to his or her body and to the other body. . . . Difference would be a bunch of new differences."[28]

Current circumstances are forcing all of us, albeit for different reasons, to reconsider our investments in sexuality and to confront the historically specific alignment between sex and death in our age. In this context, Cixous's claims about phallocentrism being deadly take on a whole new meaning. In the end, I think that Foucault and Cixous are both right. We do talk about sex more than anything else, and we still need to talk about it. If such talk is to be capable of transforming our relations to our bodies and our pleasures, such talk must work to incite as well as to represent those pleasures. That possibility will depend, as both Cixous and Foucault suggest, on developing a disclosure capable of instigating proliferative and imaginative powers, including the power of laughter, which, at least in my story, is sometimes powerful enough to cut off the head of the king.

Notes

1. Hélène Cixous, "The Laugh of the Medusa," trans. Keith Cohen and Paula Cohen, *Signs* 1, no. 4 (1976): 875–93.

2. Michel Foucault, *The History of Sexuality,* Volume I, An Introduction, trans. Robert Huxley (New York: Vintage Books, 1980), 33.

3. Ibid., 159.

4. For a discussion of the polyvalency of "*jouissance*" as it operates in Cixous's text, see Betsy Wing's discussion in her translation of Hélène Cixous and Catherine Clement, *The Newly Born Woman* (Minneapolis: University of Minnesota Press, 1986), 165.

5. Cixous, "The Laugh of the Medusa," 879. The context is a discussion of liberating "the New Woman."

6. Foucault, *The History of Sexuality,* Volume 1, 93.

7. Ibid., 100.

8. Ibid., 157.

9. Ibid., 48.

10. Ibid., 88.

11. Ibid., 99. The context for these remarks is Foucault's discussion of "the rule of continual variations" one of four "cautionary prescriptions" he offers for future analyses of sex and power.

12. Cixous, "The Laugh of the Medusa," 887.

13. Hélène Cixous, "Castration or Decapitation?" trans. Annette Kuhn, *Signs* 7 (1981): 46.

14. Ibid., 44.

15. Cixous and Clement, *The Newly Born Woman,* 6.

16. For Cixous, the consequence of this is that feminine texts are not predictable, because they are engaged in an emergence for which patriarchal logic has no room. See: "Castration or Decapitation?" 53.

17. Ibid., 52.

18. Cixous, "The Laugh of the Medusa," 881.

19. This is the title of part one of Foucault, *The History of Sexuality,* Volume 1.

20. For a fuller discussion of the difference, see Cixous, *The Newly Born Woman,* 83–100.

21. See Cixous, "Castration or Decapitation?" 48–50, and *The Newly Born Woman,* 70–78.

22. Cixous, "The Laugh of the Medusa," 882.

23. See Foucault, *The History of Sexuality,* Volume 1, part four.

24. Cixous, "Castration or Decapitation?" 43.

25. Ibid., 42.

26. Foucault, 157.

27. Cixous, "Castration or Decapitation?" 51.

28. Cixous, *The Newly Born Woman,* 83.

4

Defusing the Canon: Feminist Rereading and Textual Politics

One thing that feminist philosophers have in common with their colleagues is that they have read many of the same books. One thing that distinguishes them from their colleagues is that they do not read, or have not always read, them in the same way. The configuration of this identity in difference is significant for two reasons: it is not coincidental or accidental, and it is not reciprocal. This nonreciprocity is evidenced by the fact that most philosophers have not read and have not had to read those texts that are central to the feminist enterprise.

The nonaccidental aspect of this asymmetry can be explained, in part, by reference to the conventional nature of philosophical training and certification. Although philosophers often attempt to define the boundaries of their discipline by reference to common processes, aims, or questions that are designated as specifically "philosophical," in practice the unity or hegemony of philosophy is constituted intertextually, that is, by reference to a body of writing that collectively comprises what philosophers refer to as *the* history of philosophy. The semantic operation of the "the" in "the history of philosophy" suggests a singular, seamless history, which lends to the texts collected under this rubric a canonical status, a status which another authoritative text, the *Oxford English Dictionary,* defines as "of the nature of a canon or rule; or admitted authority, excellence, or supremacy; authoritative; orthodox, accepted; standard." The term "canon" is also therein defined as "a general rule, fundamental principle, aphorism, or axiom governing the systematic or scientific treatment of a subject" and as designating "any sacred set of books."

Those texts collected under the rubric of "the history of philosophy" come to assume a privileged position as those that set the standard for what is philosophi-

From *The Question of the Other: Essays in Contemporary Continental Philosophy,* Arleen B. Dallery and Charles E. Scott, eds. (Albany: SUNY Press, 1989). Reprinted with permission.

cal, and in terms of which philosophy defines itself to itself and to other disciplines. Therefore, to be certified as a philosopher, one must demonstrate one's mastery of the canon, and, by extension, of the synthetic chronology of issues and positions that emerges from it. Competence with respect to this history is in no way optional. It is rather presented as an epistemological imperative and as a moral obligation, as well as a condition for professional certification. From this canonical standpoint, however, feminist writing is given only optional status, as the sort of thing one can pursue in addition to and often only after one has demonstrated one's entitlement by a mastery of the canon. Conversely, and this is especially significant from the standpoint of feminists, those texts and only those texts that are granted canonical status in the discipline's self-definition are the work of white European or American men, a fact the referential rhetoric of "the history of philosophy" tends to conceal.

The rhetoric of "the history of philosophy" suggests a seamless chronology that effaces the mechanism of its construction, as well as the principles of inclusion, exclusion, and their justification in terms of an ultimately circular logic. It would seem that to determine what counts as part of the history of philosophy one would need to determine what philosophy was, yet philosophy is ultimately defined in terms of that which is acknowledged or presented as its history. Such language therefore tends to conceal the fact that there are or were potentially other candidates for membership. Describing the intertextual universe of philosophy in terms of a canon, by contrast, connotes a collection that has been formed and solidified legislatively and therefore which could, at least in principle, be otherwise.

Hence it should not be surprising that those most likely to speak of a philosophical "canon," rather than a seamless history, are those thinkers identified with the issues, texts, and discourses, like feminism, that have been excluded from that history and from the sphere of authority and privilege afforded it. To represent the unity of philosophy in canonical terms, as many feminists do, is already to adopt a critical posture toward the history of philosophy and the privilege it claims for itself as the master discourse with the power to legislate the conceptual foundations of other disciplines. It is also to bring to the foreground that which is probably the greatest source of philosophical anxiety—the recognition of philosophy's own contingency and hence its groundlessness. If philosophy lacks a necessary foundation, it is reduced to the status of just another idiolect or genre and hence loses its supremacy and legislative authority. The threat posed by feminism is substantial in that it calls into question the very nature of philosophy as such; as French theorist Jean-François Lyotard argues, for philosophy to affirm its contingency is "to turn away from the task of speculation and cease philosophizing."[1]

This helps to explain why feminism has largely been excluded from the history of philosophy, and why this exclusion is neither accidental nor coincidental. It also helps explain the argumentative strategies employed to justify this exclusion.

In her article subtitled "Sexism in the Philosophic Establishment,"[2] Shelia Ruth provides a summary of those arguments that operate by attempting to prove that feminism fails to satisfy the conditions necessary for "real" philosophy:

Feminism is a specialized pursuit, not part of the "mainstream" of philosophy.

Philosophy is universal in scope, dealing with all mankind (sic), but feminism applies to a segment of the population.

Feminist issues are trivial compared to the ultimate questions philosophers ought to address.

Feminist concerns are transient, bound to a particular time and place; philosophy transcends particular time and place.

Feminism is sociological, political, or anthropological; it asks no genuinely philosophic questions.

Feminists haven't yet learned to argue properly; they have not learned to give proper evidence for their claims; no general principles, just vignettes and metaphors.

Philosophy is neutral in its analysis. Feminism is a bias.

That such arguments have had their effect is evidenced by the longstanding exclusion of feminist texts from journals, conference programs, and university curricula.[3] *The Philosopher's Index* does not acknowledge feminism as a subject classification until 1973, and until 1980 less than ten articles per year are listed under that heading. Far more are listed under the more neutral heading "Woman," which gives some sense of the high-minded logic underlying philosophic classification. Since then some significant progress has been made. In 1986, for example, ninety-six articles are listed under "Feminism," and panels devoted to feminist theory appear more frequently on conference programs than they used to. But such progress is likely less a function of the abandonment of phallocentric bias by the philosophical establishment than of the concerted and sustained organized political activity of feminists, as well as of their continued commitment to produce work in this area, a substantial portion of which has been devoted to the rereading of the philosophical canon.

Given the way in which appeals to the canon have been used against feminism to marginalize or exclude it, it seems reasonable to ask why feminists have been motivated to reread the canon in the first place, especially since it would seem that any attempt to engage it, even critically, would involve contradictions and paradoxes of legitimacy, authority, entitlement, and desire. Why have we sought to return to the site of our own exile, and what do we hope to accomplish through that return? Can we hope to win or seduce legitimacy by engaging the mechanisms that have been used to exclude us, and if we can, what is that kind of legitimacy good for, especially if it is also something we seek to question and undermine? Can or should we hope to enjoy the pleasures and privileges of mastery, if that is precisely what we want to transform, not only, but at least in part, because it has been denied us? Can we hope to wear the emperor's clothes by revealing that he himself has none?

Any attempt to articulate the desires operationalized in feminist rereadings is subject to the dilemma and dynamics of overdetermination. There are so many reasons why feminists choose to engage the history of philosophy, many of them obvious, but such reasons ultimately fail to be either definitive or explanatory, at least in some deeper sense. But before we can address the strategic value of this practice, it is necessary to provide at least some skeletal account of the motivational logic underlying it, as a clue to the value it has had for its practitioners.

One reason why feminist philosophers reread the canon is precisely because we have already read it as part of our training as philosophers. Because acquaintance with the canon has been part of every feminist philosopher's initiation, it is not surprising that it will continue to function as a threshold and context for our activity, even as we progressively come to question its authority, and to situate our work more and more independently of it or in resistance to it. But this historical explanation leads only to further questions, namely, why were we motivated to read it in the first place?, and how, or from what position, were we able to read it, given that the discourse marginalized or excluded us as women in the first place? Since philosophical training is neither obligatory nor coerced, nor is it a usual pursuit for women, any woman who has read the canon has done so as a consequence of some deliberate choice or decision, a choice that often must be continually reaffirmed in the face of resistance or hostility from teachers, peers, and, sometimes, family.

To sustain the interest and discipline that philosophical training requires, especially in light of the minimum prospects for economic or social rewards, one must believe in the intrinsic value of the enterprise as such. One must, at least in some sense, be seduced by the promises of philosophy, even if one also hopes to use those to subvert or transform it. What is most seductive about philosophy, I think, is its appearance of being or promising to become a self-rectifying discourse, a discourse capable of recognizing its limits and lacunae and of reforming itself in light of these recognitions. It is not so hard to understand why this should appear so attractive to feminists, who recognize that there is much to be reformed and rectified in ourselves and in the world. Philosophy is seductive because it seems to offer a mechanism both for isolating what needs to be changed and for changing it; rather than resigning ourselves merely to desiring or imagining a transformed world, we can also gain access to the rational means for constructing another one.

To the extent that one has studied and continues to study philosophy, one is invested, to varying degrees, in its promissory and optimistic economy, especially with respect to the prospects of power and authority it offers. This is especially seductive to women, because such power is represented in what appear to be gender-neutral terms, terms in which women are not by definition disadvantaged, because such power is said to arise not from contingently gendered bodies, but from minds and from a logic that transcend incarnation and dependence on the arbitrary. Philosophy appeals to some women because it offers access to that which we are otherwise denied because we are women, namely, the possibilities of self-transcendence and empowerment. Since philosophy is a discipline that advocates truth and knowledge as the foundation of power, it provides to women the prospect of empowerment and emancipation through knowing.

Such appeal is amplified by virtue of its affinity with the process by which most feminists are made, namely, the process of consciousness raising, which presupposes a similar positive correlation between knowledge, power, and self-transcendence. Part of what is liberating about consciousness raising is the process by which one comes to understand one's situation and the reasons for it in ways that were previously unavailable. Consciousness raising and philosophy are two enterprises where it is still assumed that the truth can set you free. It is therefore not surprising that some women become attracted to a discipline that defines itself in terms of the pursuit of truth, nor that we will pursue it by reading those texts in which it is allegedly lodged or in process.

But despite this affinity between philosophical and feminist practice, insofar as one is a feminist, one also stands in a problematic relationship to the history of philosophy, precisely because it is the history of one's own subjugation, as well as to the discourse that has provided many of the grounds and justifications for that subjugation. It is also a discourse that marks women's difference in a way that is problematic existentially, conceptually, and professionally. In this sense, being a feminist necessarily entails a critical or ambivalent stance toward the promissory dimension of philosophy, since one is forced to recognize that philosophy also withholds that which it promises, namely, a truth that mitigates or overcomes the disadvantages accruing to women in patriarchy. Philosophy acquaints feminists with the logic of the fathers that has produced and kept us in our place, as well as with the mechanisms by which that operation and its consequences are perpetually effaced. To approach philosophy as a feminist is also to confront a place from which one has always already been exiled.

The recognition of this situation of exile also produces the desire to return, to take up or make up one's own place, a room of one's own. It is this desire that I believe lies at the motivational core of feminist rereadings. Given the quantity and quality of feminist rereadings that have already been produced, it seems clear that this desire must be taken seriously. But I think that feminist theory has also reached a degree of maturity that makes it a legitimate place from which to question the strategic value of continuing to pursue this practice. Such assessment is made in a context that is necessarily relative, that is, judged in light of competing values and priorities. Given the wealth of work to be done in areas of concern to feminists, the question I wish to pursue is whether continuing to reread the canon is the best way for feminists to direct their energies, or whether this practice has, in some sense, outlived its usefulness and thus should occupy only a relatively subsidiary place in feminist theoretical priorities.

In posing the question this way, I do not mean to devalue or dismiss the significance of the work that has already been done. For a number of reasons which will soon be made explicit, I believe that this practice has resulted in much very good work that has also had important political and theoretical consequences for professional philosophy as a whole and for feminist theory in particular. The trajectory of my question is rather aimed at a future that feminists will have a role in constructing. I will pursue this question by examining the different kinds of rereading practices currently in operation, and assessing the political implications of the interpretative strategies each employs. Without tipping my hand too much at this preliminary stage, I hope to raise questions about the dependence of feminist philosophy on the canon, and to indicate that such dependence may no longer be necessary, in part because of the successes feminism has already achieved.

The first point to be made is that feminist rereadings are no more monolithic in strategy or intent than is feminist theory in general. My discussion will focus on three different kinds of rereadings that differ in intent, interpretative logic, and conceptual consequences. Each has its practitioners and its critics. The first kind of rereadings are those that approach the history of philosophy in search of the "conceptual forefathers" of feminism. In this kind of reading, one returns to the history of philosophy in order to find or confirm the existence of earlier expressions of feminist sentiments or principles in philosophers whose work predates the rise of feminism as a social movement. One thus rereads Plato (who, incidentally, is the philosopher who has thus far been subjected to more feminist readings than any other) in order to recover his advocacy of education for women, or John Stuart Mill as an early advocate of equal rights for women, or Kant as a spokesman for equal treatment under law. Part of the intent of such readings is to show that some of what feminists are trying to do has already been done for us by the fathers themselves. We can be good daughters because we have had some good fathers. This kind of reading hopes to amplify the prospects for success in achieving feminist goals by finding the traces that already exist, making the path to liberation that much more navigable because it has already been marked for us. As a consequence of the success of these kinds of readings there is emerging a revisionist history of philosophy liberally populated with proto-feminists and feminist advocates.

It is not hard to understand the appeal of this strategy for its practitioners or, for that matter, for its audience. First, such readings help to restore faith in the rational benevolence and gender neutrality of philosophical discourse. Sexual difference therefore need no longer be seen as threatening to limit the scope, entitlement, or authority of philosophy to speak for all of us, because male philosophy can and in fact has spoken for women, and in many cases well in advance of explicitly feminist discourse. It also helps support an alternative mythos, namely, that, as David Krell says of Nietzsche, male philosophers can "write with the hand of a woman."[4] This allows for the emergence of the politically useful implication that there is therefore no particular need for women to speak for themselves, nor for philosophy to make explicit room for feminism as a separate discourse, because the fathers can and have already spoken for us, and perhaps better than we could speak for ourselves, since they are also the bearers of the argumentative acumen feminist theory is often said to lack. The strategic logic underlying such readings is to help to legitimate feminist sentiments by finding them articulated by voices that are already taken to be authoritative.

This strategy is understandable, particularly as a response to a time when the legitimacy of feminist scholarship was far more tenuous, and when intervention into a well-known tradition offered a way to introduce what would otherwise have likely been rejected as irrelevant issues. Before a profession is educated to a new language and a new literature, it is often necessary to speak in the terms that are already available, if one wishes to be understood. Because this crisis of legitimacy affected not only professional relationships but also had impact on feminists' own sense of entitlement, it is logical that feminists sought authorization for their concerns by writing within the frameworks which they had already been socialized to privilege. Returning to the canon as a forum for feminist expression was, and probably still is, one way for feminist theorists to assure themselves that they are still philosophers, and that philosophy can still be a viable enterprise. Discovering a sympathetic forefather is also one way to mitigate the contradictions that often arise between one's philosophical and feminist commitments. To the extent that such readings allow feminists to continue to work, they are valuable as survival strategies that ought not be easily dismissed.

But despite the value of these readings as self-authorizing practices, I am concerned about the misleading effects of the revisionist history that seems to be emerging from them, a history that I think misrepresents the development of phallocentric discourse and the development of feminism as a historically specific discourse of resistance. In this rewritten history, sexism, misogyny, and male privilege become phantasmic, untethered from historical roots. Masculine supremacy is a position held by no one, defended by no one. Plato is already a feminist, even though there were no women in the *agora* to hear and benefit by his insights. The discourses that have been used historically to justify women's subjugation emerge from nowhere because they belong to no one. Not only does this remove any possibility of accountability, but it also misleads us about the way philosophy has understood itself and the ways it has been appropriated by other authoritative discourses. If feminist readings end up erasing phallocentrism from the history of philosophy, we play into the hands of those who would encourage our uncritical complicity with it. With such acts of erasure, we have no way of understanding either the logic of male dominance or the possibilities of resisting it. We also help to undermine the significance of feminism as a historically specific discourse of women's resolve, by obscuring recognition of the social conditions that helped produce it and that will be necessary to sustain it. If feminism is severed from the historically specific activities and struggles of women and is treated as just another philosophical leitmotif, we lose access to the means of establishing the grounds for our entitlement in terms of our difference from the operative hegemony as well as diminish our will and power to resist it. A feminist theory envisioned even by its advocates as separable from the concrete political activities of courageous and committed women willing to pursue the unprecedented because it is unprecedented, is a feminist theory that has already lost its reason for being. It is a feminist theory that is already domesticated, capable of taking up residence in the structures the fathers have already built for us.

To the extent that we as feminists still rely on the *maître-penseurs* for ground and support, we are still dependent upon, and therefore contained by, a phallocentric economy of approval. By remaining dutiful daughters, we limit our vision as well as our strategic options for resistance. This tactic is also problematic because it conveys a mixed message to those colleagues still unwilling to grant legitimacy to the feminist enterprise. By remaining on turf they already claim as their own, we reaffirm their hegemony through our practices, while largely relieving them of the pressure to learn to speak our language and to read the writing that does not find inclusion within the canon as currently constituted. If we continue to accommodate the existing levels of professional ignorance and indifference by sublating our difference from it, we diminish our potential for changing the rules of the game, as well as for changing the lineup of players. If we don't assume and expand the sphere of our own legitimacy, no one else will, either.

A second kind of rereading (which at this stage may be the dominant one, at least in quantitative terms, in part because in some sense it is the hardest to resist) are critical/combative readings that operate with a strategy exactly opposed to the first kind of readings. Rather than searching for predecessors, this sort of reading aims to challenge what the history of philosophy has had to say about women on the grounds that such discourse amounts to a self-interested effort on the part of men to construct women in their absence, as well as to try to justify an indefensible logic of male privilege by embedding it in codes that lend to these prejudices the force of philosophic legitimacy and authority. This kind of reading has served and may continue to serve the crucial function of establishing a basis for feminist grievances as well as helping to clarify just what we are up against. The collective effect of the work produced from this kind of reading is to intensify or revalidate our sense of the necessity and urgency for sustained feminist theory and practice, even though the styles and forms of rationale offered for male supremacy may vary historically. It also has some value in the context of enlisting other women not yet engaged in feminist struggle, by demonstrating the ways in which the history of philosophy persistently fails in its claim to be gender neutral. These critical readings help to make problematic what for many remains a persistent hope, that things will be all right if one can just find the right adopted father. Taken collectively, the force of these critical rereadings is to minimize the possibility that there is some place within traditional philosophical discourse to dwell or to hide.

Beyond the value these readings have for the community, they also serve a very vital function for the reader herself which ought not be ignored. Such rereadings often provide a way to articulate and validate what were once intuitions—intuitions of alienation, displacement, the sense of not really being addressed by the texts we spent our time examining and attempting to understand as students and as teachers. What began for many of us as a nagging self-doubt about the limits of these texts with respect to our own experience, a doubt that more likely than not we initially turned on ourselves, in the form of fear of our limitations, now gains critical expression and becomes empowering, because doubt is now directed where it belongs, onto texts that either deliberately or uncritically reproduce the conditions of female absence as central to the structures of rationality as such. We can, as a consequence of engagement in this critical enterprise, come to understand better why, if rationality is predicated on women's absence, we so often thought or feared that we were crazy. We can also understand why our distress so often went unrecognized or misidentified.

But as crucial as such strategies may be in the course of a feminist's development, I do not think we ought to conceive of this strategy as a place to dwell or take root, conceptually or professionally. For one thing, such a strategy, too long pursued, tends to bog one down in the eternal return of the same—the same motifs, the same logic, the same absence. Continuing to reiterate narratives of exile does not really address the problem of where we as feminists can dwell. Continuing the discourse of absence cannot by itself produce a way to intervene and make a place for ourselves, nor can it help us to determine where we want to be. As long as one remains tied to a position of challenging the history of philosophy on more or less its own turf, we may get recognition for our grievances, but we also risk succumbing to the numbness that accrues from repetition, and thereby end up lending our energies to intensifying the force of the dominant hegemony, while diminishing our capacity to envision, demand, and produce significant alternatives. We may move from being grateful good daughters to the position of rebellious ones, but our identity and our logic still remain dependent on the discourse of the fathers.

The last and most recent strategy for rereading the canon is that which endeavors to read texts "against the grain."[5] Tactics employed in this kind of reading differ significantly from those discussed previously and are in some sense more radical, because they aim to intervene and subvert the textual mechanisms operative in phallocentric texts. Rather than addressing texts at the propositional level and extracting an explicit discourse of origins or of refusals, this kind of reading speaks against this thematic grain in order to reveal gaps and lacunae, which leave room for an interventionist activity of rewriting that introduces a feminist voice which the logic of the text is powerless to control. Philosophy is an especially important target for such tactics because, as one exemplary reader-against-the-grain Luce Irigaray puts it, "It is indeed philosophical discourse one must question and disturb because it lays down the law for all the others, because it constitutes the discourse of discourses."[6]

Reading against the grain constitutes an intervention into the phallocentric dynamic of authoritative textual closure. By reading a text in terms other than those it explicitly poses, by using one's position of difference to disclose the text's conflicts and contradictions, such readings work to disrupt the self-suturing operations used to marginalize or displace feminine voices. Often linked to the larger practice of deconstructive reading, this interpretative strategy works to call into question the self-authorizing discourse of rationality in which it is assumed that texts can and do say only what they claim to say, and with that the presumptions of traditional logocentricism to legislate the forms of interpretation and circulation to which it is subject. I have characterized these readings as radical, because they challenge the foundations of traditional reading practices, while making operational an alternative model of interpretative authority. Such readings undermine the prospect of significatory univocity by demonstrating its limits, most specifically the failure of these texts to contain and thereby dominate all that falls within their frame of reference. One consequence of this kind of textual subversion is to demonstrate that the logic that has been used to contain and domesticate women cannot in fact deliver what it promises. If the obstacles are rendered inoperative, then we need no longer think of ourselves as bound to or by them. If "phallogocentrism" can be ruptured in the process of reading, and if the text can be recognized to be complicitous with the process of its dismemberments, then these readings also open the possibility that phallocentric domination can be ruptured in other ways as well.

Feminist readings against the grain have resulted in some very insightful and, to many, unsettling scholarship. Those who are unsettled by this practice recognize its challenge to the terms upon which philosophic hegemony has been constructed and circulated as an authoritative discourse. Those readers are therefore right to be unsettled because it challenges the foundations of the privileges enjoyed by systematic rationality. The capacity of such readings to produce unease about that which philosophy has historically taken most for granted is one of its major strengths as a tactic. The question I wish to pose with respect to these readings is a strategic one, that centers around their utility as ongoing practices. Is this a strategy that feminists should expect to normalize as a competing hegemony, or should this rather be conceived as a specific tactic of accommodation to circumstances that feminists must work harder, in other ways and through other means, to change, so as to render obsolete the conditions that necessitate such reading?

My concerns about institutionalizing reading against the grain as a strategy of feminist hegemony are twofold. The first recapitulates the questions I raised in response to rereadings that aim to retrieve conceptual forefathers of feminism. Even though the logic and intentions of these two kinds of readings differ fundamentally, readings against the grain that locate or retrieve suppressed feminine voices also run the risk of severing feminism from its historically specific roots in women's deliberate and self-initiated political struggles. If a text can be read as giving voice to essentially feminist sentiments, even against its will or better judgments, the efforts of women to discover or produce the difference in their own voices is somehow devalued or effaced. If a text can be feminist in spite of itself, what happens to feminist commitment and the courage it takes to sustain it? Has the myth of authorial intentionalism been displaced only to recover the myth of the good father under another guise?

My second concern lies with the extent to which reading against the grain is still dependent, conceptually and epistemologically, on that which it operates against, specifically, the canon and its traditions of interpretation. Perhaps such readings, despite their intention to do otherwise, end up revalidating the force of the canon, by attributing to it more power and authority than it has or deserves. Reading against the grain, however, also makes room for another far more empowering and politically viable alternative that distinguishes it positively from readings of the first two types. The interventionist strategies at work in such readings authorize the recognition that the sympathetic voices emerging through this process can be affirmed not because they belong to the good father but rather to the good reader. They are thus attributable not to the canon, but rather to the gestures that work to diffuse it. It is, therefore, the act of reading and not the self-sealed text that produces these voices, allows them to speak and to speak with authority. Those voices can, therefore, also rightfully be described as feminist without risk of anachronistic misdescription because they are very much our own, a product of our labor. This gesture of reappropriation not only extends and affirms the sphere of feminist discourse, it also provides a space and a way of raising what may be the most subversive and fundamental question about the relationship between feminism and canonical philosophy, namely, the question of who exactly has given birth to whom.[7]

Reading against the grain is no easy feat, not only because one must overcome deeply engrained habits of thought and protocols of readings, but also because one chooses to operate on conspicuously unstable turf, without appeal to pre-established codes of validation and verification. What is the strength of such rereadings may also turn out to be a strategic limit, namely, the decision to chart some radically new courses through old and apparently established territory. Given the political urgencies and conceptual lacunae facing contemporary feminist theory, might not the effort, ingenuity, and insight entailed in rereading be better spent trying to map some new spaces, rather than doing battle with issues and conundrums that in many respects are not of our own making? Reading against the grain may very well be the best way for feminists to reread philosophy. But at this stage of our development, there may also be other more important things to do.

This call for a new agenda that moves feminism into some new territories carries with it the desire and expectation of some specification of just what or where those new terrains are. Although I recognize the legitimacy of that desire and feel in some sense obligated to respond to it, I also recognize the problems entailed in attempting to address it in too substantive or determinate a way. Given all I have said about the limits of the discourse of prescriptive mastery, I cannot and will not try to assume the position of the legislator, authoritatively determining the direction feminist theory ought to take. To refuse to respond at all, however, would place me in the unhappy position of uncritically reproducing the dynamic of withholding the promises for which I have criticized traditional philosophy. So, like so many of my feminist foresisters, I find myself in a potentially explosive situation. The cannon I am attempting to help defuse may very well blow up in my face.

My reservations about continuing to focus on the canon lie not only with the potentially infantalizing father-daughter dynamics produced thereby, but also, pursuing this familial metaphor, with the sibling rivalries that also emerge between the sisters in such discussions, rivalries over just whose father is the best father. This does not mean that feminists ought not to engage in struggle with one another. But the struggles in which we engage ought to occur around the issues arising from the feminist theory and practice that drew us together in the first place. Rather than casting our differences in terms of a canonical logic that will always be inadequate to our needs because it systematically excludes them, we ought be articulating and working through our differences with respect to the conceptual, epistemological, and ethical questions that emerge and have already emerged in the context of our theoretical and political activities as feminists. We need to address the questions we have produced ourselves, rather than those we have inherited.

Suppose, for example, we divest ourselves of the traditional trappings and codes of authority: how is our own discourse to be authorized and legitimated? What, if anything, entitles us to speak for or on behalf of other women? Is feminist politics possible without some form of legislative and articulatory authority? If we succeed in undermining, at least for ourselves, the hegemonic relation between knowledge and power, how ought this relationship to be reconstituted? What model of truth ought to underlie liberatory discourse? How is such truth to be produced, validated, criticized? What kind of model is appropriate for feminists to advocate or exercise? In what relationship does or should this model stand to truth and knowledge? Should feminism aim to consolidate its force as another local hegemony? If so, on what basis? Does any discourse of foundationalism reproduce the dynamics of exclusion we ourselves have criticized? If feminists cannot constitute some common ground, how is political activity in its name possible? What would feminism be if separated from the possibilities of mobilizing women's energies and commitments?

In suggesting a move into new territories I do not mean to imply that feminists are free to ignore or dissociate themselves from their own intellectual histories, or from the larger forms of thought that have produced them as well as the possibility of feminist theory as a historically specific response. Insofar as feminist theory emerges within patriarchy as a form of resistance, it is to that extent also dependent, conceptually and genetically, upon it. One can no more simply declare oneself free of one's conceptual heritage than one can choose to think of oneself as free of the influence of parental and familial heritage (much as we would sometimes like to). We are all the daughters of fathers, many of whom were in close enough proximity to us as we were growing up to have been influential factors in determining directly and indirectly the kind of people we have since become. But though these influences persist, happily and unhappily, we have grown up and moved out of our fathers' houses to homes and offices of our own. Though we may sometimes feel haunted by their presence, sensing dimly or clearly how they continue to work in us, we have also managed to get on with it, in part by struggling to take from that inheritance what we can use, and leaving as much as possible of the rest behind. We have developed the power and resources to separate our agendas from theirs and get on with them.

Feminist theory is growing up as well. The volume and quality of the work we have produced and continue to produce serves as testimony to the nonnegotiable legitimacy of our enterprise. We are becoming less dependent on canonical codes of recognition and validation as a consequence of the progress we have made in developing a forum for the kind of work we want to do. As feminists we may be at a place where the dependency we once felt, and which was perhaps appropriate, is no longer necessary or desirable for our own survival—existentially, conceptually, or professionally. We may already be in a better position than we realize, a position from which we are empowered to ask our own questions, rather than continuing to try to respond to those we have been left with. Such questions are vital not because they liberate us from the effects of this past, but because the answers we produce together will help determine our future.

Notes

1. Jean-Francois Lyotard, *Le Différent* (Paris: Minuit, 1983).

2. Shelia Ruth, "Methodocracy, Misogyny and Bad Faith: Sexism in the Philosophic Establishment," *Metaphilosophy* 10:1 (1979): 49.

3. This determination is made on a quantitative analysis of the articles classified under "feminism" in *The Philosopher's Index* (1973–1986).

4. David Farrell Krell, *Postponements* (Bloomington: Indiana University Press, 1986), p. 10; see also p. 85.

5. For a discussion of the different strategies employed by feminists reading "against the grain," see Toril Moi, *Sexual/Textual Politics: Feminist Literary Theory* (London and New York: Methuen, 1985).

6. Luce Irigaray, *Speculum de l'autre femme* (Paris: Mouton, 1974), p. 72.

7. I am indebted for this formulation to friend and colleague Kristina Straub, Department of English, Miami University, who offered it in the context of a reading of a draft of this paper, against the grain.

5

Just Say No: Repression, Anti-Sex, and the New Film

It should come as no surprise that the AIDS epidemic and the cultural discourse surrounding it has produced, at least for the time being, a change in the terms of sexual exchange, and with it, a change in erotic climate. The '80s have ushered in a new sexual aesthetic which Richard Goldsmith of the *Village Voice* has dubbed "the new sobriety," an umbrella term which points toward changes in sexual behavior as well as toward larger shifts in how sexuality is culturally valued, represented and circulated. Abstinence or monogamous domesticated sexuality has become fashionable, or at least respectable again. Sex educators and policy makers rally round the promise that the sexual epidemic can be abated if one is willing to "just say no."

The AIDS epidemic is, of course, not singularly responsible for having revivified the discourse of anti-sex, nor has it been the sole occasion for arousing concern about the relationship between representations of sex and erotic material, and sexual behavior. Long before AIDS became a central social preoccupation, groups from the Moral Majority to Women Against Pornography advocated restrictions on sexual representations and their circulation. Long before AIDS there were voices raised to argue that popular media, from films to television and rock and roll, had become too permissive, i.e., too willing to capitalize on the public's desire to consume images of sexuality, images which were questionable on moral and aesthetic grounds. Both the moralistic New Right and the anti-pornography feminists seemed to agree, despite their rather significant differences, that sexual imagery encouraged, even induced, mimetic behavior. The result of this behavioral consequentialist logic was a strategy focused on targeting undesirable representations, i.e., representations which it was thought or feared resulted in undesirable behavior. Feminists, who are primarily concerned with

From *Sexual Politics and Popular Culture*, ed. Diane Raymond (Bowling Green: Bowling Green State University Popular Press, 1990). Reprinted with permission.

representations of violence and abuse of women, focus the bulk of their attention on the more marginal pornography and skin trade markets. The New Right, by contrast, focuses on mainstream media, like television and rock and roll.

Because the circulation of sexual representations is governed by the logic of commodity culture, we can expect that the decisions made by those in the industry of producing and circulating such material will be governed by the logic of the market. Part of that logic includes consideration of demographics. The rock and roll industry has been able thus far to most successfully resist, largely by ignoring, the demands for negative labeling, at least in part, because that part of the population which is represented by the New Right is not a significant segment of their market to begin with. This is far less true for television, where advertisers aim primarily at familial households, and thus are concerned about appearing indifferent to familially based concerns about the welfare of children. Consequently, television has been far more vulnerable or responsive to the regulation of sexual images in general, regulations dominated by a self-imposed aesthetic of restraint and indirection with the ways sexual issues are represented.

The film industry, since the days of the Hays Code, has been sensitive to how and what kinds of sexuality are represented. In an effort to avoid external intervention, the industry currently employs an internal regulatory system, which rates and marks films for sex and violence. But the film industry's attempts to accommodate the revived anti-sex discourse is complicated by the law of the commodity market, which demands accommodation to a diverse and polyvalent/contradictory consumer psychology. With respect to the consumption of sexual imagery, market patterns are often contradictory. On the one hand, public opinion surveys consistently reflect a perception that there is too much sex and violence in popular media. On the other hand, such offerings are often the most popular, as reflected in television ratings and movie box office receipts. Teenagers, for example, are often especially loathe to patronize films with G and PG ratings. Furthermore, the public has become accustomed to seeing sex at the movies, at least in some form. Certain traditional Hollywood genre, like the western, from which representations of sexuality were almost always entirely absent, are not very popular with contemporary filmgoers. And sexual scenes have become a regular element in other film genres like science fiction and war stories which traditionally also avoided sexual motifs. John Wayne never took his boots off. Sylvester Stallone does (a lot). He also takes off a lot more.

In general, therefore, the film industry's accommodations to the antisex discourse have not taken the form of explicit excision. Most Hollywood films include some representations of sexual activity. A conspicuous counterexample is the recent yuppie comedy *Broadway News*. In that case, sex is resisted not on moral grounds, but because the protagonist, a news producer played by Holly Hunter, is simply too busy. The displacement of sex onto work is also an element in the sexual economy represented in *Baby Boom*, where sex between the corporate cohabitants is carefully scheduled and timed.

Baby Boom also operationalizes another strategy of accommodation that has become a recurring theme in several recent Hollywood films, namely the domesti-fication of sex in reproduction. In *Baby Boom* the protagonist inherits the baby that changes her life from that of NY corporate consultant to country entrepreneur. Much of the comedic effect in this film is supposed to flow from the character's ineptitude and unpreparedness for motherhood. Her work in a male-dominated competitive corporate milieu has not encouraged or rewarded the development of her nurturing skills. Similarly, Hollywood has attempted to exploit conditions of unlikely parenthood for comedic effect in *For Keeps* and *She's Having a Baby*, where the parents are teenagers, and the very popular *Three Men and A Baby*, the American remake of the French film *Three Men and A Cradle*, which was also very popular. Paternity/fatherhood is a source of interest, perhaps, because it is so exotic. (Remember the success of Dustin Hoffman as primary parent in *Kramer vs. Kramer*). Even Woody Allen, no great sentimentalist on this score, has included father-son scenes in several films, including *Manhattan, Radio Days* and *Hannah and Her Sisters*.

These representations of paternal activity have a double strategic edge in terms of the contemporary sexual economy. On the one hand, they work to valorize paternity at a time when more and more men are choosing to desert their families, and are failing to contribute to the support of their children. On the other hand, they re-enforce the traditional double standard by virtue of which anything men do, even or maybe especially when it is gender atypical, is infinitely interesting. Watching women mother, except ineptly, is not so terribly interesting because it is so socially ubiquitous. Men engaged in active parenting is interesting because it is not. At a time when there is social urgency attached to limiting multiple and unregulated sexual exchanges, there is social utility in valorizing fatherhood, and at least attempting to glamorize the familial organization of sexuality.

A more complicated, and if box office is any indication, successful example of accommodating the anxiety induced by the sexual epidemic is *Fatal Attraction*. I want to examine *Fatal Attraction* at some length for several reasons. First, its popularity suggests it hit some kind of nerve and thus may serve as some sort of impressionistic barometer of the sex-pol climate in the age of epidemic. Secondly, its tropic function is being confirmed through replication. Television offered several major productions with similar themes and titles (like *Deadly Attraction* and *Fatal Infatuation*), reflecting the mass media logic that there is never too much of a good thing.

The questions I wish to raise about *Fatal Attraction* all revolve around the nature and significance of the kind of pleasure this film induced for its substantial audience. What is so attractive, at this particular time, about a film in which sexual attraction is also figured as fatal? For whom or what is attraction fatal, and what larger utilities are accommodated or recuperated thereby? What is the effect of eroticizing the connection between pleasure and danger? What, if anything, is ideologically significant about the ways in which *Fatal Attraction* mobilizes and organizes its audiences' desires and satisfactions?

The question of pleasure and object relations in the cinema, as elsewhere, is an extremely complex question and one to which I cannot possibly do justice in this context. Nevertheless, if you will pardon the pun, I want to take a stab at it and suggest that at least part of why *Fatal Attraction* was so interesting to the large number of Americans who were willing to invest time and money in it, was the way this film managed a nexus of contemporary sexual anxieties surrounding changes in the family, alternation in the cultural theory and practice of femininity, and transformations in the erotic climate induced by the contemporary sexual epidemic, which raises the risks entailed in sexual exchanges. One way to summarize this shift in the erotic economy was suggested by Arthur and Marilouise Kroker, who characterize the contemporary sexual hegemony as an aesthetic of "panic sex," in which sexuality is increasingly represented as a site of "disaccumulation, loss and sacrifice." Panic sex operates affectively "between a melancholy sense of fatalism and a triumphant sense of immunity." Representationally, this hegemony works to produce eroticism as a "scene of a violent and frenzied implosion where sexual activity is coded by the logic of extremism, where consciousness is marked by an intense fear of ruined surfaces . . . [I]t is just the hint of catastrophe that makes sex bearable" (*Panic Sex in America*, p. 14).

The intuition I tend to elaborate is that *Fatal Attraction's* success is attributable, at least in part, to the ways it represents and resolves the forms of sexual anxiety it both exploits and produces. The whole economy and narrative development of *Fatal Attraction* work to link sex and loss—loss of stability, security, respect, family and property. At one point, the image of the daughter's dead pet rabbit is offered to us as a carnal image of sacrifice, a motif also represented through the recurring imagery of spilled blood. The narrative unfolds in the direction of increasing catastrophe. The temporal economy of the film works to conflate the pleasures attached to sexual adventurism, restricting their representations to the first reel. After that the fun is definitely over, and the rest of the film is devoted to expanding the concentric circles of consequences following from a husband's one night stand with another woman. As the plot unfolds, representations of pleasure are progressively displaced by images of panic, hysteria, destruction and eventually death. *Fatal Attraction* develops as a narrative of sexual panic, but in a way that also produces pleasure for its audience.

Fatal Attraction works to create its specific forms of pleasure in danger by figuring sexual catastrophe in a way that both draws upon and manages the anxieties induced by contemporary sexual conditions. One major mechanism operative in achieving this effect is that of displacement. Within the diegetic logic of the film, social factors, like the decline in nuclear families, the changing position of women, AIDS, are displaced entirely from the frame of reference, and are instead condensed into individuals whose conflicts can then be resolved within an atomistic dramatic framework. But the operations of displacement and condensation also transfigure those anxieties, and thereby the terms of their recuperation. In the case of *Fatal Attraction* the effect is to make the anxieties more manageable and thereby more susceptible to a satisfying resolution, either by being eliminated or by being re-directed in ways that are more productive viz. the existing systems of social utility.

Fatal Attraction is not the only film that attempted to draw upon the connection between pleasure and danger operative in situations of sexual catastrophe. Some of the other recent entries in the mainstream genre of "dangerous sex" films include *Body Heat, The Postman Always Rings Twice* (a remake), *Thief of Hearts, Angel Heart, No Way, Out, Black Widow,* and *Falling in Love.* None of these films was nearly as successful at the box office as was *Fatal Attraction.* The film in this group to which it is closest in terms of subject matter is *Falling in Love.* Both films figure sexual catastrophe in terms of the dissolution of what otherwise seem to be well-functioning marriages. I think a quick comparison will provide some clues to the specific representational strategies that help account for the former's success, and which, I think also constitute the core of its ideological significance as a discourse influencing contemporary sexual politics.

In *Falling in Love,* a series of chance encounters between two middle-class suburban commuters results in an attraction that eventually disrupts both their marriages. Moreover, the infatuation that comes to take hold of their situation functions without benefit of coitus as lubricant or motive. Both characters are represented as guilty about the prospect of infidelity. Their behavior toward one another is callow, almost adolescent in its awkwardness and indirection. Neither one is living life in the fast lane, but are rather contrasted with peers who cannot understand their reticence in pursuing one another more directly. Both are shown as otherwise devoted to their spouse and in the case of the DeNiro character, his children. Neither one is to blame. Whatever it is that draws them out of their marriages and towards one another is vague, unstable, and thereby produces an anxiety that cannot be contained, resolved or relieved. *Falling in Love* ended up leaving its audience uneasy, having tapped into a circuitry of anxiety about marital stability and the dynamics of desire that it cannot or does not suture.

Fatal Attraction also opens with images of a well-running nuclear family. The couple, played by Michael Douglas and Anne Archer, and their young daughter are healthy, attractive and well dressed. Their apartment is clean and well furnished, and by Hollywood standards is scaled small enough to encourage belief in its verisimilitude. The initial sequence shows Douglas and Archer preparing for an evening out, which suggests both that they have an interesting social life, and also allows the couple to engage in gestures that reveal sexual interest between them. Douglas is shown to be a warm and attentive father. As a lawyer, he is also a representative of middle-class respectability and stability. His identification with the law will later become a figure of irony, as this position will be shown to offer little protection against a force that will eventually threaten not only his well-being but the stability of his family as well.

The effect of this opening sequence is to establish the familial economy as a diegetic threshold, an image of stability designed to elicit an identificatory or desirous investment from the audience. It also works to position sexual threat as a force from without, and as a gratuitous, hence unjustified, invasion by the alien or outsider, rather than as a dynamic already operative within the family. By eliciting audience belief in the family's stability, the film mobilizes the audience's investments in the form of a desire for the restitution of the family and the organization of desire it represents, a desire that the film fulfills with its closing shot of the framed family portrait, an image of the family romance recuperated.

The film is capable of satisfying its audience's desire for the restitution of the family because that which threatens family stability is figured as a singular alien force from without. In *Fatal Attraction*, the family is positioned as the major target of sexual risk, the major victim of the economy of pleasure in danger. Within its diegetic logic, that which threatens the family takes the form of a woman, specifically the "other woman" who disrupts a stable erotic economy by challenging the wife's claim to undivided sexual possession of her husband. In this case, the other woman is an attractive, unmarried New York career woman played by Glenn Close. This construction of sexual threat in the form of an aggressive transgressive female sexuality is certainly not a new diegetic strategy. But in the case of *Fatal Attraction* the figure of female transgression is put to some rather historically specific ideological and narrative use value that I think is worth elaborating as a way of understanding this film's mass appeal.

Dramatically, the figure of Alex provides a kind clarity that was lacking in *Falling in Love*. In *Fatal Attraction*, even if there are no heroes, there is a villain, and therefore a specifiable site of disruption and threat subject to specific mechanisms of containment and eventual elimination. Because sexual threat is figured as a sexually predatory woman, audience sympathies can be mobilized on behalf of the male character who comes to occupy the position of victim, and on behalf of the order of family and law with which he is symbolically linked.

Because I think the construction and development of the character of Alex is crucial to the way the film organizes its audience's expectations, I want to examine it at some length. The establishing shots of Alex work to glamorize her, and thus position her as a culturally decipherable object of desire. She is attractively dressed and beautifully lit. We see her first when Douglas does, at the cocktail party where they engage in brief flirtation, and thus we are encouraged to see her as he does. In this sequence she is shown as poised, confident, as a woman who is accustomed to the attention of men. Her persona is further glamorized when she is shown working for a publisher with which Douglas has legal business. These stylistic and contextual codes establish Alex in terms of the contemporary stereotype of the new age career woman—independent, successful, and sexually sophisticated. The appropriation of this contemporary cultural fiction has dual effects. On the one hand, it makes Douglas's interest in her understandable, even forgivable. After all, this was a desirable woman, desirable in part because she is positioned as an alternative to the traditional full-time wife and mother he has at home, desirable, in other words, because she is not like his woman. Given the way the character of Alex is established, neither Douglas nor the audience can be expected to foresee the disastrous consequences that follow from Douglas's submission to desire. The problem or risk as figured by *Fatal Attraction* is not Douglas's desire, as such, but its object. His mistake was to have picked the wrong woman. In the logic established by the film, such an error is understandable because the objects are women, creatures of appearance which, in this case, are ultimately deceiving.

This factor allows for Douglas, and the male position he comes to represent, to be removed from the primary sphere of culpability for marital infidelity and its more disastrous social consequences on the one hand. On the other hand, it allows the film to engage in some feminist backlash and misogynist tactics, by offering a woman that the film will make it all too easy to hate, by placing the blame for familial destabilization clearly on the backs of non-traditional women. Certainly this film does not invent feminist backlash. But it does exploit it by developing a narrative logic such that the solution to the problem will appear to be the elimination of woman, or at least of a particular kind of woman. The strategic beauty of this solution, from a hegemonic perspective, is that even though the male character is positioned as the victim, it is the transgressive woman that pays the price. Even though *Fatal Attraction* mobilizes audience sympathy on behalf of the man and the family he represents, it is the women in this film, both Alex and the betrayed wife, that suffer the consequences. Furthermore, this suffering is presented in a way that the audience is induced to take pleasure in it. On the two occasions I saw this film, the scene of Alex's death at the hands of another woman was greeted with tremendous satisfaction.

Part of the pleasure at this climactic moment, to which I will return later, is dependent upon the way in which the character of Alex is transformed from that of being an object of desire to that of castrating predator. This transformation begins with the encounter which results in their one night stand. Given the way this encounter is written and staged, Alex appears to be so much in charge of the situation that every one of her moves appears to be calculated. Douglas's character is made to appear callow, almost innocent by comparison. He represents his interest in her as clearly supplemental. He assures her of the quality of his marriage, which elicits her ironic comment, "then what are you doing here with me?" When he agrees to go home with her, he is operating under the assumption that she understands and agrees to the limited conditions of their involvement. Though both parties acknowledge the importance of discretion, i.e., secrecy about such matters, that part of the bargain is the one which Alex eventually chooses to betray.

The transformation of Alex from glamorous vixen to terrifying bitch begins almost as soon as the two leave the restaurant and return to her loft apartment. Its location within New York's meat market district links Alex with the economy of the sexual meat market. The disarray in her apartment clearly marks her as the nondomestic type, in sharp contrast with the kind of home that Douglas's wife, who is away for the weekend, has provided for him. Her sexual habits also mark her as transgressive, as she begins moving in on Douglas in the elevator, an encounter that culminates in the infamous sex-in-the-sink sequence. This is hardly the good housekeeping kitchen. The appearance of the knife in this sequence also functions as an image of foreboding. It is an instrument that the female protagonist, true to the masochistic tropes of femininity, initially wields on herself in a suicide attempt the morning after when Douglas is getting ready to leave. The knife, as we will later discover, will eventually be aimed at other targets.

As the plot develops, Alex becomes progressively detached from any orienting or stabilizing milieu. There are no more scenes of Alex at work. The film gives us no indication that she has any other interpersonal connections with friends or family. Her wardrobe changes as well. To visually mark her progress toward increasingly predatory behavior, Close begins dressing in black leather, which, at least according to Hollywood stylistic codes, is apparently the preferred fabric choice of sadists. Because Alex appears to belong nowhere, she seems to appear everywhere, in subway stations, on the telephone, and eventually at the male protagonists' apartment, under the guise of a prospective buyer for their condo. When the family moves to the suburbs, she follows them, and begins to shift her attention to the wife and daughter. The course of events works to construct Alex as a threat that is ever more polymorphous and present, an uncontained, unbound female agent in a masculinist social order.

Because the logic/motivation behind Close's pursuit of Douglas remains ambiguous within the diegesis, it is thereby also made to seem all the more terrifying and irrational. At one point, Alex tells Douglas that she is pregnant and that the child is his. Although the film provides ample occasion for the viewer to question its truth, the issue is never diegetically clarified or resolved. Given the forms of deceit of which Alex is shown to be amply capable, the viewer is left with the impression that she very well might be lying about this as well. At another point in the same conversation, she rails at Douglas that she is not just a one night stand. But nothing we have seen from Close and her way of approaching Douglas would suggest she could have expected more from him. Given the directness with which she pursued him, her moral outrage is made to seem irrational, and excessive. By keeping her motivation ambiguous, the logic of the film works to position Alex as an excessive alien threat, to the family, stability, and rationality itself. The development of this anxious economy induces along with it a desire for her elimination, a desire the diegesis satisfies in the final sequence when Alex is, quite completely, eliminated.

Part of what is interesting about *Fatal Attraction* is the way it displaces the threat to masculinity onto a contest between women. Ultimately it is the betrayed wife who must come to the defense of the household. This is because she and not her husband has become Alex's eventual target. The final showdown in the bathroom is the culmination of a series of sequences in which Alex moves in on Douglas's family. The women have been positioned oppositionally from the beginning of the film: housewife versus career woman, dark haired versus light haired, married versus single, mother versus childless. At one point Alex says she wants the child she is supposedly carrying, and thus all of a sudden seems to want everything the wife has, despite the fact that we are given every indication prior to this that Alex very deliberately is leading another kind of life. When Alex goes after Douglas's wife and child, the transparent logic of this replacement makes her seem all the more insane. On the other hand, it also has the effect of letting the Douglas character off the hook. The really serious consequences of his transgression will accrue to others, and to the innocent.

By the time Alex confronts her rival, the threat Alex poses is literally overflowing, as the water leaks through the floor to the ceiling below, threatening the integrity of the house's structure. By this time, everything in the situation calls for her elimination. In the economy of justice established by the film, it is only appropriate that she who is really threatened, she who represents the stability of the family and the world of "good women" should be the one to eliminate Alex and the threat she poses. Both times I saw the film, the moment of Alex's demise was greeted with great pleasure from the audience. Indeed the film has worked carefully to produce that effect, and anticipates it, by allowing the camera to linger on Alex's bloody body, which is now dressed in a white sweat shirt ensemble that makes her body look almost naked, revealed, bloodied (perhaps evoking menstrual blood, indicating Alex was not even pregnant after all). The audience's pleasure at Alex's elimination is further stoked by the film's final image, a close-up of a family portrait which assures us that the order represented by the family has been restored.

The figuring of the threat to the family as a female homewrecker, is certainly not new to Hollywood film (indeed the word "homewrecker" is a term almost exclusively applied to women). This construction has persisted as a satisfying fiction because it serves several ideological and psychological functions. Most significantly, in this context, the fiction of the female figuration of sexual temptation helps assure men of their sexual mobility, while also allowing them the assumption of their wife's fidelity, through her containment and conflation within the family. (That is why in this film the wife must stand as protector of the family. She is the family, or stands in the place of it, especially when, in this case it is the only social space the character of the wife is shown to occupy. Though Anne Archer is represented as attractive, she is never shown operating as an independent sexual agent.) Through the consumption of such images, men can empower themselves with this fiction of the perpetual accessibility of women outside the family, without having to confront the anxiety about its loss within.

For women spectators, by contrast, I think this fiction works quite differently. The figure of the "other woman" becomes associated not with the promise of plentitude/excess but rather explicitly with the threat of loss. The other woman is made other to and for women. She threatens loss of the woman's key possession—her man. As rival, the other woman can function as a projective screen for a variety of anxieties, resentments and angers, because she is a symptom or emblem of male marital discontent, which is also likely to be perceived as a real threat to women. The figure of the other woman allows the woman spectator to displace her fears of male marital discontent onto women who come to be blamed as its cause. This allows for a reading where it is female and not male transgression that is responsible for the dissolution of marriage and the family. The utility of this kind of fiction for the maintenance of male hegemony cannot be overemphasized, especially at a time in history when the nuclear family is in a state of decline or at least transformation, and contemporary conditions motivate a repackaging of the family as the latest safe sex prophylactic device. The genius of *Fatal Attraction* is the way it works to displace this anxiety onto the bodies and presence of women, especially women who occupy non-traditional roles.

Even though Alex is figured as threatening and therefore as an object of anxiety and/or contempt she is also made to seem attractive. In doing so, the film also works to eroticize and glamorize the threat she represents. Alex is a figure of sex laced with danger. For the audience, of course, this is pleasure at a safe distance. Such a figure is a very fitting one for the era of sexual epidemic, allowing for the appropriation of pleasure in danger, while at the same time promising that the threat it represents will also ultimately be contained, neutralized or eliminated. In this way, *Fatal Attraction* provides for its audience a resolution of the anxiety it induces, a resolution that takes a form which is very well suited to the current mood—militaristic combat. *Fatal Attraction* offers what to many is the pleasurable fiction that we can directly combat the forces which threaten us. It also promises that we can do that by directing our combative mechanisms at socially acceptable targets, the bodies of women, and that furthermore the agents of this combat will also be female.

According to the story told by this film, attraction is fatal in the end to and for women. It is they who pay the ultimate price for male transgressions, and they are also the ones who will have to clean up the mess afterward. *Fatal Attraction* can be read as a cautionary tale, or as an exercise in cost-benefit management of sexual risk. Read from the perspective of a female spectator, this indeed is a cautionary tale, alerting us not only to the risks we are all likely to want to displace, but also to the need to be protected from that which also often poses as protection.

6

Feminism and Postmodernism

The expression "feminism and postmodernism," as it often operates in a contemporary context, makes a proposal, a proposal of conjunction. In the face of the ubiquity of this expression, especially within the discourse of professional scholars, and the intensity that usually accompanies discussion of this subject, I have been tempted to interrogate the nature of the linkage being offered, to think about the conceptual strategic and theoretical function of this "and." What is the nature of the proposal being made? What desires are invested in this formulation? What agendas are enacted in proposing or resisting this conjunction of "isms"? How does one who finds herself in some relationship of both affiliation and distance from these signifiers position herself in order to both pose and respond to these questions?

If one is endeavoring to address this nexus of issues from something like an indigenous perspective—that is, from a position of both acquaintance and sympathy or attraction to a variety of the discourses and practices collected under these umbrella signifiers—it is clear at the outset that none of the questions can be answered in the singular. It is both ironic and paradoxical that the terminology of "feminism" and "postmodernism" works dramatically against the grain of much of the writing, theory, and practice to which they are supposed to refer, since such terminological collection works to occlude, deny, or obscure the very differences, particularities, and specificities upon which feminist and postmodern projects so often insist. The viability and credibility of paradigmatic designators like "feminism" and "postmodernism" depend upon the production and circulation of some system or criteria of linkage, which establishes circuits of inclusion and exclusion. Yet as the indigenous literature of feminism and postmodernism both asserts and symptomatizes, such foundations are entirely phantasmatic, present

From *Feminists Theorize the Political*, Judith Butler and Joan W. Scott, eds. (New York and London: Routledge, 1992).

only as perpetual absence, as that which can never be adequately articulated or represented. Insofar as both "feminism" and "postmodernism" operate not only as textual designators but also as forms or contexts for social production and exchange, the surplus signification attached to these signifiers is in a perpetual process of formulation and revision. In both contexts, not only is there little agreement among practitioners of that which they may in any sense be said to have or enjoy in common, but the terms, apparatus, and scope of these signifiers are very much a matter of open and intense confrontation. Such historical specificities will further complicate the question of articulating the nature of the proposal being made when conjoining "postmodernism" with "feminism." How does one do justice to the diversity of viewpoints, voices, and textual strategies that is signified by these terms, while also trying to isolate specific sites of conjunction, consensus, or agreement?

The question of justice or doing justice is but one of the issues that arises in the consideration of the proliferation of attempts to find some site of conjunction between postmodernism and feminism. The question of desire is another. What lack is being aimed at in these gestures, what needs are proleptically satiated when such linkage is achieved, even episodically, or ideolectively? What sort of pleasure is written into the text of "feminism and postmodernism," and what sort of pleasures flow from our readings of it?

The erotic underpinnings of the text of "feminism and postmodernism" that I am pursuing are distinguishable from all those particular texts which symptomatize or betray the influence of feminist and postmodern writing. With these latter texts, the relationship between "feminism" and "postmodernism" is one of an informal and often unthematized cross-fertilization, symptomatized by choices of language, register, and textual strategies. But the text of "feminism and postmodernism" asserts/desires a far stronger and more highly articulated connection—a connection with legislative force and authority to establish a sort of intertextual social contract. The force behind this contract is that which aims at writing or inscribing limits discursively, epistemically, and strategically. The outcome projected is some sort of alliance, and recognition of reciprocal indebtedness, that can be represented and practiced systematically for its exponents and the audiences their work addresses.

The desire to legislate or construct some paradigmatic protocol for the linkage of postmodern and feminist theory bespeaks/symptomatizes a desire inherited from a far earlier phase in "the history of theory." The libidinal formation I see at work in this contemporary enterprise has much in common with "the Cartesian complex," that historically specific albeit long-standing desire to unify and consolidate knowledge through a series of methodological prescriptions, and through the establishment of some definitive frame of relevance. Although the object of desire pursued by contemporary theorists is other than what it was for Descartes, whose work pursued an ideal of objectively necessary truth of a kind immune to erosion or dispersal through doubt, the Cartesian impulse toward systematic consolidation through establishment of connections of coherence remains in force. Such impulses toward systematicity are particularly ironic in a contemporary context, however, given the postmodern fixation on the phenomena of endings— the end of metaphysics, history, humanism, art, and the era of the subject, each of which radically forecloses any promise of closure offered by the ideal of systems. In the work of postmodernists like Jean-François Lyotard and Jean Baudrillard, for example, the notion of system modeled (as it was for Descartes) on the orderly relationships inherent in a rational and divinely originated world are displaced by the more episodic and unpredictable connections of network— modeled on information and communication networks which disperse, circulate, and proliferate exchanges in a way that belies any myths of unitary origins, foundations, or essences.

From the standpoint of a range of feminist theories, from both sides of the Atlantic, which have also focused on eroding or undermining the stabilization effects of the systems of nature, essences, and patriarchy, the impulse to establish some privileged relationship with postmodern discourse which is intended to have regulative impact on the conduct of feminist theory and practice is also surprising. Part of the history of feminist theory has been a progressive series of attempts to frame or pursue feminist issues under the regulatory and strategic practices initiated by some other theoretical paradigm. Over the last thirty years, for example, proposals have been made in the direction of Marxism, socialism, phenomenology, psychoanalysis, and semiotics, among others. The motives and rationales for these specific conjunctions have varied. But with each successive attempt, there has always emerged, almost in tandem, discourse of resistance to prescriptions, either on the grounds of the inadequacy of the particular paradigm being proposed, or on the level of resistance to alliance with the project of "grand theory" in general, that is, a critique of the impulse to systematize and consolidate knowledge, and through it power.

Given both the theoretical and rhetorical privilege given to notions of dispersal and differences, and given both discourses' investments in anti-essentialist episte-mology, the nature of the impulse which prompts contemporary movements of consolidation and coalition both within and between these paradigmatic enter-prises calls for further interrogation of its motives, independently of questions of feasibility or utility. Given the extent to which such movements run counter to the thematic and rhetorical postures assumed by both discourses (in a variety of stylistic and ideolective variations), I think the question of motive or desire must be pursued indirectly, that is, by examining the strategies by which such linkages are made, rather than through an analysis of the substantive reasons and arguments offered in support/defense.

To interrogate desire is already to assume a relationship of transferential ambiguity with the interrogated, and hence to risk being sutured, caught up in the figures and formations from which one also needs to keep some critical interpretive distance. In this case it means I will operate in some unhappy alliance with the totalizing tendencies of the legislative discourse I am working to problematize or dismantle. In order to foreground what I see as three of the dominant strategies for pursuing the linkage of feminism and postmodernism, I will be operating from a somewhat globalizing stance, which will diminish awareness of the specificities of these strategic pursuits, their particularities and differences. That which is resisted returns to the resistor. The text that follows cannot entirely resist its own totalizing tendencies in articulating three ways in which the linkage between feminism and postmodernism is being figured or metaphorized in contemporary writing. But such consolidating effects will only be temporary, destabilized by a conclusion which speaks in the imaginary voice, the voice of the imaginary other, which both situates and problematizes whatever globalizing gestures might already have been set in place.

One strategy employed to link feminism and postmodernism has been a kind of metonymic analysis, in which some particular perspective or set of texts is made to stand in for or represent "feminism" or "postmodernism" writ large. In this case, the offer being made is much like a proposal of marriage—a linkage of individuals marked by proper names in a relationship of exchange of asymmetrical and differentiated obligations and desires. Such conjunctions are often motivated, like marriage proposals, by a situation of perceived need. One attempts to conjoin perspectives because Foucault's analysis of power needs to be informed by more specific attention to the operation of sexual difference, as articulated by feminists like Luce Irigaray or Simone de Beauvoir, or because American feminist theorists like Adrienne Rich or Andrea Dworkin are said to need a theory of split subjectivity like that provided by Lacan. Such atomistic unions occur throughout the literature, and, as good marriages should, continue to produce a variety of hybrid offspring with polymorphous paradigmatic affiliations, the new breed of "hyphenated" feminists and postmodernists.

At this level, therefore, there is evidence of a certain kind of marital conjunction of postmodernism and feminism in the work of all of those who have been influenced and interpolated by texts that are placed in these two different camps. In these cases, conjunction is elective, selective, and, therefore, circumscribed in its scope and impact. There is ample evidence of a multifaceted exchange of concepts, problematics, and language in a range of writers and writings, but it is not clear how such particular strategic inscriptions bear on the question of paradigmatic conjunction. Some marriages work, others don't. Some seductions are reciprocated, others resisted. Any form of elective engagement can also be refused. Argumentatively, one can make a stronger or weaker case for the possibilities and prospects of such elective affiliations depending on one's choice of proper names, on who is brought in to stand for "feminism" or "postmodernism."

Even when such marriages seem to work as sites of production and fertility, such unions have no legislative or regulatory status with respect to other texts and positions which resist acknowledging the legitimacy or desirability of such unions of convenience. At best, these marital conjunctions of feminism and postmodernism offer evidence of affiliation in an episodic intertextual mode, but cannot adequately address the question of whether such unions are merely fortuitous, or are in some way paradigmatically binding, necessary, or desirable. Such evidence is also vastly inadequate to the task of trying to persuade a resistor to such unions, since such a person has easy access to a range of counterexamples. Divorces, abuses, and cases of incompatibility make regular appearances in our intertextual judicial systems.

For these reasons, the demand or expectation of romantic exclusivity and/or marital fidelity between feminism and postmodernism seems woefully misplaced. Furthermore, as in the traditional marriage contract, expectations about purity and fidelity are unequally distributed, in this case weighing more heavily on the developmental course of feminist theory than on postmodernism. Both from within and from outside feminist discourse, there reemerges with regularity these days a cautionary invective with respect to appropriation of the language concepts and rhetoric—like that of the subject or personal identity—which has been placed in a problematized epistemic suspension by postmodern tactics of deconstruction. While such cautionary considerations are not without merit (and many, at least to my mind, are truly compelling), it is both presumptuous and preemptive to assume that such considerations must occupy some privileged position with respect to the development of feminist theory in the range and breadth of its concerns and approaches. Any attempt to totalize the theoretical resources of contemporary feminism under the sign of postmodernism seems on the face of it to speak from a distinctly nonpostmodern place, which may help explain why the demand is seldom made in reverse: that postmodernism necessarily take feminist concerns into consideration in developing its theory. Insofar as feminism and postmodernism call attention to the way in which discourse is situationally articulated (by conditions of reception, the specificities of the text's addresses, and so forth), any prospect of radical paradigmatic loyalty/affiliation is or should be read as foreclosed. There can be no arranged marriage between feminism and postmodernism. Hence their conjunction might be better thought in other ways.

One alternative formulation of the conjunction of "feminism" and "postmodernism" has been that of a kinship or family resemblance. The relationship is thus like that of siblings who share common genetic origins, and yet also are placed in a differential familial semiotic characterized by division of labor, accompanied by a certain rivalry. Considered in this light, it is possible to construct a narrative of common origins or parentage for feminism and postmodernism in post-Hegelian critical traditions of thought like Marxism, existentialism, and psychoanalysis. They can also be read as the offspring produced by the kind of critical cultural practices that commanded social visibility, especially in France and the United States, during the late 1960s. One theme that recurs with variations in each of these critical paradigmatic spheres is an explicit discursive strategy of challenging the terms, conventions, and symbols of hegemonic authority in ways that fore-ground the explicitly transgressive character of this enterprise.

In conspicuous opposition to canonical philosophy and systematic metaphysics which operate with the assumption that this is the best or most rational of all possible worlds, critical philosophy emerges from a recognition of lack, and from the desire to force acknowledgment that things are not as they should be. With this critical enterprise emerges a different set of strategies, protocols and conven-tions for theoretical writing. Rather than endeavoring to represent what is or to provide the foundations for that which is known as "common sense," the critical traditions that are crucial to the genesis of both feminist and postmodern dis-courses pose as conspicuous affronts to and violations of the hegemonic common sense, as it is variously configured. Part of the tradition of critical writing that postmodernism and feminism inherit, albeit in ways that are differentially specified, is a tradition of writing as a form of resistance, writing which works not to confirm cohesion, but rather to disrupt, destabilize, denaturalize.

Part of what can also be said to constitute the family resemblance linking postmodern and feminist theory and practice is their respective ways of resisting and challenging established forms of power by undermining the legitimacy and validity of the mechanisms by which that power is sustained. What allies these particular incursions into the political economy of knowledge is a strategy of disclosing that things are not as they should be by also exposing all the ways in which things are not as we say they are. Both feminist and postmodern writing depend upon relativizing, ironizing, and circumscribing the mechanisms and tactics by which dominant authorities entrench themselves, legitimated by the totalizing voice of what Kierkegaard called "the ethical universal," which speaks from nowhere to everyone, sufficiently disinterested so as to be undifferentiated and globalizing in its effects. Like the critical traditions that preceded them, feminist and postmodern discourse disrupt the project of closure by consensus, by insisting on exposing how differences inscribe themselves, even when they are explicitly refused or denied. The voice of rationality is shown to be riddled with contradictions it cannot exclude.

This insistence on difference, while in some senses allying feminism and postmodernism as discourses challenging the hegemonic dominance of a legisla-tive rationality, also pose serious problems when trying to pursue their connection in other than this postural sense. In other words, those very differences—in emphasis, strategy, and concern—can become bones of contention and sibling rivalry. There is no shorthand way to characterize these differences—nor could such an account be sufficiently totalized so as to do justice to the range of relationships between feminist and postmodernist enterprises. And I, for one, would want to resist what is often offered as a facile distinction between femi-nism's political engagement and postmodernism's aestheticized self-absorption.

That there are sites of serious contention between them is episodically and intertextually overdetermined like any sibling rivalry.

The rivalrous tensions which are characteristic of all familial relationships also differentially position feminism and postmodern ambivalences about their respective ancestries and origins in the intertextual nexus of relationships that constitutes "Western culture." Postmodern discourse can both claim origins in canonical culture (Nietzsche, Heidegger, modernist aesthetics) and therefore also displace the anxiety this arouses by focusing not on origins but on "ends"—the end of history, philosophy, art and so on. Feminist discourse, by contrast, tends to begin from a relationship of exclusion and exile with respect to these same institutions. This may be why some feminists are drawn to postmodernism's claim that all this is in some sense over, ended. But one can also read in this recognition a counter impulse/desire—not to ironize but to retrieve that of which one has been deprived: To speak not in the language of death and ends, but rather to focus on births and beginnings, lost origins, and to do so with more *jouissance* than irony. Feminist discourse is precisely not a member of the old boys clubs which can tire of their games and call an end to them. Not that feminist discourse can claim to be immune from the effects of this game playing, and its sociosymbolic imaginary; but because so much of that imaginary has produced discernible effects, of the kind that, on many occasions, merit outrage, judgment, indignation—just the kind of tone and frame that postmodern cool works so hard to avoid.

Outrage and irony are two very different sorts of responses, affectively and strategically, but they are not mutually exclusive. Neither irony nor political enthusiasm can expect, or be expected, to function as the transcendent tonal frame for discourses of resistance. To focus on this difference is not to try to reach some essentialist site of fixed division, nor is it clear that all feminist and postmodern writing could be fairly characterized by this division. The focus in this context is strategic, with respect to the concerns about potential hegemonic paradigmatic domination of one of these discourses by the other, as well as out of concern for understanding the affective and stylistic frame in which many of the sites of contention are drawn. Because outrage and irony are not foundational authorizing grounds, but rather matters of discursive and argumentative strategy that also bespeak differences in the positional nature of these discourses, such focus helps to amplify a sense of kinship relation between them that does not, at least in principle, amount to a relationship of dominance and submission. Outrage and irony are not only not mutually exclusive, but also produce a kinship of effects with respect to the objects so addressed. Both can work as forms of resistance to a dominant hegemonic rationality, and to the forms of knowledge and power they produce. Hence, although the relationship between postmodernism and feminism can be read as a familial relationship of allied resistance, this conjunction enjoys or operates with no regulative or legislative force/authority with respect to the course and development of these particular forms of critical discourse. Rather, both feminism and postmodernism problematize the prospects of preemptive consensus, as well as interrogating the desires which set this expectation in motion. Though allied both through their choices of targets, and to a lesser degree through their sense of common parentage, feminism and postmodernism cannot be expected to develop in some sort of lock-step symmetry with one another, since each emerges from an interpretation and appropriation of origins and historical positions that are specific and nontransferable.

Born of a similar intertextual legacy, feminism and postmodernism have been invested in rather different sets of priorities, and in establishing different kinds of claims. The kinship that exists between feminism and postmodernism neither implies nor inscribes any particular disciplinary agendas or accommodations— except as these are electively explored and exploited in particular and localized modes. The kinship between postmodernism and feminism cannot be formulated as some localizing set of Kantian imperatives—except perhaps by those who seek through oversimplification and reduction to discredit the authority and fecundity of these discourses in their differences.

The kinship metaphor, however, suffers from some of the same limits as that of the marital model. One may post the question of which feminists are kin to which postmodernists. In some cases, these family resemblances will be more readily apparent than in others. And it is clear to anyone engaged in these enterprises that neither feminism nor postmodernism operates as one big happy family. A kinship system establishes linkage marked by a system of proper names and ritualized exchanges. Yet as signifiers of the paradigmatic imperative to resist preemptive totalization and condensation, feminism and postmodernism are not really proper names marking individuals linked by preestablished relationships like kinship. Rather, postmodernism and feminism operate more like the names given those fictive entities known as corporations, under whose auspices a wide range of enterprises are organized and collected in ways that consolidate and maximize their profitability without assuming any essential relationship between them. This form of strategic conjunction, born of a logic of maximizing utilities, may be a better way of metaphorizing the motives for the conjunctive relationship in which feminism and postmodernism are currently placed. Corporate mergers are not undertaken as romantic projects of desire, or out of the need for some form of mystical communion. They are strategic unions born of an interest in consolidating competition, diversifying one's assets, or operating from a greater position of strength and viability in the market place.

The advantage of this metaphor over the marital and kinship proposals is that a model of corporate merger assumes, and in fact proceeds from, a recognition of the diversity and division of the function between and among the two entities to be merged, without the expectation of some unifying principle or medium of identity or unification, like those which have traditionally been assumed about persons. Furthermore, the nature of the desire is recast from that which might be said to emerge indigenously from the needs or desires of the parties themselves, and instead displaces the motive onto a larger and nonclosable logic of a political economy of production, distribution, and exchange. In its more optimistic formulations, the prospect of a merger between corporations is undertaken as a way of intensifying and enhancing the value of each entity taken separately. More ominously, as recent events have disclosed, such "mergers" can ultimately amount to "takeovers" in which one entity is subsumed and subjected to the demands of the other. It is these dual possibilities that help fuel the debate about the desirability of such conjunctions and anxiety about their possible consequences.

Some of the proposed linkages between postmodernism and feminism emerge from a modification of this corporate metaphor. The hope is that the viability of these enterprises will be enhanced by a pooling of resources—which in this case are mostly conceptual and strategic currencies. But beyond the value emergent from these exchanges, one of postmodernism's and feminism's major assets is the audiences and intertextual networks and institutions this work has collected and solidified over the years. Hence we should not be surprised that many writers, journals, and publishers are interested in paradigmatic crossovers—texts that address multiple, already established spheres of sensibility as one strategy for expanding potential readership. For while the audiences for those overlap—they are also distinct. At this historical moment, feminism and postmodernism seem to be a relatively "hot," marketable duo.

Part of its appeal as a new line of commodity is that "postmodernism" is saturated by the signification of "newness," functioning as a substitutable signifier for that which used to be called "the avant-garde." It is this associative signification and the complex of needs and desires condensed by it that help explain why, at a time when the word "revolutionary" is now more often attached to commodities than to mass social movements, feminism and postmodernism are ultimately recuperated in the forms of market logic and rationality they both work to disrupt, if not with the promise of revolutionary transcendence, then at least with critical, outraged, and ironic discourse which displaces and destabilizes that logic and rationality with respect to its own mythologies and master narratives. "Newness" sells, even to consumers already acculturated to anticipate the eternal return of the same, in the form of next year's model.

Some of those waiting poised on the cusp of newness are writers, academics, and cultural critics, even those who claim no longer to have been seduced by belief in the coherence or truth value of such a position. The suspended belief in the novelty of some corporate conjunction between feminism and postmodernism serves a double, albeit also contradictory, purpose. It is that which both sells texts and motivates their censorship. It moves toward proliferative productions, and is used to justify more restriction on the production and distribution of writing and other forms of cultural production. It is a conjunction that is not true or grounded, necessary or verifiable. It is a conjunction made in the name of truth and freedom on the one hand, ignorance as the restrictive deployment of hegemonic force on the other. But for those who are somehow positioned/ interpolated explicitly by these paradigmatic signifiers, and the collection and contradictions of historical forces they gather, the proposal of conjunction prompts reflection on that space between and on what it means to take up one's place there. My intuition, and one in which I take a certain amount of pleasure, is that part of the appeal of this conjunction is that it represents some moment of convergence and reciprocal recognition of the need for work which resists a climate where cultural production and pedagogy are being regulated in the interest of buttressing the legitimacy of a progressively more suspect and unjust social order.

For someone like Allan Bloom, feminism and postmodernism are but two of a group of suspects which must be rounded up and herded out of academic pedagogy and scholarly legitimacy, so that the one great conversation that constitutes the Western cultural tradition can go on undisrupted and undisturbed. Although feminist and postmodern interventions threaten the fluency and common language of that conversation in different ways, for different reasons, and with differential consequences, I think that the polymorphous fracturing set in play by these writings and practices in their very diversity has been intensive enough in its effects to prompt an explicit mandate for the reimposition of some supposed classical values, and cultural literacy. Figures like William Bennett and E. D. Hirsch, who no longer try to conceal the political agenda inscribed with the construction and promulgation of a canonical cultural consensus, can be taken as some of the stranger hybrid offspring of this conjunction between feminist and postmodern discourse. The need to reassert the necessity for establishing arbitrary canonical points of cultural reference, assimilation, and interpolation only emerges when the centrality and hegemony of those markers have been seriously challenged or eroded.

Feminist and postmodern theory and practices have done much to reconfigure the Western cultural imaginary in ways that authorize and legitimate the enactment of differences as an explicitly critical enterprise and hence are conjoined, perhaps beyond any elective enterprise of intention or desire, by the enemies they make, and the forms of challenge and resistance they provoke. Both feminism and postmodernism have been subjected in recent years to conservative reductionist critiques, which operate by constructing each as a monolithic dogmatic discourse, opaque to outsiders, organized by arcane rhetoric and rituals from within. This reductionism aims at organizing social outrage and anxiety against these perceived threats, and thus serves many of the same strategic purposes as did the myth of the monolithic communism in the 1950s, by providing an impetus for a sentimentalized return to the familiar, the canonical, the classic.

The conjunction of feminism and postmodernism helps sustain for many of us the prospect of some multipronged, albeit uncoordinated, counterculture—some intertextual network of resistance to those forces which seek to appropriate cultural artifacts as pedagogical instruments of authoritarianism and acculturation to dominance. At a time when even liberal appeals for tolerance seem to go unheeded by those at the NEA and NEH and the Department of Human Resources, among others, conspicuous gestures of resistance take on added import—whether or not these efforts take the form of some particular substantive agenda. That may be why feminism and postmodernism are often conjoined more easily by their opponents than by their practitioners, as members of the New Right's hit list—along with other offenders—like racial, ethnic, and gay studies. Their connotative force speaks absent any specific content or rhetoric.

So as I've been thinking about the fates of postmodernism and feminism in their current configurations, I also imagine the Bush-Reagan cultural power-brokers and their hired pens thinking about the same thing and fretting that the stable world of official culture over which they assume regulatory and preservative responsibility is currently being reassembled and rewritten in ways that even the most explicit forms of censorship cannot contain. I imagine their concern in contemplating the conspiracy of forces that is working to displace their cultural icons, and thereby dismantling the hegemonic forms of cultural literacy from which, presumably, much of their power and privilege stems. I envision rooms of cryptographers working to translate these feminist and postmodern texts—in efforts to break these conspiratorial codes. I imagine their frustration as these hieroglyphics clog their binary circuitry.

Those of us who operate in the postmodernist and feminist universes can laugh with Medusa's glee at the thought of feminists and postmodernists locked in some disciplinary long march toward some already specified "great beyond." Not all of us are yet infected by the eliminationist imaginary that seems to dominate the power elite. But in our moments we need also to recognize that our fears of paradigmatic encroachment from another critical strategy are not very well placed and that the major threats to discourses of resistance come from those who seek to still the play of differences with regulative canonical devices. What tends to resist any specifiable resolution of relationship between feminism and postmodernism is that their argument cannot be formulated or expected to take the form of some dogmatic positional/legislative discourse. The thematic and strategic interplay between these paradigms and their opposition tends to work against any mechanism of unification. The "and" therefore keeps open a site for strategic engagement. The "and" is a place holder, which is to say, it holds a place open, free from being filled substantively or prescriptively. The "and" holds/preserves the differences between and among themselves. To try to fix that space by mapping it—setting landmarks, establishing fixed points of conjunction-directionality—is precisely to miss the point of a conjunction which is also always already nothing. Just as problematic as attempting to fix some site of connection would be the attempt to definitively prohibit intercourse between feminism and postmodernism, especially if one takes into account the historical process in which the contours and integrities of both paradigms are constantly being revised, rewritten, reformed. There is little need to organize some form of mass resistance to the conjunction of feminism and postmodernism—since the substantive and juridical nature of the connection is in itself empty—and exists only as written or deployed or rewritten.

We can recognize the eternal return of our master narratives of control through insight, through freedom which lifts the veil of untruth only, as those pre-postmodernists like Nietzsche wrote, at great cost and at great risk. This is complicated by our own multiple investments in forms of knowledge and fictions, and in forms of writing designed for legislation, that finds itself confronted with forms of power immune to legislation. But as makers and readers of stories, we also recognize the possibilities of contradictory interpretation, multiple readings, and effects. So, if the fiction of some conspiratorial connection between feminists and postmodernists engenders anxiety in the hearts and heads of the hegemonically powerful and institutionally entrenched—this might be a story that is worth repeating—at least until such time as such stories are no longer necessary.

Other Works by the Author

"Feminism and Postmodernism," in *Feminists Theorize the Political,* eds. Judith Butler and Joan W. Scott (New York: Routledge, 1992). (Reprinted in this volume.)

"Recalling a Community at Loose Ends," in *Community at Loose Ends* (Minneapolis: University of Minnesota Press, 1991).

"Just Say No: Repression, Anti-Sex, and the New Film," in *Sexual Politics and Popular Culture,* ed. Diane Raymond (Bowling Green, OH: Bowling Green State University Popular Press, 1990). (Reprinted in this volume.)

"Eye, Mind and Screen," in *Quarterly Review of Film and Video,* Fall 1990.

"Bodies—Pleasures—Powers," in *Differences: A Journal of Feminist Cultural Studies,* Vol. 1, Winter 1989. (Reprinted in this volume.)

"Defusing the Canon: Feminist Rereading and Textual Politics," in *The Question of the Other: Essays in Contemporary Continental Philosophy,* eds. Arleen B. Dallery and Charles E. Scott (Albany: SUNY Press, 1989). (Reprinted in this volume.)

"True Confessions: Cixous and Foucault on Sexuality and Power," in *The Thinking Muse,* eds. Jeffner Allen and Iris Young (Bloomington: Indiana University Press, 1989). (Reprinted in this volume.)

"Power, Gender, Value: Do We Need a Different Voice?" in *Power, Gender, Values,* ed. Judith Genova (Edmonton, Canada: Academic Printing and Publishing, 1987).

"Interpretation and Retrieval: Rereading Beauvoir," in *Women's Studies International Forum,* Vol. 8, No. 3, 1985. Reprinted in *Hypatia Reborn: Essays in Feminist Philosophy,* eds. Azizah Al-Hibri and Margaret A. Simons (Bloomington: Indiana University Press, 1990). (Reprinted in this volume.)

"Nietzschean Mythologies: The Inversion of Value and the War Against Women," in *Soundings,* Fall 1983.

"A Studio of One's Own: The Question of Feminist Cinema," in *Dialectics and Humanism.*

"We Still Need the Eggs: Hollywood Love Fetishes for the Eighties," in *Objects of Special*

Devotion: Fetishes and Fetishism in Popular Culture, ed. Ray B. Browne (Bowling Green, OH: Bowling Green State University Popular Press, 1982).

"Merleau-Ponty on the Concept of Style," in *Man and World,* Vol. 14, No. 2, 1981.

Review, *The Existentialist Critique of Freud* by Gerald Izenberg, in *International Studies in Philosophy,* 1979, pp. 195–6.

Works Cited in Part I

Altman, Dennis. *AIDS in the Mind of America*, Garden City, N.Y.: Anchor/Doubleday, 1986; *The Homosexualization of America*, New York: St. Martin's, 1982.

Althusser, Louis. *Lenin and Philosophy and Other Essays*, New York: Monthly Review Press, 1971.

Atkinson, Ti-Grace. *Amazon Odyssey*, New York: Links Books, 1974.

Barry, Kathleen. *Female Sexual Slavery*, Englewood Cliffs, N.J.: Prentice-Hall, 1979.

Baudrillard, Jean. *Selected Writings*, ed. Mark Poster, Stanford: Stanford University Press, 1988; *The Mirror of Production*, tr. Mark Poster, Saint Louis: Telos Press, 1975; *Fatal Strategies*, ed. Jim Fleming, tr. Philip Beitchman, Autonomedia, 1990.

Beauvoir, Simone de. *The Second Sex*, tr. H.M. Parshley, New York: Random House, 1952.

Brandt, Allan M. *No Magic Bullet: A Social History of Venereal Disease in the United States since 1990*, New York: Oxford University Press, 1987.

Camus, Albert. *The Plague*, tr. Stuart Gilbert, New York: Vintage-Random, 1972.

Cixous, Hélène. "The Laugh of the Medusa," trans. Keith Cohen and Paula Cohen, *Signs* 1, no. 4, 1976, pp. 875–93; "Castration or Decapitation?" tr. Annette Kuhn, *Signs* 7, no. 46, 1981; and Catherine Clement, *The Newly Born Woman*, tr. Betsy Wing, Minneapolis: University of Minnesota Press, 1986.

Delacoste, Frederique, and Alexander, Priscilla. *Sex Work; Writings by Women in the Sex Industry*, Pittsburgh: Cleis Press, 1987.

Deleuze, Gilles, and Guattari, Felix. *Anti-Oedipus: Capitalism and Schizophrenia*, tr. Robert Hurley, Mark Seem, and Helen R. Lane, Minneapolis: University of Minnesota Press, 1983.

Dworkin, Andrea. *Intercourse*, New York: Free Press, 1987.

Ehrenreich, Barbara. *Remaking Love: The Feminization of Sex*, Garden City: Anchor Doubleday, 1986.

Firestone, Shulamith. *The Dialectic of Sex: The Case for Feminist Revolution*, New York: Morrow, 1970.

Freud, Sigmund. *Civilization and its Discontents*, tr. James Strachey, New York: Norton, 1989.

Foucault, Michel. *The History of Sexuality*, Vol. I, tr. Robert Hurley, New York: Vintage, 1980; Vol. II, *The Use of Pleasure*, tr. Robert Hurley, New York: Pantheon, 1985; Vol. III, *The Care of the Self*, tr. Robert Hurley, New York: Pantheon, 1986; *Discipline and Punish: The Birth of the Prison*, tr. Alan Sheridan, New York: Vintage, 1979; *The Birth of the Clinic: An Archaeology of Medical Perception*, tr. A.M. Sheridan Smith, New York: Pantheon, 1973.

Fromm, Erich. *The Anatomy of Human Destructiveness*, New York; Holt, Rinehart, and Winston, 1973; *Escape from Freedom*, New York: Avon, 1982.

Fumento, Michael. *The Myth of Heterosexual AIDS*, New York: Basic Books, 1990.

Gay, Peter. *Freud: A Life for Our Time*, New York: Norton, 1988.

Gallop, Jane. *The Daughter's Seduction: Feminism and Psychoanalysis*, Ithaca: Cornell University Press, 1982.

Heath, Stephen. "Notes on Suture," *Screen*, Winter 1977/78, Vol. 18, no. 4, pp. 55–56; *The Sexual Fix*, London: Macmillan, 1982.

Irigaray, Luce. *Speculum of the Other Woman*, tr. Gillian C. Gill, Ithaca: Cornell University Press, 1985.

Kroker, Arthur, and Kroker, Marilouise. eds. *Panic Sex in America*, New York: St. Martin's, 1987.

Lacan, Jacques. "The Subversion of the Subject and the Dialectic of Desire in the Freudian Unconscious," in *Écrits*, tr. Alan Sheridan, New York: W.W. Norton, 1977.

Laclau, Ernesto, and Mouffe, Chantal. *Hegemony and Socialist Strategy*, tr. Winston Moore and Paul Cammack, London: Verso, 1985.

Lévi-Strauss, Claude. *The Elementary Structures of Kinship*, Boston: Beacon Press, 1969.

Lyotard, Jean-François. *The Differend: Phrases in Dispute*, tr. George Van Den Abbeele, Minneapolis: University of Minnesota Press, 1988.

Malraux, André. *Man's Fate*, New York: Random House, 1969.

Marcuse, Herbert. *Eros and Civilization: A Philosophical Inquiry into Freud*, Boston: Beacon Press, 1955; *One-Dimensional Man*, Boston: Beacon Press, 1964.

Moore, Gloria. *Margaret Sanger and the Birth Control Movement, a Bibliography, 1911– 1884*, Metuchen, N.J.: Scarecrow Press, 1986.

Morgan, Marabel. *The Total Woman*, New York: Pocket Books, 1975.

Nancy, Jean-Luc. *La communauté désoevrée*, Paris: Christian Bourgeois Editeur, 1986; *The Inoperative Community*, tr. Peter Connor, Minneapolis: University of Minnesota Press, 1990; *The Literary Absolute: The Theory of Literature in German Romanticism*, and Philippe Lacoue-Labarthe, Albany: SUNY Press, 1988.

Nietzsche, Friedrich. *On the Geneaology of Morals*, tr. Walter Kaufmann, New York: Vintage, 1969.

Patton, Cindy. *Sex and Germs: The Politics of AIDS*, Boston: South End Press, 1985.

Reich, Wilhelm. *The Function of the Orgasm: Sex-Economic Problems of Biological Energy*, tr. Vincent R. Carfango, New York: Farrar, Straus, & Giroux, 1973; *The Mass Psychology of Fascism*, tr. Vincent R. Carfagno, New York: Farrar, Straus & Giroux, 1970; *Sex-pol, Essays, 1929–34*, ed. Lee Baxandall, New York: Vintage, 1972.

Risse, Guenter B. *Hospital Life in Enlightenment Scotland: Care and Teaching at the Royal Infirmary of Edinburgh*, Cambridge and New York: Cambridge University Press, 1986; see also Guenter. ed. with Victoria A. Harden, *AIDS and the Historian*, Proceedings of a Conference at the National Institutes of Health, 20–21 March, 1989, Washington, D.C.: U.S. Department of Health and Human Services, Public Health Service, National Institutes of Health (NIH publication 91-1584), 1991.

Scarry, Elaine. *The Body in Pain: The Making and Unmaking of the World*, New York: Oxford University Press, 1985.

Slater, Philip. *The Pursuit of Loneliness: American Culture at the Breaking Point*, Boston: Beacon Press, 1976.

Sontag, Susan. *AIDS and Its Metaphors*, New York: Farrar, Straus, & Giroux, 1989.

Stern, William M. *Baby M Case: The Complete Trial Transcripts*, Superior Court of New Jersey, Chancery Division, Family Part, Bergen County, Indexed by Sara Robbins, Buffalo, N.Y.: W.S. Hein Co., 1988.

Sullivan, Janet Grady. *The West Side Spirit*, August 21, 1988.

Vance, Carole S., ed. *Pleasure and Danger; Exploring Female Sexuality*, Boston: Routledge & Kegan Paul, 1984.

Watney, Simon. *Policing Desire: Pornograhy, AIDS, and the Media*, Minneapolis: University of Minnesota Press, 1987.

Weeks, Jeffrey. *Sexuality and Its Discontents: Meanings, Myths and Modern Sexualities*, London: Routledge, 1985.

Willis, Ellen. "Coming Down Again: After the Age of Excess." in *Salmagundi*, no. 81, Winter 1989.

Vreeland, Diana. *Allure*, with Christopher Hemphill, Garden City, N.Y.: Doubleday, 1980.

Index

Abortion, 99, 114
ACT UP, 105
Addiction, 38–39, 44–45
Adolescence, 138–39
Advertising
  mobilization and proliferation of desire, 29–30
  sexuality and late capitalism, 37–38
Advocacy, patient, 11–12
Affirmative action, 120
AIDS
  anti-sex discourse, 177
  commodification of sexuality, 58–60
  cost-benefit logic and sexuality, 40
  cultural and economic implications of epidemic, 7
  epidemic logic and interventionist and regulatory practices, 30–31
  erasure of women as victims, 84
  history of institutional responses, 117–18
  hospitalization, 100–106
  images of erotic access and mobility, 29
  logic of contagion, 6
  marketing, pornography, and epidemic logic, 38–39
  panic logic as disciplinary response, 10–11
  rise in sexually transmitted diseases in 1980s, 113–14
  safe-sex techniques and gay community, 83–84
Allocation, resource, 105
Anxiety
  Falling in Love and sexual, 181

Fatal Attraction and sexual, 180, 186
  logic of epidemic, 29
Atkinson, Ti-Grace, 52–54
Audience, 21–22
Authors and authorship
  Cixous's advocacy of women's writing, 147–49, 153–55
  different tropes of feminine, 25–26
  problematic of feminine, 4–5, 19–25
  silence and women, 153
Authority
  Cixous's textual strategies, 158
  conservatives and sexual epidemic, 118
  epidemics and reinstitution of hegemonic lines of, 31
  Foucault's textual strategies, 157

Baby Boom, 178–79
Baby M case
  epidemic logic, 11
  logic and politics of parental privilege, 126–28
  reproductive regulation and sexual epidemic, 88–99
Bakker, Jim, 50
Bandita, 22–24
Baudrillard, Jean, 9, 41
Beauvoir, Simone de
  gendered bodies and sexual difference, 78
  rereading of, 131–43
  Singer on sex/gender distinction, 10
  trope of feminine author, 25–26
Bennett, William, 196

Binary oppositions, 7
Bloom, Allan, 196
Body
  body building, 123
  epidemics and sexual politics, 116–29
  regulation of and destabilizing effects of
    sexual epidemic, 27–28
  sexual difference and substitutability, 77–78
Broadway News, 178

Camus, Albert
  plague as ontological crisis, 29, 31, 119
  sexual politics and plague, 69
  Singer and existentialism, 3
Cancer, 11–12
Canon, philosophical, 163–75
Capitalism
  disciplining of pleasure, 72–82
  male privilege and reproductive technolo-
    gies, 86–87
  regulatory and disciplinary practices and he-
    gemonic structures, 8
  sexuality and logic of late, 34–60
  workers and new sobriety, 123
Castration, 158, 161
Catholic Church, 120
Child abuse, 42, 43
Choice
  arguments for legalization of prostitution, 56
  marriage and prostitution, 51
  medical authorities and treatment, 2–3, 5
Christianity, 63–64, 120
Cixous, Hélène
  asymmetrical distribution of pleasure and male
    dominance, 78
  Foucault on sexuality and power, 145–61
  history of philosophy as chain of fathers, 22
  politics of pleasure, 72
Class
  Baby M case, 94–95, 128
  criminal sexuality and recognition of differ-
    ence, 43
  marketing of motherhood, 125
Confessions, 150
Consciousness raising, 167
Conservatives, political
  epidemics and reinstitution of hegemonic
    lines of authority, 31–32
  epidemics and sexual politics, 118–19
  failure of traditional liberalism to provide al-
    ternative, 120

reductionist critiques of feminism and post-
    modernism, 196–97
Constructions, authors as, 23
Contraception, 99, 125–26
Control, 3–5, 31. *See also* Regulation
Courts, 96. *See also* Legal system
Criminality, 42, 43–44

Death
  sexual epidemic and politics, 129
  Singer and, 3, 5
Decapitation, 158, 159
Decision-making, 2–3, 5
Deconstruction, 143n.2
Demographics, 178
Descartes, René, 188–89
Desire
  epidemic and changes in sexual exchange,
    122
  notion of erotic welfare, 28
  philosophy and power, 32–33n.1
  postmodernism and feminism, 188, 189
Difference
  Beauvoir and concept of freedom, 132–43
  Beauvoir's discourse of, 143n.2
  Cixous and Foucault and textual politics,
    155–58
  problematic of feminine author, 20
Disease, 43. *See also* AIDS; Epidemics; Vene-
    real diseases
Divorce
  economics of marriage and prostitution, 51,
    52
  single motherhood and nuclear family, 80
Drug abuse, 38–39
Dworkin, Andre, 55

Economics. *See also* Capitalism
  marriage and prostitution, 51–52
  nuclear family and reproduction, 79–80
  paternity and demographics of poverty, 92
  sexuality as political, 34–35
Ehrenreich, Barbara, 46, 48
Epidemics. *See also* AIDS; Sexual epidemic
  Cixous and Foucault on problem of sexual
    discourse, 145–61
  hospitalization as structure of logic, 100–
    105
  logic and production of anxiety, 29
  radical interventionist policies by state, 11
  sexuality and late capitalism, 37–60

as socially authoritative discourse, 30–31
sociopolitical implications of term, 27
sociopolitical results of cultural and economic production, 6
Escort services, 47
Ethics
  Beauvoir's concept of freedom, 140–43
  gender and decision-making, 133–34
  Sartre's concept of freedom, 136
Existentialism
  Beauvoir's concept of freedom, 132
  ethics and social behavior, 142
  Singer and death, 3
Exploitation
  commodification of sexual services, 57–58
  reproduction and women, 96–97

Falling in Love, 181
Family
  Baby M case, 89–90
  Fatal Attraction and images, 181–82, 185–86
  paternal capitalism and disciplining of pleasure, 78–80
  safe sex and remarketing of nuclear, 68
  sexuality and hegemonic social structures, 8
  value-laden social forms and criminality, 42
  women's sexual safety and social organization, 85–86
Family romance, 79
Fatal Attraction, 179–86
Femininity
  Beauvoir's identification with, 144n.4
  Cixous on classic narratives and symbols of, 154
  problematic of feminine author, 21
  Singer's method of feminist inquiry, 4–5
Feminism
  backlash in *Fatal Attraction*, 183
  Foucault on sex and power, 146–47
  philosophical canon and textual politics, 163–75
  postmodernism and, 187–98
  repressive hypothesis and feminist discourse, 152
  sexual imagery and mimetic behavior, 177–78
  Singer as philosopher, 12–13
  Singer's method of inquiry, 1
Fetishism, 74–75
Film, 177–86

Foucault, Michel
  body and power, 123–24
  Cixous on sexuality and power, 145–61
  epidemics and power, 117
  liberation from power through sex as fiction, 77
  new forms of sexual political discourse, 120–21
  politics of pleasure, 71, 72
  power and disciplinary mechanisms, 69
  regulatory force of epidemics, 30
  sexuality and hegemonic institutional utilities, 59
  Singer and view of power, 3–4, 9
  society of "talking sex," 47
Freedom
  Beauvoir and concept of, 132–43
  pleasure and hegemonic power, 8–9
Freud, Sigmund, 34, 68–69

Gender
  Baby M case, 94–95
  capitalism and legal system, 97
  ethics and decision-making, 133–34
  feminist critique of humanism, 10
  women and management of bodies, 123–29
  women and regulatory strategies, 114
Gilligan, Carol, 133
Goldsmith, Richard, 177
Goldstein, Richard, 62

Hefner, Hugh, 40
Hegemony, 129n.1
Herpes virus, 113–14
Hirsch, E. D., 196
History of philosophy, 72, 163–75
Hobbes, Thomas, 55
Hospitalization, 100–106. *See also* Medical system; Patient
Humanism, 10, 120

Informed consent, 102–103
Institutions, 100–105
Irigaray, Luce, 172

Janeway, Elizabeth, 133
Justice, 188

Kant, Emmanuel, 168
Kierkegaard, Søren, 192
Knowledge, 122

Krell, David, 169
Kristeva, Julia, 78
Kroker, Arthur and Marilouise, 62, 180

Labor
    capitalism and legal system, 97
    marriage and women's unpaid, 51–52
    prostitution and manipulation of women, 49
    sexuality and late capitalism, 36–37, 39
    workers and new sobriety, 123
Lacan, Jacques, 10
Language
    capitalism and pleasure, 74–75
    Cixous on sexual difference, 154–55
    inexpressibility of pain, 71
Legal system
    arguments for legalization of prostitution,
        56–57
    marriage and prostitution, 54–55
    selective limitation of women's rights and
        privileges, 96
    women as providers of sexual services, 127
Leisure, 36
Lévi-Strauss, Claude, 39–40, 63
Liberalism, 120
Liberation
    potential of pleasure, 71
    sexual disclosure and, 151
    sexual revolution and politics of ectasy, 115
Lyotard, Jean François, 164

Mapping, 24
Marcuse, Herbert, 59, 64
Marketing
    marriage compared to prostitution, 50–51
    mobilization and proliferation of desire, 29–
        30
    motherhood and target populations, 124–25
    sexuality and late capitalism, 38–39, 46–48
    sexual politics in 1980s, 113
Marriage
    as form of sex work, 42
    prostitution and traditional bourgeois, 50–56
Marx, Karl, 34
Media, 43–44. See also Film industry; Tele-
    vision
Medical system, 2–3, 5. See also Hospitaliza-
    tion; Patient
Mill, John Stuart, 168
Misogyny, 140, 183
Monarchy, 151

Morgan, Mirabelle, 46
Motherhood
    Baby M case, 88–99, 126–28
    Beauvoir's concept of freedom, 137
    film industry, 179
    marketing to target female population, 124–
        25
    revisions of popular images, 79
Music industry, 178

Narcissism, 138
New Right
    authoritarian social agenda, 85
    epidemics and sexual politics, 118, 119
    exploitation of AIDS phenomena, 31
    feminism and postmodernism, 197
    sexual imagery and mimetic behavior, 177–
        78
New sobriety
    AIDS epidemic and cultural discourse, 177
    sexual epidemic and political strategies,
        121, 122–23
Nietzsche, Friedrich Wilhelm, 63, 169

Origins, 137–38

Pain, 71, 74
Panic sex, 180
Paranoia, 104
Paternity
    Baby M case, 88–99, 127–28
    film industry and sexual imagery, 179
Patient
    consumer model of rights and patient
        agency, 12
    contemporary politicization of, 105–106
Patriarchy
    absence of discursive forms representing
        women's pleasures, 147–48
    disciplining of pleasure, 72, 76–82
    reproductive technologies and exploitation
        of women, 98
Phallocentrism
    absence of discursive forms representing
        women's pleasures, 147–48
    asymetrical organization of sexual differ-
        ence, 78
    Cixous's and Foucault's textual strategies,
        161
    male hegemony and AIDS discourse, 84
The Philosopher's Index, 165

Philosophy
  Beauvoir and philosophical canon, 131,
    140–43
  feminist rereading of canon and textual poli-
    tics, 163–75
  power and desire, 32–33.n.1
  problematic of woman philosopher, 21–22,
    24
  sexual epidemic and relationship between
    sex and power, 26–27
  Singer as feminist philosopher, 12–13
Planned Parenthood, 125
Plato, 168, 169
Pleasure
  absence of discursive forms representing
    women's, 147–48
  anxiety and danger, 186
  disciplinary apparatus and regulation of, 9
  epidemics and sexual politics, 116–29
  freedom and hegemonic power, 8–9
  object relations in cinema, 179–80, 180–81
  sexual epidemic and regulation, 62–82
Policy, social
  AIDS and discourse, 105
  sexual epidemic and reversal of, 120
Politics
  AIDS and patienthood, 105–106
  Cixous's and Foucault's textual strategies,
    155–58
  feminist rereading of philosophical canon,
    163–75
  pleasure in age of sexual epidemic, 70
  problematic of pleasure, 66–67
  sexual in 1980s, 113–29
  sexuality and late capitalism, 44
Pornography
  feminism and behavioral consequentialist
    logic, 177–78
  marketing and epidemic logic, 39
  mass-marketing techniques, 46
  sexuality and late capitalism, 37–38, 44
Possession, 74–75
Postmodernism, 24, 187–98
Power
  Cixous and Foucault on sexuality and, 145–
    61
  desire and philosophy, 32–33n.1
  epidemics and sexual politics, 116–29
  feminism and postmodernism, 192
  hospitals and informed consent, 103
  marketing of sexual services, 48–49

  politics of pleasure, 71–72
  problematic of feminine author, 20
  Singer's method of feminist inquiry, 3–5
  women and study of philosophy, 166–67
Pre-nuptial contracts, 54
Privacy, 102, 103–104
Production, 35
Profit, 35–36
Property rights, 127
Prostitution
  arguments for legalization, 56–57
  institutional forms for capitalizing on sexu-
    ality, 39–40, 44
  laws protecting consumers rather than pro-
    viders of sexual services, 127
  marketing of sexual services and power, 48–
    50
  traditional bourgeois marriage, 50–56

Race, 125
Readers
  author and question of audience, 19, 21–22
  Cixous's and Foucault's textual strategies,
    156–57
  pornography and theory of reading, 38
Reagan administration, 67
Reductionism, 196
Regulation
  AIDS and sexuality, 7
  binary system of, 42
  body and destabilizing effects of sexual epi-
    demic, 27–28
  epidemic as socially authoritative discourse,
    30–31
  sexual epidemic and disciplining of plea-
    sure, 62–82
  sexual epidemic and reproduction, 88–99
  sexual epidemic and women, 83–87
  as theme in Singer, 3–5
Relationships
  Beauvoir's concept of freedom, 139–40,
    142
  Satre's concept of freedom, 135–36
Repression
  film industry and sexuality, 177–86
  logic of and discussions of prostitution, 55–
    56
  politics of sexual revolution, 115–16
Repressive hypothesis
  feminist discourse, 152
  liberation and sexual discourse, 151

relationship between sex and power, 149
Reproduction
    commodification of functions, 57
    male control of technologies, 86–87
    management of female body in 1980s, 123–29
    marriage and women's unpaid labor, 51–52
    nuclear family as socially cost-effective means of, 78–79
    regulation in age of sexual epidemic, 88–99
    sexual politics in 1980s, 113
Resistance
    AIDS and politics, 106
    Singer's method of feminist inquiry, 3–5
Responsibility, 141
Ruth, Sheila, 165

Safe sex
    contemporary politics of pleasure, 67–68
    epidemic conditions and hegemonic social structures, 8
    relationship between pleasure and discipline, 80–82
    sexual epidemic and political strategies, 121–22
    value-laden social forms and criminality, 42
    women's sexual health and safety, 85–86
Sanger, Margaret, 67
Sartre, Jean-Paul
    authorship and audience, 21
    Beauvoir and concept of freedom, 132, 134, 135–37, 141
    power and difference, 20
Scarcity, 35, 41
Scarry, Elaine, 71, 72
Scheherazade, 19–22, 26
Secular humanism, 120
Self-censorship, 153
Service economy, 35
Sex crimes, 42–43
Sex industry, 46, 77. See also Prostitution
Sexual disclosure, 151
Sexual epidemic. See also AIDS; Epidemics
    contemporary as political construct, 27
    as hegemonic construct, 129n.1
    images of erotic access and mobility, 28–29

disciplining of pleasure, 62–82
    logic and language of and sexual politics in 1980s, 113–29
    regulation of bodies and destabilizing effects, 27–28
    regulation of reproduction, 88–99
    regulation of women, 83–87
Sexuality. See also Sexual epidemic
    Cixous and Foucault on power and, 145–61
    construction of women's, 7–8
    film industry and repression, 177–86
    importance of sexual politics, 129
    logic of late capitalism, 34–60
    patriarchy and disciplining of pleasure, 76–82
    as social currency, 9–10
    use of term, 28
    viability of alternative in post-liberatory erotic climate, 8–9
Sexual revolution, 115–16
Sexual services, 45–48
Singer, Linda, 1–13, 111–12
Sontag, Susan, 43
Stories, sexual, 159–61
Style, 75–76
Sullivan, Janet Grady, 58
Surrogate motherhood
    Baby M case and logic and politics of parental privilege, 126, 127–28
    Baby M case and reproductive regulation, 88–99

Taste, 75
Teenage pregnancy, 125
Telephone sex industry, 41, 47
Television, 113, 178
Truth, 21

Utilitarianism, 73–74

Venereal diseases, 117
Victorian era, 156

Watney, Simon, 69–70, 82
Welfare, 28
Writing. See Authors